HOMO IDIOTICUS

WHY WE ARE STUPID *and* WHAT TO DO ABOUT IT

CEZARY PIETRASIK

BELVEDERE MEDIA

© 2025, Cezary Pietrasik. All rights reserved.
Published by Belvedere Media, San Francisco, California

www.cezarypietrasik.com

Homo Idioticus: Why we are stupid and what to do about it

ISBN 979-8-9924108-1-5 (paperback)
ISBN 979-8-9924108-2-2 (hardcover)
ISBN 979 979-8-9924108-0-8 (eBook)
Library of Congress Control Number: 2025904547

Without limiting the rights under copyright reserved above, no part of this publication may be reproduced, stored in or introduced into a retrieval system, or transmitted in any form or by any means (electronic, mechanical, photocopying, recording, or otherwise, whether now or hereafter known), without the prior written permission of both the copyright owner and the above publisher of this book, except by a reviewer who wishes to quote brief passages in connection with a review written for insertion in a magazine, newspaper, broadcast, website, blog, or other outlet in conformity with United States and International Fair Use or comparable guidelines to such copyright exceptions.

This book is intended to provide accurate information with regard to its subject matter and reflects the opinion and perspective of the author. However, in times of rapid change, ensuring all information provided is entirely accurate and up-to-date at all times is not always possible. Therefore, the author and publisher accept no responsibility for inaccuracies or omissions and specifically disclaim any liability, loss, or risk, personal, professional, or otherwise, which may be incurred as a consequence, directly or indirectly, of the use and/or application of any of the contents of this book.

To Mercedes Blanco, for your everlasting love, encouragement, and support.

"Two things are infinite:
The universe and human stupidity;
and I'm not sure about the universe."

Albert Einstein
(allegedly)

CONTENTS

Introduction 1

PART I: HOW? 11
Individual Stupidity 13
Societal Stupidity 23
Political Stupidity 59
Technological Stupidity 72
Economic Stupidity 86
Beautiful Stupidity 103

PART II: WHY? 121
Biology 123
Psychology 144
Sociology 160
Institutions 226

PART III: WHAT TO DO ABOUT IT? 243
Education 246
Mindset 256
Structural Solutions 271
Concluding Thoughts 291

Acknowledgments 303
Notes 305
About the Author 327

INTRODUCTION

Humans conquered the earth and became the dominant species on our planet about 12,000 years ago. This happened mostly because of our phenomenal brains, which are capable of processing 11 million bits of information per second and storing about 2.5 petabytes, the equivalent of around 500 billion pages of text.[1] This brainpower, which we learned how to use over millennia, catapulted humans into the powerful position of overlords of this planet. We now decide which other forms of life can or cannot live; we shape, literally *and* figuratively, the face of the planet; we even change the climate.

Along the way, we mastered fire and invented the wheel. We developed agriculture and writing and turned wolves into great pets. We constructed the pyramids and the Great Wall of China. We harnessed electricity, penicillin, nuclear power, and flight. We put people on the moon and split the atom. We made *The Marriage of Figaro* and "Ode to Joy." We developed quantum mechanics, democracy, and ethics. We mapped the human brain and DNA. And quite soon, *Homo sapiens* will become a multiplanetary species.

Yet, on many occasions, we cannot escape the feeling that we are still ... so very stupid. In other words, we are still idiots, some intermediary form we can call: *Homo idioticus*.

The term *Homo sapiens* is Latin for "wise man."

Does that describe most of the people *you* encounter every day? Is it truly the designation we deserve?

In this book, we will find many examples to suggest otherwise.

Just as a preview, please note the following:

- Roughly 10% of Americans think the world is flat.[2] In other words, one in ten Americans defies a fact that can be simply proved by catching a plane from the US to Europe over the Atlantic Ocean, and then flying to Asia, and then coming back to the US over the Pacific Ocean.
- About 40% of Americans still believe God created humans in our current form about 5,000 years ago—rejecting the evidence of the well-preserved skeletons or naturally mummified bodies of earlier human species, which often can be easily checked out in local museums.[3]
- Approximately 56% of Americans believe we should *not* teach Arabic numerals at US schools. Yet Arabic numerals (1, 2, 3, 5, 10, etc.) are what we use every day. (Almost nobody in America can use a different numerical system.)
- Approximately 86% of American teens cannot reliably distinguish fact from fiction.
- In 1954, the Soviets detonated an atomic bomb at Totskoye in the Ural Mountains as a test and then ordered 45,000 soldiers to advance through this area to "check what impact it would have on them."
- In 1994, extremist Hutu militias in Rwanda killed, in only one hundred days, almost one million Tutsis and moderate Hutus in probably the fastest genocides in modern history, despite the recent memories of the Holocaust.

- The effects of global climate change are observable to the naked eye year after year, yet we're still arguing over whether the threat is real.

So, despite all this unbelievable brain power, huge chunks of the population (often among the most powerful and relatively well-educated citizens in all of human history) can still be, clearly, pretty dumb.

All that stupidity largely includes those of us who live in *optimal* conditions—relative wealth, peace, education, and full access to the information base of our civilization (libraries, museums, the internet, etc.). If we were to strip ourselves of our civilization's benefits (institutions, education, access to technology) the results would be even more devastating.

In 1867, a group of hunters in the Bulandshahr district of India found a young boy in a cave, a child of maybe six who seemed to be living on his own with a pack of wolves. He walked on all fours, could not speak, and ate raw meat like an animal. The boy was turned over to the Sikandra Mission Orphanage and subjected to a process of "rehabilitation" to reintegrate him into society. But despite the caretakers' energetic efforts, the results of the "rehabilitation" proved quite disappointing: The boy never mastered basic vocabulary (although he still made the sounds of a wolf), only with great reluctance allowed himself to be clothed, never formed deep relationships with other people... and continued the habit of gnawing at bones. (Interestingly, he also picked up smoking and became a chain smoker.)

Homo sapiens can go from the height of civilization back to being almost animals—in just one generation. Or, apparently, just six years.

The difference between us being "animalistic" and being human can therefore be attributed mostly to the benefits of civilization. However, as you will see shortly, even with full access to civilization, we still behave more like *Homo idioticus* a lot of the time. Even smart, highly sophisticated individuals who rule the most powerful, civilized countries are susceptible to complete idiocy, acting in ways that risk the total annihilation of humankind.

Take October 27, 1962.

The world was at the height of the Cuban Missile Crisis as the United States and the Soviet Union played geopolitical chess over the island of Cuba. The Soviets had recently sent ships with nuclear missiles to Cuba so it could build a more convenient missile launch station to achieve parity with the US (which had earlier placed similar missiles next door to Russia, in Western Europe and Turkey). The young President John F. Kennedy, deciding to demonstrate his strong leadership and play hardball, announced a naval blockade of Cuba. Unbeknownst to Kennedy, Soviet Foxtrot-class submarines had already entered Cuban waters, armed with nuclear missiles. Kennedy had ordered that any Soviet submarines discovered by US forces be forced to the surface by deploying "practice" depth charges as "signals" of warning. A major problem here was that the Soviet submarine crews did not know what "warning" depth charges meant.

On this fateful Saturday, Captain Valentin Savitsky and his B-59 submarine received a hit from a "practice depth charge" dropped by a US destroyer, which damaged its depth steering wheel. The crew of the B-59 assumed they were under attack. So, on board this one Soviet ship, one of humankind's most important conversations happened in less-than-optimal conditions.

The Soviet submarine was not designed for such warm waters—these were subs designed for the cold Arctic Circle—and its ventilators had broken days ago. This drove the temperature on the sub to 120–140 degrees Fahrenheit (50–60 degrees Celsius) and the level of carbon dioxide was critically close to poisonous. In this extreme environment, Captain Savitsky had a hot (!) debate with his political officer, Ivan Maslennikov, about what they should do. They agreed they were under attack. Given their latest briefings, the lack of communication with Moscow, their awareness of the potential nuclear conflict, the incredible political pressure—and temperatures reaching 120 degrees Fahrenheit—they concluded that World War III had already begun. They decided the best course of action was to fire their nuclear weapons toward the battle group of US Navy ships above them.[4]

Normally, the decision to fire a nuclear missile required the decision of the ship's captain and the political officer, each of whom had half of the key to launch the weapon. However—randomly, on this one ship—there happened to be *one more* senior officer aboard: Second Captain Vasily Arkhipov. Fortunately, in just such an event, Soviet military procedures required *his* consent as well. All three men had to give the collective thumbs-up.

If he had, the most likely turn of events would have been as follows: An unexplained nuclear explosion over the Caribbean and elimination of part of the US Navy would be interpreted as an undetected missile attack from Cuba. This action, as announced by President Kennedy on October 22, would have led to a *full-scale US nuclear attack on the Soviet Union*. This, in turn, would have triggered a Soviet attack on the US. The combined power of 30,000 nuclear warheads in the arsenal of those two countries would have caused the immediate death of around 500 million people. Even worse, such powerful detonations would have blown a huge volume of ashes into the atmosphere, obscuring the sunlight. Through obstruction of photosynthesis because of a prolonged period (ten years) without sunlight, most plants would have died, which would have starved all animal herds and created a decade of famine. That would almost certainly have killed the *rest* of humanity—if the radioactive ashes and winds hadn't done it already.

Fortunately for the whole of humanity, despite the crankiness caused by temperatures of more than 120 degrees Fahrenheit and pressure from his two overzealous colleagues, Vasily Arkhipov refused to fire the nuclear weapons. Using reasoned judgment and focusing on strict adherence to military protocol, the second captain could not justify the all-out response. Instead, the B-59 limped away and surfaced safely again out in the Atlantic. The Soviet Union and the United States didn't end the world.

"I was just doing my job," Vasily Arkhipov said 40 years later. He had nothing more to say about the afternoon he saved humanity from itself.

Crazy, isn't it? The mere presence of this coolheaded man potentially saved the world from total obliteration in 1962. This provides such a startling contrast to what we see today. President Vladimir Putin of Russia regularly threatens to use nuclear weapons against Ukraine and other Western countries because of the disappointing performance of his conventional forces in Ukraine. A powerful, educated man is risking the very existence of humanity because... his pride was humbled.

Why? Why do we make such stupid decisions?

It is mostly because our brains are still optimized for surviving in the African savanna, rather than modern jungles of steel and glass. It is because our herd-culture mentality creates huge biases that are very difficult to overcome; because our institutions have ingrained in us certain behaviors; because we subconsciously love authority and grandeur as opposed to hard truths and balance.

The topic of human stupidity (my own included) has fascinated me for years. The paradox of having the most sophisticated brainpower in the whole animal kingdom while also behaving so erratically and foolishly does not fail to mesmerize. From individuals to societies, the size of our stupidity is limitless, astonishing.

But so is our potential for overcoming those same follies.

In *Homo idioticus*, we will explore our own absurdities and show how fighting our own stupidity is a noble and worthy pursuit—one that will literally save humanity from its own self-destruction.

* * *

Twenty years ago, I was named the Best Economics Student of Poland, and it eventually led to work with grand investment banks, consulting companies, and mighty private equity firms, which I later quit to create a mission-driven health start-up in Silicon Valley that was meant to save one million lives. Finally, I switched to building a behavioral artificial intelligence company, which taught me how easy it is to predict human actions. Today, I am investing in visionary start-ups, learning about the brave new world every day.

All of this experience has afforded me the gift of spending time with people with different backgrounds and different mentalities from all over the world. Living in 7 different countries and traveling to more than 80 has helped me gather diverse perspectives.

Wherever I go, I'm struck by the paradox that humans have the most sophisticated brainpower in the animal kingdom, yet still behave so erratically. Understanding this paradox and its causes became a bit of an obsession for me, and I am proud to share some of the results of those studies in the form of this book.

Why bother to look at human stupidity at all, you may ask? Isn't it all too painful and depressing? Well, self-realization is the first step. Then we can agree on how to improve.

Therefore, let's dive into the sea of human stupidity: finding the key patterns and underlying causes, drawing conclusions, and then suggesting solutions. We really can get better, much better!

This examination is split into three parts:

- **How?** A brief exercise in mapping out human stupidity—providing a taxonomy that arranges it into well-defined categories.
- **Why?** A deep dive into the reasons for our idiocy. In short, it's rather complex—a combination of biological, psychological, sociological, and institutional factors. We'll go from purely medical explanations of our inner body workings to analysis of our group behavior paradigms and institutional shapers of our silliness.
- **What to do about it?** A more action-oriented segment that shows what we can all do to temper and even reverse human stupidity.

For the purposes of this journey, we will define stupidity as a relatively broad term, encompassing irrational behavior that produces suboptimal results for humans given the available data, knowledge, and circumstances. So *stupid* here can mean anything from irrational to illogical; uneducated to unnecessarily aggressive; primitive or backward to overconfident to wasteful.

We shall not equalize stupidity with low IQ, or lack of stupidity with high IQ. There are countless examples of people with very high IQs displaying the utmost in stupidity (such as, say, the usually clever Napoleon, who infamously marched his army to death in Russia).

In this book, I use a lot of references to the USA, the UK, and Poland—three countries that I have lived in for a long time, know the best, and care about a lot. So readers might get the impression that I'm overly harsh toward those countries or the West in general, criticizing them excessively. The fact is that I love them, and my fervent critique is a call to action and a sign of how much I care about fixing them. (Also, I've never lived in Asia or Africa and my knowledge of those cultures is limited.)

In any case, if we can point to so many stupidities in relatively well-organized, wealthy, developed, and seemingly well-functioning states, the outlook for the rest of the world does not look great.

Another thing to remember: We are all in this together.

When I say "We are stupid," I wholly include myself in this statement. And quite likely... you, dear reader. The author of this book has made a huge number of stupid decisions and avoidable mistakes, and fallen victim to all kinds of fallacies—many of which I will include here. *Where was my brain when I made those mistakes?* Hmm, probably switched off, snoozing, saving battery for the "important things." I write so assuredly about our stupidity because I've lived so much of it myself.

You and I should not be afraid of admitting foolhardiness, as many respectable people—from Isaac Newton and Steve Jobs to Mozart, Gandhi, and Margaret Thatcher—have made terrible decisions too.

It is a part of being human.

This is a story of how stupid we are, why we are stupid, *and* how we can fight it. So, let's map out this millennia-long phenomenon—explain the *why*, hypothesize how to combat it, and show that fighting it is a noble, worthy cause, sometimes (as exhibited above) literally saving the world from self-destruction.

If you've ever been the "only one" in the room who thinks everyone else is mad... that is not necessarily a fallacy. Maybe YOU are the next coolheaded person who will save the world from death by its own folly.

Welcome to the world of *Homo idioticus.*

HOW?

"Think of how stupid the average person is and realize half of them are stupider than that."

George Carlin

INDIVIDUAL STUPIDITY

While humanity has produced some incredible specimens—such as Marie Sklodowska-Curie, Leonardo da Vinci, William Shakespeare, Michelangelo, Nikola Tesla, and Albert Einstein—overall we are not that impressive intellectually.

I am not referring here to specific, isolated individuals—those who exhibit stupidity deserving of the annual Darwin Awards. (The Frenchman, for instance, who filled a cement mixer with water to use it as a swimming pool and was sucked into the mixer and drowned; or the "Fumigator" German who tried to fumigate his house by filling it with pesticide and then lighting a match to "spread the fumes." The resulting explosion vaporized his house *and* the German.)

I am more interested in showing that *as a whole, on average*, the human race is not that smart. In this book, I focus on societal-level *systemic* stupidity, rather than individual aberrations.

So let's start with some statistics to show us where we stand:

- Fewer than 7% of the world's population had a college degree as of 2020.[1] While a college degree is by no means a measure of one's intellectual powers, it often gives some directional approximation. More often than not, college degrees are correlated with a higher level of intellectual attainment.

- Close to 40% of the world's population has not completed high school—an even better approximation of intellectual advancement—as of 2020.[2] People who do not complete high school typically miss important verbal and numerical skills. They also have a poorer understanding of the surrounding world.
- Approximately 14% of the world's population cannot read or write.[3] While this may seem like a small proportion, in absolute terms this is more than a billion people!

Functional Illiteracy

A far scarier trend than actual illiteracy is the problem of so-called *functional illiteracy*.

This phenomenon has many definitions, but the best approximation is the inability to read and write at a level sufficient to accomplish basic daily tasks. Even the most well-developed, privileged, and richest countries have very large populations that are functionally illiterate.

Here is an example from the United Kingdom:

> *You are buying a television for £250. Which of these options is better for you:*
>
> 1) 10% discount
>
> 2) £30 discount

Obviously, you are better off with a £30 discount, which is greater than 10% of £250 (i.e., £25). However, 1 in 10 Britons didn't understand that.[4] To them, the 10% "sounded" or "seemed" like a better deal.

It is estimated that in the European Union, between 8% (best case: Sweden) and 40% (worst case: Portugal and Romania) of adults are functionally illiterate.[5] In 2006, about 47% of children in the UK who left school at age 16 didn't have a basic level of functional mathematics, and 42% failed to achieve a basic level of functional English.[6] In the US, 45 million Americans cannot read above a fifth-grade level. In Russia, only 33% of high school graduates can comprehend the content of scientific and literary texts, per a 2015 study.[7]

That is very sad news indeed, as it either shows a decline in cognitive skills *or* reveals the failure of formal education to teach basic skills.

Even more shocking, a 2018 Pew Research study discovered that only 26% of Americans were able to reliably distinguish fact from opinion. That number drops to less than 14% when looking at American 15-year-olds, according to a Programme for International Student Assessment study.

Welcome to the world of deep fakes, post-truth, influencers and TikTokers, and Kim Kardashian as the next US president!

The Negative Flynn Effect

We are going downhill intellectually.

This statement is not rhetorical. It is, in fact, called the *negative Flynn effect*, named after James R. Flynn, a New Zealand intelligence researcher. In the 1980s, Flynn argued that IQs were actually going *up* across the world; this was dubbed the Flynn effect. More recently, however, he observed the opposite.

An intelligence quotient (IQ) is a standard measurement of cognitive abilities. (IQ tests began in the early 20th century in France with Alfred Binet's work, which was designed to identify students needing extra educational support. Later, Lewis Terman adapted Binet's test into the Stanford-Binet IQ test in the US. These tests have evolved over time to measure cognitive abilities and intelligence across various domains.)

The basic IQ test assesses logical reasoning, verbal and mathematical aptitude, and the ability to identify patterns and sequences. The results are typically in the 0-200 range, with 90-110 being the average result. For example, in the US, 68% of the population has an IQ between 85 and 115.[8]

IQ is also considered a highly imperfect measurement. It misses a number of dimensions (including emotional, social, and creative), and, therefore, a person with a "low IQ" may demonstrate surprisingly exceptional ability in their domain. (I am strongly against using IQ as a sole measure of stupidity. There are many incredibly wise people with "low IQ.")

However, it is a measurement that gives us *some* information—so we will use it as one of our metrics.

In the 1990s and 2000s, researchers in the most advanced countries observed an unexpected *decline* in IQ among younger people. The Flynn effect, as it were, in reverse.

This was first observed in Norway.

Due to the risk of Russian aggression, Norway has a compulsory military service, and during the draft, all conscripts (males ages 18-19) must take a mandatory IQ test. As a result, Norway has a huge longitudinal database of 730,000 male recruits from 1962 to the present day. Based on analysis of this data, scientists have observed a decline in IQ of about 7 points *per generation* since the mid-1990s.[9] For Norway, intelligence peaked for individuals born around 1975 and then started declining slowly.

In 2008, the same trend was observed by James R. Flynn himself in the UK, where he concluded British teenagers had lower IQs than their counterparts 30 years earlier.[10]

So what is happening?

One prevailing hypothesis is that changes in our lifestyles are behind this phenomenon. It has to do with how we educate our children these days, what types of play they engage in, whether they read books, and so on. Our current culture is much more visually oriented—full of computer games, easy solutions, and 30-second TikTok spots, all of which make us highly attention-deficit prone. The teachers at schools are "teaching the tests," rather than imparting real skills and problem-solving. Constant bombardment by emails and texts alone is estimated to reduce IQ temporarily by 10 points.[11]

Nowadays we consume a ton of irrelevant, intellectually unstimulating content—posts by idiotic influencers, videos created by not-that-impressive peers, unnecessary emails, bloggers, and the like.

Before the era of social media, we used to read and follow the best brains on this planet. Writing a book and going through the publishing process was a natural filter that weeded out a lot of poor-quality content. Now we don't have those natural selection mechanisms and we consume *what's available*—not necessarily what's good.

As they say, "We are what we eat."

(Lack of) Understanding of the World

We humans live in a world surrounded by incredible feats of civilizational achievement. However, the reality is that we built it as a group. One person knows a little about a narrow field, and this "little" is added to another person's narrow knowledge, and so on. This ultimately produces incredible things like skyscrapers, bullet trains, the internet, the metaverse, and artificial intelligence. Yet most individuals do not understand the contemporary world.

I spent several years as a mergers-and-acquisitions banker at J.P. Morgan, advising on complex international mobile telecoms deals; but I really do not understand how mobile telephony works. I can give a superficial explanation, but very quickly I'm at a loss to explain in depth why you can pack more and more data into different frequencies of spectrum bands, how trees and walls cause interference, and so forth.

Similarly, most people can't explain how basic tools work. For instance, why do you tip over and fall off a bike when you're at a standstill, but not when you're moving? Why does a pan burn when it's empty, but not when you put something in it?

Most people know only about their close surroundings or country and have little or no idea about overseas. In 2022, famous experiments were conducted in America in which citizens were asked to identify Ukraine on a map; 66% were not able to do so correctly.

FIGURE 1. Can you place Ukraine on the map?[12]

Even in such basic, fundamental things like procreation, we have no clue. Countless studies reveal misconceptions about how pregnancy occurs, widespread misunderstandings about birth control methods, lack of knowledge about sexually transmitted diseases, and confusion about sexual anatomy and function.

Most women do not understand how the male body works. (The vast majority do not know that men cannot control their erection (i.e., keeping the penis hard is beyond their conscious control). The muscles that make up the penis are under the control of the autonomic nervous system and act involuntarily; that's why a man can get an erection at an embarrassing moment and often cannot tell his penis to relax.)

Similarly, most men do not understand how the female menstrual cycle works. Most could not tell you how many days a woman is fertile each month or how long she likely menstruates. (A female friend of mine was dating a sophisticated, financially successful man in New York who believed that "a woman is dirty 15 days a month.") Hardly any men know that women produce eggs only while still in their mother's womb and do not produce any after they are born. As an adult, a woman releases only the eggs she produced as a fetus.

A survey conducted by the American Sexual Health Association found that a notable percentage of respondents were unfamiliar with the location and function of the clitoris. (A conclusion that is perhaps not all too surprising to many of you.)

Love of Conspiracy Theories

As a species, we evolved and flourished through gossiping.

This is how we created the first stories, shared beliefs, abstract thinking, and ultimately our myths and religions. However, it is clear that our appetite for talking about lion-headed people, mermaids, and other fantasies is not going away.

In 2016, ahead of the US presidential election pitting Hillary Clinton against Donald Trump, a conspiracy theory went viral that alleged Clinton had used Comet Ping Pong, a pizzeria in Washington, DC, for child sex trafficking. The absurd story, which became known as "Pizzagate," spread so widely that a man from North Carolina traveled there, threatened to kill the staff, and shot his rifle inside the restaurant to search for hidden bodies. Fortunately, no one was injured, and the gunman was apprehended by police. Still, his behavior was representative of real concerns at that time for a large chunk of American society.

A lot of us still behave like our prehistoric ancestors—sitting around the bonfire with stunned eyes, looking at shamans who are talking about the most improbable phantasmagorias. We love conspiracy theories, often the more absurd, the better. For example, 16% of Americans believe the moon landing is a hoax. And 10% of Americans do not believe climate change is happening, and another 15% are unsure about it.[13]

Think about all those conspiracy theories you have heard of: 5G health risks, QAnon, flat Earth, Holocaust denial, climate change denial, reptilian humanoid rulers, FEMA concentration camps, Bill Gates putting microchips in vaccines, the Rothschild family, George Soros....

If you are a skilled politician, you throw out an absurd conspiracy theory and ... it will stick. At least partially. Typically, 5%–15% of people in modern societies with developed economies will buy the most absurd accusations on any topic. Sometimes this is more than enough to get elected. (See the chapter on the US political system later in the book.)

Aggression

In our broad definition of *stupid*, we must include unnecessary aggression as one of its manifestations.

While sometimes aggression is useful or needed in our daily lives to repel an attack, defend the family, or stand up to injustice, in most situations this characteristic has clear negative connotations and negative consequences. In the "Why?" section of this book, in the "Biology" chapter, we will dive into the reasons for aggression and point out that we are making good progress in reducing it. However, current levels of aggression are not looking good at all.

About 8% of Americans have anger-control issues.[14] This means that little things make them so angry that they lose control. They have temper outbursts, or they hit people or throw things at them when they are upset.

Violence against a romantic partner, in particular, is widespread globally and typically involves males behaving aggressively toward females. About 35% of women in Afghanistan and Congo experienced violence from their romantic partner in the last 12 months. In another 27 countries, more than 1 in 5 women experienced such aggression in the last year.[15] Domestic violence is highly correlated with low income and education levels. A startling statistic is that globally, 137 women are *killed every day* by a romantic partner or relative.[16]

Many societies in the world have extremely violent cultures, where simple conflicts quickly escalate into bloody vendettas, shootings, and assaults. Machismo and payback culture coupled with availability of weapons causes real carnage in many societies today.

For example, in El Salvador, before Nayib Bukele became president, a male aged 15–49 faced about a 7% chance of being intentionally killed. Yes, you heard it right. In other words, if you were a man between the ages of 15 and 49, you had a 1 in 14 chance of being killed, not as a result of disease or accident but as a result of intentional violence.[17]

Many more countries in Latin America or Africa have a similar problem. From 2007 to 2014, more civilians died violently in Mexico than in the Iraq and Afghanistan Wars.[18] As a reminder, these were major wars with long-standing insurgency campaigns. Mexico, meanwhile, kills its own citizens in everyday acts, repetitively, as part of normal "peacetime" violence.

The ultimate price of aggression disproportionately falls on men. In Mexico, about 88% of all victims of violence are male (almost all murdered by other men).[19] In 2022, 75% of those murdered in the US were men; in Russia, 80% were men.

While these are terrifying statistics, it is encouraging that we are actually improving compared to our ancestors; so at least our trajectory is good. In the past, we have been much worse.

SOCIETAL STUPIDITY

The stupidity of individuals gets vastly aggregated at a societal level.

If one member of *Homo idioticus* can be stupid, just imagine when millions are at it. Since prehistoric days, foolishness always seems to escalate exponentially. While societies—from Mesopotamia to the British Empire—have been the major force in the advancement of our species, in many instances, they are also bastions of backwardness.

The most typical flavor of this stupidity is a blind adherence to tradition. Poet T. S. Eliot observed, "A tradition without intelligence is not worth having." He was so right!

While most societal rules have contributed to our progress, all too many of the bad ones are propagated by an unjustified respect for what has come before.

Rules That No Longer Make Sense

Imagine you're a smart, lovely, dynamic Brazilian lady, age 25, who just graduated from university. You've had the same boyfriend, an equally splendid person, for three years, and things are going great. You are maybe ready to live together, get a dog, have some kids, and live happily ever after. Most people at this stage would likely consider getting married.

Not Brazilians. For many, it just doesn't make financial sense.

In Brazil, if your father entered the Brazilian military before 2001, upon his death, you, as an unmarried daughter, are entitled to his pension for the rest of your life.[20] Thus, Brazil's military personnel have an abnormally high percentage of unmarried daughters. It is not because these ladies are unloved, chaste, or man haters. It's because of the pension rules.

If *you* could live your whole life on a nice army pension without ever doing one day of work—or enjoy a "side hustle" that's probably worth more than your real job—*why wouldn't you?*

This is just the tip of the iceberg.

You might be lucky enough to have ancestors who fought in the Paraguay War of 1864–70. (Also known as the War of the Triple Alliance, this one featured Paraguay unexpectedly attacking Brazil, Argentina, and Uruguay, resulting in the death of 90% of Paraguay's males—yes, 90%.) According to the Brazilian pension system, the descendants of that massacre more than 150 years ago are still entitled to *lifetime pensions!*

Generous, isn't it? Damn, wouldn't it be great to have a great-great-great-grandfather in the Brazilian military?

No wonder Brazil is in permanent economic crisis. In 1999, the average Brazilian retired at age 49. Who's there to earn all those pensions for the citizens retiring at 49? Seems like the 20-to-48-year-olds have a lot of extra mouths to feed.

So perhaps the country folk are harder working? Not really. There are cases of Brazilian farm workers retiring at 33 because, *technically*, they have already satisfied the formal national auditor test of having "worked for 30 years"—as they had been helping on the family farm since they were ... 3 years old.

Thanks to the morons in the Brazilian government in the 19th century who invented these rules without doing the related math, the Brazilian pension system today is on the edge of collapse. Recent reforms have improved it a bit, but it is still exorbitantly overgenerous.

A completely different perspective on "because somebody said so a long time ago" comes from Massachusetts.

This US state often evokes an image of a liberal, intellectual, highly educated, left-leaning society, with its famous Harvard University, Massachusetts Institute of Technology, and the large urban population in Boston. Nonetheless, until the early 2000s, it was technically illegal to have oral sex there.

Yes, you read it right. Until 2003, it was officially illegal to have oral sex with a consenting adult partner in the privacy of your bedroom, in one of the most liberal states in the United States of America.

As of late 2022, eleven US states—including Massachusetts, Maryland, Alabama, Louisiana, Florida, and Michigan—*still* formally had "antisodomy laws,"[21] which prohibit nonprocreational sex. These laws were enacted in the 17th to 19th centuries, targeting mostly same-sex couples.

This legislation often refers to *sodomy*, a biblical term derived from the story of Sodom and Gomorrah in the book of Genesis. But the definition of sodomy includes *any* sexual intercourse that is not for procreation, covering such broad activities as oral sex or anal sex.

My hypothesis is that the legislators who originally enacted those laws were most likely shy, puritanical characters who blushed when talking about such hot topics. Therefore, they wanted to use a dignified term, one not involving too many graphic descriptions (which would make them uncomfortable), so they used the biblical term *sodomy*.

As a result, you *can* be persecuted in these states for giving "nonprocreation-related" pleasure to your wife or husband at home. Isn't it crazy? Shouldn't what we do in our bedrooms with our romantic partners be our own private matter, as long as both parties consent? Sexuality is a beautiful world of our own creativity; why should the state have a right to peek into our bedrooms?

Well, because some stupid, not-that-well-informed dudes from the 19th century enacted some law a long time ago that is still in place because it is embarrassing for contemporary politicians to talk about nonvaginal sex.

In 2003, the US Supreme Court ruled the Texas antisodomy law unconstitutional, so, at present, these laws are practically unenforceable in other states. However, there are still some incidental, nonsensical examples that illustrate that those laws are not entirely dead (e.g., a 2008 case in North Carolina where two men were arrested by the Raleigh Police Department for having consensual sex ("crimes against nature") in private[22]).

Another shocking example of stupid rules invented by some moron a long time ago, but in use until recently, is from Indonesia.

Until recently, the Indonesian army required female army recruits to undergo a virginity test.[23] In August 2021, they finally decided to scrap this rule—well done! But why was it ever there in the first place? Apparently, the requirement for virginity was introduced to ensure that women in uniform are "moral." Interesting that such tests were not required for men. The assumption was, perhaps, that men who have sex before joining the army are still moral, while women aren't.

Can you believe this rule survived until 2021?

One final "because someone a long time ago said so" example: The US has more guns owned by the public than any other country in the world—one aspect of US society that is particularly shocking for most foreigners.

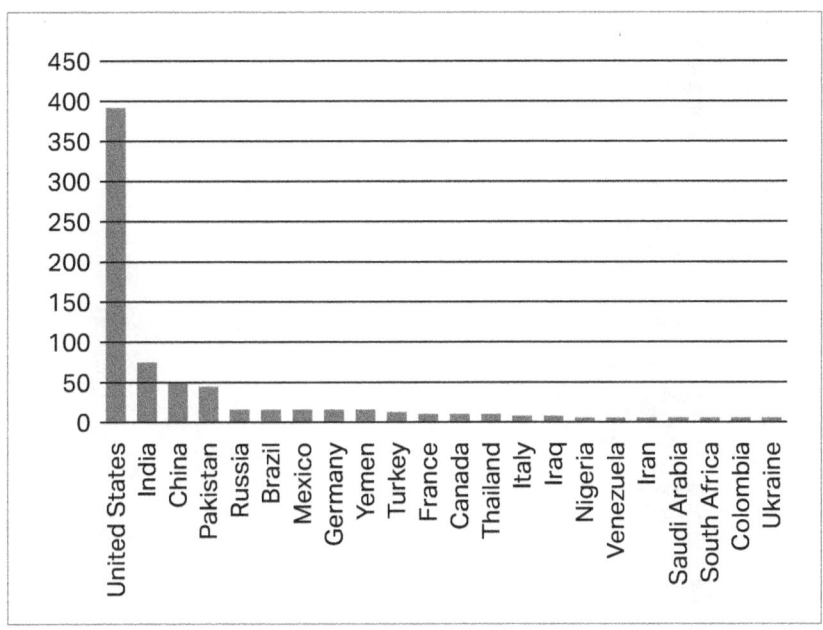

FIGURE 2. Number of guns owned per country (in millions)[24]

Americans own approximately 400 million guns, enough to arm every single US citizen, including every woman and child, with still enough to spare for the whole of Canada, and even *then* some still to spare.

Despite India and China having populations approximately 4 times greater than the US, America still has 5–8 times more guns in absolute terms! Close to half of all guns in the world are in the US.

On a per-population basis, this statistic is also an outlier. The US has more than 120 firearms per 100 citizens, with not even half that many in the second sovereign state on the list (Yemen). (Yemen is a failed "third-world" state, a country at war, with a broken society.) Gun ownership in all other developed nations is a fraction of that in America—on average, below 10 per 100 citizens, 12 times lower than in the US!

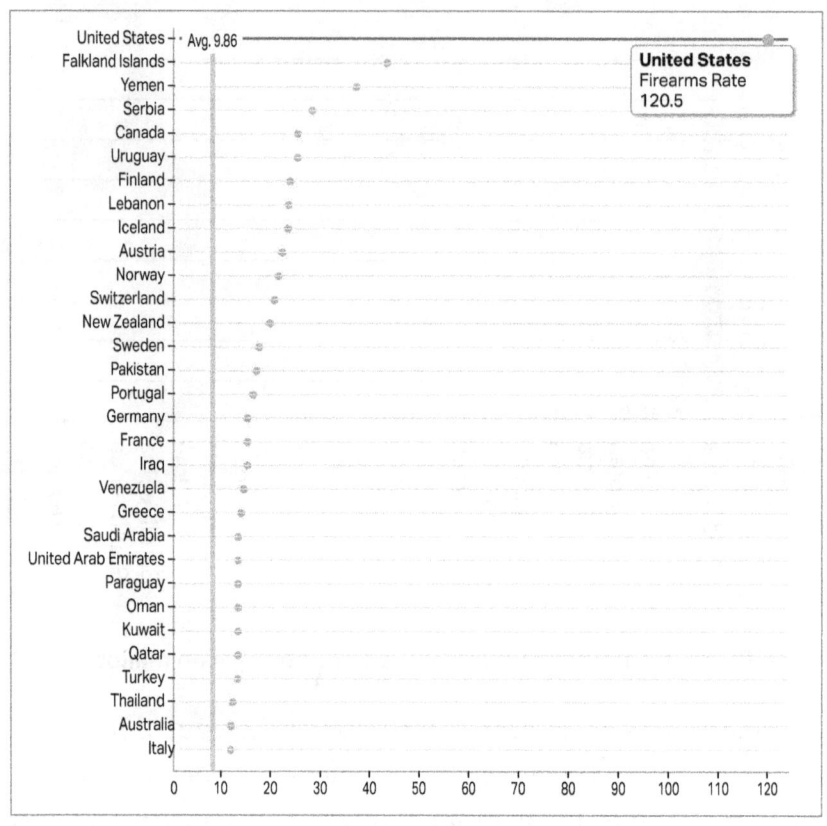

FIGURE 3. Gun ownership per 100 citizens[25]

To be fair, the origins of gun ownership in the US are logical and well-understood. It was a pioneer culture, a country of immigrants who would move inland and settle the country. Firearms were used on such journeys for hunting, protection against other settlers, or fighting Indigenous peoples. The US also largely depended on community militias during its colonial period. Hence, the guaranteed right to own a gun has been enshrined in the US Constitution (in the Second Amendment) since 1791.

Perhaps at that time it was justified, but it is no longer justified in the 2020s. This is only another example of a societal rule that somebody agreed to a long time ago, and while it is not valid anymore, we keep doing it.

As to the three original reasons for owning guns in 1791:

- Most of the US population no longer gets its meat from hunting or needs firearms for protection from wild animals. The share of the US population living in rural areas, where attacks by animals typically happen, is among the lowest in the world (17% versus 44% globally).
- The US population is not at risk of attacks from local hostile populations. Indigenous peoples were killed or absorbed and integrated into the overall society.
- The US population is no longer at risk of being called up to join militia units to defend its country from the British Redcoats. The US has a large, professional, incredibly effective and powerful military that can deal with any external security threat. No need to call militias armed with rifles and pistols when the US Army has airplanes, tanks, drones, and professional foot soldiers who can do tough work on the ground.

However, Americans still own a lot of guns, and each year, they buy more and more of them. Gun ownership laws are incredibly lax: You can buy a gun legally at age 18, while you cannot buy a beer until you are 21. So you can legally shoot at other people (if you are in the military or police) at 18, but you cannot rent a car or have a shot of vodka.

Pervasive gun ownership leads to a huge number of homicides, mass shootings, and simple accidents.

In Japan, in 2021, there was only one murder using a gun. One.

In the US, in 2022, there were 220 murders during the Fourth of July weekend alone.[26] From 2009 to 2018, there were 288 school shootings in the US, while in Canada there were 2, and none in the United Kingdom and Poland.[27] Every day in the US, about 12 children die from gun violence.[28]

The table in Figure 4 shows the number of gun-related deaths per 100,000 people in a few selected countries with varying degrees of violence.

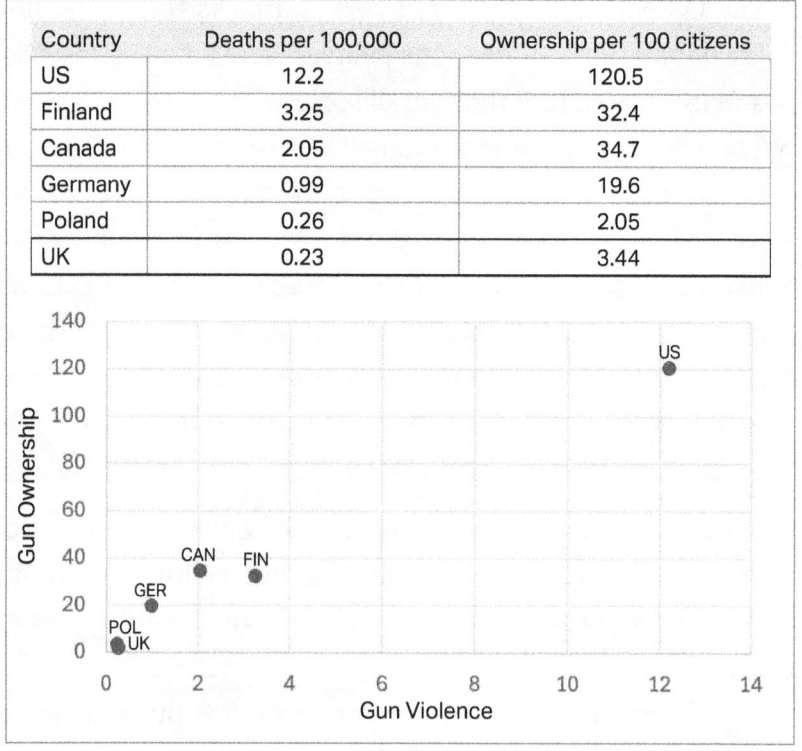

FIGURE 4. Correlation between gun violence and gun ownership[29]

The US tops the league, with an average of 12 people killed by firearms per every 100,000 people per year (including suicides, homicides, and accidents). On the opposite end of the spectrum are Poland and the UK, which have minuscule levels of gun violence, with around 0.2 dying per 100,000 people per year (same definition). When we plot those deaths against gun ownership, we see a clear correlation, visible even to the naked eye (see the graph in Figure 4). To be exact, for this table, the correlation coefficient (which measures the statistical relationship between two variables) is 99%!

The availability of guns makes shooting people easier. This seems intuitively right, and the math above fully supports that premise. The fewer guns we have, the safer our society.

The US, as a country—year after year, day after day—makes a conscious decision that it is acceptable to pay the price in innocent lives for the privilege of high gun ownership. The link between gun murders and the ease of obtaining the guns is undeniable, but American society prefers to frame it as "I need a gun because I need to protect myself from others owning a gun." *How about if none of you had guns?* You would not need anything to protect yourself. Does that sound rational?

Perhaps too many Americans are merely clinging to ideas from almost 250 years ago and blindly following traditions?

Too Many Rules

The longer social structures exist, the higher the risk of creating silly rules. Simply put, the continuum of existing rules and new rules created over time almost always leads to true idiocy.

This is particularly relevant for countries without written constitutions, which typically force law-making to be coordinated in some way. Therefore, in many revered geographies, legal acts pile on top of each other over centuries without much coordination or reflection.

A country that illustrates this predicament very well is the United Kingdom, which hasn't been successfully invaded since 1066. As a result, we find some marvelously ridiculous rules there, rules that are technically still valid:

- It is illegal to dress as a sailor or soldier for a costume party, according to the Seamen's and Soldiers' False Character Act of 1906. I think I violated this rule a couple of times.
- Wearing a suit of armor has not been allowed in the UK Houses of Parliament since 1313 (and this law has still not been repealed).
- Per the Act of Settlement of 1701, no Roman Catholic or person married to a Roman Catholic can ascend to the British throne. This rule, from over 300 years ago, still might determine the dating preferences of the British royal family, although there is clearly no reason for it anymore.

Another example is the US tax code. Clarifying the rules, particularly those that refer to numbers and require logic and consistency, is *very* difficult. One needs to understand the ample related laws, dependencies, consequences, varied scope of definitions, concepts such as "mutually exclusive, collectively exhaustive," "circular reference," and so on. Almost nobody wants to do that hard job, and frankly, with the volume of legislation, probably nobody *can* do it anymore—comprehending the US tax code in its entirety is an insurmountable task.

The US tax code grew from 409,000 words in 1955 to 1.395 million words in 2001 to 3.7 million words in 2008. In 2012, it was estimated at around 4 million words in 2012—equivalent to about 6,550 pages of text. If you include the related IRS documentation and tax case law, we're talking about 60,000 pages of text.[30] How can you be proficient in a law that takes 60,000 pages to describe?

So we end up with a practice of piling up one rule over another, simply adding more requirements, more laws, and more exceptions, even if they are inconsistent, unclear, and ambiguous, given their lack of connectivity with previous laws.

This creates absurdities such as lack of clarity on even simple concepts such as: "Is the qualified small business stock (QSBS) exemption limited only to me, or can it be doubled if I file together with my wife?" This question should be easily answered, but even the 60,000 pages are unclear on this. (For non–Silicon Valley–based readers: QSBS is a big deal. It's an exemption that allows you not to pay capital tax on the first $10 million (!) of proceeds from the sale of a start-up.) In a start-up nation such as the US, the fact that it is not entirely clear whether this rule applies to one person or can be doubled for a married couple is mind-boggling.

There are so many rules, we're not entirely sure anymore what some of them even mean. When you don't understand something well, the tendency is to be strict.

Rules That Are Too Strict

Let's start with the severest rules for theft. Probably all of us agree that reducing or even eradicating theft is a great idea. It increases trust in society, makes it more cohesive, and encourages cooperation and—in the long term, perhaps—sharing of resources. So from an evolutionary point of view, it's a good thing that we have had, for thousands of years, strict laws against theft.

However, isn't cutting someone's hand off a bit too harsh a punishment for stealing some lipstick or a pair of Bluetooth headphones? Such punishment feels like it belongs to a darker, more medieval past. However, several countries today still practice this cruel justice of amputation, including Yemen, Saudi Arabia, Sudan, and northern Nigeria. Many other forms of brutal punishment are still in use, including stoning (in Iran and Somalia), eye-blinding or eye-gouging (in Iran) and flogging (in Indonesia, Malaysia, Saudi Arabia, Brunei, and even Singapore). So when a New Yorker and a Somalian say they are "stoned," they might mean totally different things.

There are also many strict societal rules that are not laws at all—but rather, customs, traditions, or religious beliefs. These often are the most incredibly ruthless and stupid ones.

Let's start with innocent things like ... eating. Among the Hua peoples in New Guinea, for boys to be considered men, they cannot eat anything that in any way—however remote—resembles ... a vagina. This means nothing red, wet, slimy, or that has a hole or anything resembling hair.[31] How crazy!

Many people will conclude that these are the "limited, funny customs of savages from the bushes." Well, think twice. How about the food taboos in the culture YOU, perhaps, were born in?

- If you are a Hindu from Orisa, you would likely consider it disgusting for a widow to eat fish three times a week, because fish there is considered a "hot" food that increases sexual appetite. It is not considered appropriate for a widow to have a big sexual appetite because it might prevent her dead husband from reincarnating at a higher level.[32]
- If you are a Roman Catholic, you would feel guilty eating meat on Fridays, on Ash Wednesday, on Good Friday, and generally during fasting periods. If you do practice your carnivorous habits on those days, you may be ostracized by family or friends.

- If you are Muslim, you cannot eat pork, and you cannot eat or drink during Ramadan.
- If you are Jewish, you cannot eat pork or anything that "swarms upon the earth."

Still laughing about the savages in the bushes? Perhaps they are laughing at us too.

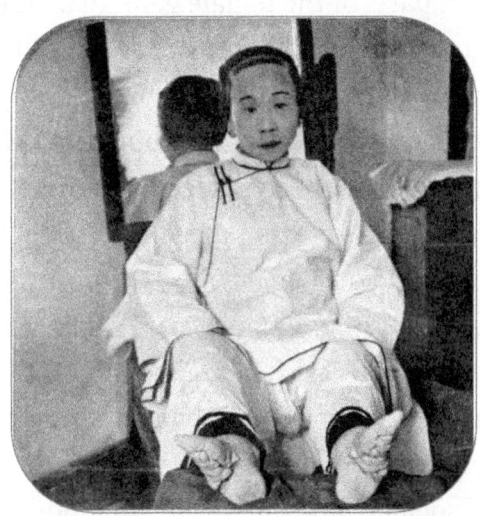

FIGURE 5. Chinese high-class woman in the early 20th century[33]

These small things quickly escalate to much harsher and brutal measures.

Did you know that until the early 20th century, foot binding remained a customary procedure for women in China, in particular among the higher classes? Foot binding is a cruel process of gradually deforming a woman's feet to cause them to have the shape of a lotus or lily, which was considered "chic." Obviously, such deformation causes enormous pain, mobility issues, and disability. Yet this didn't stop the tradition from spreading and achieving huge penetration: Up to 50% of all Chinese women and close to 100% of upper-class Han Chinese women were subjected to this procedure in the 19th century.[34] Communists in China rationally put an end to this horrific procedure post-1949.

Another example of a brutal custom that is still widespread today is that of female organ mutilation (female circumcision). This essentially involves cutting off the clitoral glands and sometimes other parts of the female genitalia. This procedure is demanded by tradition or religion and is typically done during childhood. Every year, approximately 4 million girls undergo this procedure, mostly in Africa, and approximately 200 million women living today have been subjected to this cruel act. There are no known benefits of this procedure. None. But there is a huge amount of evidence *against* it, from complications with urinating to issues with pregnancy and childbirth, reduced sexual appetite, painful sex, and mental health problems. The negative consequences and pain are obvious to the parents of any girl, but nonetheless, they continue with this brutal tradition in the name of social conformity. They do it out of fear of being different, and this fear works very well: The percentage of girls undergoing female circumcision is 99% in Somalia, 87% in Sudan, and 87% in relatively connected, "westernized" Egypt.[35]

Stirring up some controversy here: You probably rightfully think these barbaric examples are from "backward" countries. How about provoking you to reconsider a more controversial question: *male* circumcision?

It's a procedure that's widely popular not only in the Middle East but also in the United States. The studies that suggest this practice is beneficial from a hygienic point of view are actually mostly *based on sub-Saharan Africa* and don't translate well to wealthy, advanced societies with sufficient levels of hygiene and healthcare. There are heaps of evidence that this procedure is unnecessary, albeit deeply entrenched in cultural tradition. In the US, 80%–90% of male babies born in the 1960s were circumcised; according to the Centers for Disease Control and Prevention, the circumcision rate for newborns in US hospitals was still around 55%–60% in the 2010s.

Perhaps both female and male organ mutilation is wrong? Perhaps a grown-up person should decide what they want to do with their own body?

Rules That Are Too Tolerant

The opposite of the "too strict" side of stupidity in societal life is being "too tolerant." Yes, being too lenient, too generous, and too forgiving can also have very bad—sometimes tragic—consequences. Let's take San Francisco as an example.

This is a city that I know intimately, a city where I lived for many years and I care deeply about. The city is run by "progressives," who can be described as the most leftist, radical wing of the US Democratic Party. Their lofty ideas are often out of touch with reality, which ends up in a total mess.

San Francisco's leftist ideal of "protecting vulnerable populations" leads to incredibly generous policies toward the homeless and criminals. Until the 2024 election, city authorities presided over an irrational set of rules that encourage or promote criminal activities and homelessness. Just a few examples of what the city or the charities associated with the city do:

- Through Proposition 47, decriminalized theft under $950
- Provide free tents for the homeless and allow them to pitch those tents in the most prestigious, beautiful locations in the city
- Refrain from prosecuting those who defecate in public

- Refrain from prosecuting those who inject heroin or fentanyl into their veins in broad daylight
- Give free marijuana to drug addicts instead of offering rehab
- Give free needles to the homeless population so they can inject themselves with fentanyl, meth, heroin, and other hard drugs
- Prohibit police from keeping aggressive meth-intoxicated individuals in jail for a few days so they can cool down
- Prohibit the "hot pursuit" of criminals who have stolen something because of "security concerns" (So, if a police officer sees someone take a watch worth $10,000, they cannot legally chase the thief because it could be "too dangerous.")
- Forbid chasing gangs of bikers who, in broad daylight, often go through red lights in the city center, creating massive risks for traffic accidents
- In 2020, paid (!) for two billboards, created by the Harm Reduction Coalition, promoting the "safe use of drugs"[36]

The results? Approximately 8,000 homeless people terrorize 800,000 citizens of San Francisco. It seems that city authorities care more about the homeless and criminals than law-abiding, hardworking families. More than half of my friends in San Francisco have been physically or verbally attacked by the homeless, and some of them have suffered serious trauma as a consequence.

Parts of the city, including prestigious central locations next to the San Franciso City Hall, the War Memorial Opera House, the Ferry Building, and other historic buildings are ruled by the homeless. These areas are dominated by mentally ill people who do whatever they want, unconstrained and unchecked. The streets are full of human excrement, needles, broken glass from smashed car windows, garbage, and makeshift criminal workshops. Figure 6 below shows a picture taken by your author in 2020, 300 yards from City Hall (the most prestigious historical building in the city). This is a place where thieves bring stolen bikes, then dismantle them into parts to sell on the black market. In the middle of the city—practically next to its capitol—on the street, in broad daylight.

FIGURE 6. San Francisco street near city capitol
Central San Francisco, January 24, 2020, at 3:24 p.m. A makeshift disassembling station of stolen bikes, 300 yards from the capitol.

San Francisco's pharmacies are notoriously pillaged by the homeless because they aren't penalized for thefts that fall under the $950 threshold. There are examples of criminals literally walking through the aisles of the store with a calculator and stealing items worth just below $950. Most stores tell their staff to avoid confronting such criminals for the sake of their personnel's safety. Between 2016 and 2021 alone, Walgreens closed down 17 pharmacies in the city because the homeless would go in, steal less than $950 worth of goods, and leave the store unhindered because, legally, not much could be done.

Why do the homeless pillage mostly pharmacies? Because they are full of products that can be easily resold on the black market, as well as some products you can get high on.

Many shops in San Francisco hire police officers privately to protect their premises. A Lululemon (expensive athletic clothing) store in my neighborhood always has a police officer guarding it. The Apple store in San Francisco has a police officer protecting it, but it still gets raided by hooded criminals who, in broad daylight, rip off iPhones and iPads from the tables (check out the famous TikTok video from late 2022). Almost every pharmacy that's still open has a police officer or private security guard protecting it.

When you want to purchase $6 melatonin pills from the pharmacy, you need to press a call button in the aisle so a staff member can unlock a plexiglass antitheft window with a key. This requires a lot of staff, which, in turn, makes the pharmaceutical products very expensive. As a result, a lot of people do not buy needed medicines, which leads to increased mortality.

The ultimate result is that the city of San Francisco, rather than cracking down on criminals and the homeless, indirectly prefers its hardworking, law-abiding citizens to die quietly in their homes from lack of access to medicines.

Police forces can grow demotivated and dispirited. The San Francisco police are actually very capable, but their effectiveness is completely hindered by a set of stupid rules that prevent them from doing their job. I spoke with a police officer who told me that he chased a car thief in San Francisco, one who was driving extremely dangerously (most likely under the influence of drugs). This criminal crashed the car into a building and broke his leg. After this incident, the suspect sued the police officer for ... breaking his leg.

This is how empires fall.

San Francisco is one of the most expensive US cities to live in, partly because of the incompetence of its authorities. When you have to hire an off-duty police officer to stand in front of every major store (police officers make about $140,000 a year in San Francisco); when you have to take your car to the garage every few months because the windows were smashed while it was parked on the street; when your bike is stolen within hours if you leave it outside (even chained); when the window of your restaurant is broken every few months—well, then of course everything will be expensive, because you have to price those costs into the cost of doing business.

In the meantime, San Francisco promotes the "housing first" concept, which allows the homeless to get housing without meeting certain criteria (such as being sober or not high). "Housing first" has been proven ineffective again and again in multiple locations and multiple studies, such as the 1999–2002 experiment in San Francisco or the 2018 National Academies of Sciences, Engineering, and Medicine report.[37]

Most surprising of all, the city stopped requiring drug addicts to undergo obligatory rehabilitation. What's more, even the rehabilitation programs that the city of San Francisco requires are typically three months long, insufficient to prevent relapse. Most successful therapies last six months or more. Rather than increasing the length of the programs, and therefore their success rate, the city throws away a ton of money on completely unsuccessful rehab efforts.

This is simply utter incompetence. So what do you get as a city official for being so incompetent? You get a half-million-dollar salary! The average salary for the top 20 officials in San Francisco is about $500,000. Well, ultimately it *is* the capital of Silicon Valley! Good life!

The consensus in San Francisco is that you cannot speak badly about the homeless or criminals, because very shortly you will be accused of being a Nazi or racist. Unfortunately, when societies cannot talk openly about their problems, they crumble. We are close to this stage in San Francisco and California, as progressives ostracize and "cancel" anyone who opposes their views.

So, in some countries we cut off the hand of a poor man who steals a loaf of bread to feed his family, and in others, we do not punish someone at all for violently stealing $949 worth of goods to get high. Aren't those two scenarios a bit extreme?

Why can't we figure out a moderate, balanced approach somewhere in the middle?

Inertia: The Hidden Power Ruling the World

In 1968, Richard Nixon had two enemies in his bid for the US presidency: the antiwar left and America's Black population. Nixon was looking for something that could help him marginalize those two groups. He found it: marijuana.

Per John Ehrlichman, Assistant to the President for Domestic Affairs under Richard Nixon:

> We knew we couldn't make it illegal to be either against the war or Black, but by getting the public to associate the hippies with marijuana and Blacks with heroin, and then criminalizing both heavily, we could disrupt those communities. We could arrest their leaders, raid their homes, break up their meetings, and vilify them night after night on the evening news. Did we know we were lying about the drugs? Of course we did.

So, as a result of expedient political maneuvering, the laws were changed to help them play that particular political trick. The Controlled Substances Act of 1970 classified marijuana as Schedule I (on par with heroin), rather than Schedule V (which includes lighter drugs, like pain relievers). This unleashed a whole avalanche of tragic consequences. Millions of people were arrested and often incarcerated simply for possession of marijuana. Families were broken, careers ruined, education and growth plans thwarted for a substance that is less dangerous—according to most studies—than alcohol.

Between 2001 and 2010 alone, 8.2 million people were arrested in the US because of marijuana—88% of them just for possession.[38] Because of this law, an illicit drug trade industry boomed. By the mid-2010s, marijuana comprised approximately 50% of a $300 billion a year illicit drug trade.[39] This strengthened the gangs tremendously, allowing them to build financial power and political connections.

This 1970 classification was not revoked until July 2024, after more than half a century, because of the power of inertia.

Homo idioticus does not like changing things, because changing something—however small—requires explanations and political will. Most important, it requires effort and thought. As Jefferson notes at the start of the Declaration of Independence: "Experience hath shewn that mankind are more disposed to suffer, while evils are sufferable, than to right themselves by abolishing the forms to which they are accustomed."

Too often, we would rather stay miserable than make a change.

Thus, we continued with a law that was decimating US society, a law implemented by an exploitative politician who is often considered the worst president of the United States.

Anybody still not believe that inertia rules the world?

The Military

Armed forces reflect how we organize ourselves as a society. Most countries in the world maintain standing armies (with someone notable exceptions, such as Costa Rica). Those are particularly prone to limitless stupidity. An organizational design in which obedience is far more important than logical thinking creates opportunities for disasters on an epic scale. The degree of stupidity embedded in most military organizations is tantalizing.

Let me recall a few examples from modern history.

The real reason for Napoleon's defeat in Russia

One of the greatest military leaders of all time—Napoleon Bonaparte, conqueror of all of Europe—was defeated squarely at the peak of his power in 1812 in Russia by a very boring enemy: logistics.

When recollecting Napoleon in Russia, most of us immediately have an image of a mustached Imperial Guardsman lumbering through the deep snow, wrapped in dirty civilian clothes recently commandeered for warmth, repelling vicious attacks by Cossacks. Well, that's only the *end* of the story.

The real cause of the French troops' defeat was visible months earlier, when the invincible Grande Armée marching on Moscow was still in full glory, wearing new, beautiful, colorful uniforms, proudly carrying silver regimental eagles, with the sun shining and a sense of military achievement all around. But the simple mathematics of the defeat was already in front of everyone. All the French generals, including brilliant Napoleon, and all the soldiers had been watching it day by day, and ... nobody did anything.

As a result, more than half a million soldiers died, likely the biggest military catastrophe in human history up to that point. It was like a train wreck in slow motion.

Literally a train wreck, actually. A baggage train, to be exact.

How did it happen? For the invasion of Russia, Napoleon mustered the biggest army ever seen in Europe: about 600,000 Grande Armée soldiers drawn from all over Europe to overwhelm the Russian army of 200,000. Winning in battle when you have a three-to-one advantage in numbers doesn't look difficult at all, in particular when you are such a military genius as Napoleon.

But moving such a huge number of people across the continent, plus some 250,000 horses, was a challenging task, requiring thinking through details such as feeding, clothing, housing, and providing medical care to this mass of people and animals. Napoleon would make catastrophic mistakes in planning the campaign, which made him lose 80% of his army for reasons unrelated to combat.

Napoleon, until that point, was considered a master of logistics. He had an exceptional ability to identify the logistical details most important to the success of any military operation. He is credited with saying that "an Army marches on its stomach," which echoes Frederick II of Prussia: "No army is brave without supplies." In 1799, Napoleon had performed the maverick trick of landing in Egypt and conquering it from Turkey. It was an incredibly complex logistical-military feat, given the huge distances covered, the need to plan in advance for all supplies required, a different climate, and unfamiliarity with the terrain. In 1805, his Grande Armée outclassed the European coalition of Austria, Russia, and England in a spectacular, rapid maneuver, covering hundreds of miles from the English Channel to southern Germany and surrounding the Austrian army at Ulm. After such a rapid, forced march, his forces were still in great shape and performed spectacularly in the Battle of Austerlitz, his most famous victory.

Despite all this experience, however, in 1812 he still marched half a million of his soldiers to death by neglecting the basic facts—facts that were fully available to him at that point. He simply did not provide enough food for his soldiers and fodder for their horses.

The problem had two sides: the total amount of food available and the ability to distribute it to the frontline troops. Napoleon's highly skilled chief of staff, Marshal Louis-Alexandre Berthier, had organized food supplies for 4 *days* in every soldier's rucksack and a further 40 days in the battalion trains, drawn by horses. However, the campaign lasted over 5 *months*, so given the limited local supplies available in Russia, this amount was highly inadequate.

An even more catastrophic mistake was the flawed plan for food distribution: The French amassed a baggage train of 7,800 wagons to transport a humongous amount of food for its soldiers and horses. The problem was that half of those wagons (carrying probably two-thirds of the supplies) were heavy, 1.5-ton vehicles drawn by four horses. It became clear that on Russia's poor dirt roads, those vehicles would easily get stuck after it rained, or even in decent weather due to congestion.

So, about two-thirds of the transportation system's volume capacity proved to be useless. This resulted in dramatic food shortages from the first days of the campaign, further exacerbated by Napoleon's habit of using forced marches in an attempt to catch and encircle the withdrawing Russian armies. The faster Napoleon requested his infantry to march, the farther they got from their own supply depots and the more difficult it was to feed them with just one-third of the transportation capacity available. Meanwhile, the Russians cleverly implemented a "scorched earth" policy, destroying all available food supplies and housing in their line of retreat to deprive the invaders of the ability to rest and recover.

On top of the food shortages came disease. Typhus is spread by lice, which flourish in high temperatures and poor hygienic conditions. These were exactly the circumstances that the Grande Armée experienced. Columns of Napoleon's soldiers marched in the scorching sun through the Russian countryside for hours and hours, sweating profusely and then sharing crammed quarters with other soldiers in the same tents, or in the few buildings or barns that had not been burned. The French soldiers wore the same uniforms for months, which made them an ideal breeding ground for lice. This resulted in the outbreak of a huge epidemic, decimating already vulnerable, undernourished soldiers with weakened immune systems.

In 2001, builders digging trenches for telephone lines in Vilnius came across a morbid discovery: a mass grave with 2,000 French soldiers. They had been hastily buried, many still with their waist packs and some still with 20-franc coins in their pockets. French scientists from the Université de la Méditerranée in Marseille identified the men as members of the Grande Armée. They analyzed the dental pulp from their teeth and found that 29% of them had DNA traces of *Bartonella quintana* or *Rickettsia prowazekii*, bacterial species that cause typhus. Vilnius was captured on June 28, 1812, only four days after the start of the campaign ... so Napoleon's army was in deplorable shape, losing thousands of soldiers just a few days after the start of the war!

In such conditions, by some estimates, by July 28, 1812 (only one month after the start of the Russian campaign), the French and Allied invaders had lost almost half (!) of their army to disease, malnutrition, and desertion.[40] Until that time, no major battles had been fought, and the French suffered fewer than 10,000 combat casualties. Yet about 250,000 soldiers were already missing from Napoleon's ranks! Forget the frosty Russian winter—this war was already lost by the middle of the summer. The harsh Russian winter was only the finishing touch to an act of stupidity of such magnitude.

And what did Napoleon do? He pressed on, moving forward to capture Moscow, even farther from his supply lines. Didn't he know about the poor state of the Russian roads? Didn't he know he had food for only 44 days?

Well, he knew all of that very well. He had extensively studied Swedish king Charles XII's 1707–09 invasion of Russia. Moreover, he had campaigned himself against Russia in 1807 in the middle of winter, on the fringes of its empire, where he'd seen firsthand the poor roads and even wrote home to his wife that the campaigning was so hard and the logistics so difficult that in the last week he hadn't "taken the boots off my feet" and had been "eating only boiled potatoes."

Nonetheless, by ignoring the facts and not making sufficient preparations for his largest-ever campaign, he single-handedly caused what was perhaps the worst military catastrophe in human history. Out of approximately 600,000 soldiers that marched with Napoleon into Russia, only 20,000 came back alive.

Operation Market Garden

A spectacular, more recent example of human stupidity in military circles can be supplied by the British military toward the end of World War II.

After successful landings in Normandy in June 1944, the Allied armies opened the second front in France. The German defenses there crumbled under well-coordinated American and British attacks. In late July and August, the German Wehrmacht was in full retreat, causing one gigantic traffic jam in northern France as they tried to get back to Germany. This disorganized mass was harassed from the air by deadly Thunderbolt and Typhoon ground attack aircraft, which incessantly peppered convoys of withdrawing German vehicles with rockets, 20mm cannons, and machine guns. The roadsides of the French countryside were littered with burning equipment and the corpses of German soldiers and horses. The Nazi army on the Western Front was on its last breath.

Under these circumstances, Bernard Montgomery, a top British general, proposed a bold plan to bring World War II to a close by Christmas 1944. The idea was to prevent the German army from reorganizing and building a second defensive line along the Rhine River, a strong natural barrier. The plan called for the surprise capture of several critical bridges in the Netherlands, with the help of paratroopers, and pushing the Allied tank armies across those bridges into the plains of northern Germany, where there were no natural defensive positions. This would open the road to Berlin and end the war. The key to the whole plan was the element of surprise and the unpreparedness of the German troops, who were still in chaos due to their hasty withdrawal from France.

However, a few days before the start of the operation, Major Brian Urquhart (from the well-functioning British intelligence service) discovered that the Germans had moved two battle-hardened SS Panzer divisions into the city of Arnhem—the location of the bridge it was most critical for the Allies to capture. Urquhart confirmed the credibility of his critical reports with additional aerial reconnaissance and firsthand reports from the Dutch resistance forces.

These reports were highly alarming. They implied that instead of fighting demoralized, disorganized groups of retreating stragglers, the British paratroopers were to face the 9th and 10th SS Panzer Divisions—elite troops, highly trained in anti-airborne operations. (The Allied armies had gotten a painful lesson on the strength of the SS divisions only three months earlier, where they required 5–10 times the resources—troops, tanks, and other equipment—to annihilate the 12th SS Panzer Division "Hitlerjugend" in Normandy. Hitlerjugend's soldiers were 17- and 18-year-old boys who had never seen battle before. The 9th and 10th SS Panzer Divisions were composed of veterans who had seen everything). The Allied forces' biggest prize, the Arnhem bridge, was much better defended than they had anticipated.

This undeniable, and concerning, evidence was passed to Frederick Browning, the commander of the British 1st Airborne Corps, who was supposed to land at Arnhem. One would think that such a threat would encourage Browning and Montgomery to amend their plans.

Unfortunately, human stupidity demonstrated itself here in full. Not only were the plans not amended to adjust for this new information, but Major Urquhart, the intelligence officer who had correctly reported the situation, was labeled alarmist and unfit and was ordered on compulsory sick leave *by Frederick Browning*! In the same operation, Browning showed another example of stupidity by reserving 38 badly needed gliders to transport his headquarters staff and personal belongings instead of using them to bring more supplies to the fight.

Ignoring this vital intelligence was a coldly premeditated decision, made with full access to verified data. It cost the Allies dearly. Out of 12,000 British and Polish paratroopers sent into this battle, only one-third were safely evacuated. The rest were killed, wounded, or taken prisoner.

A high price to pay for ignoring rock-solid evidence, backed by aerial reconnaissance and on-the-ground witnesses.

You might wonder, did the officers responsible for this blunder suffer any consequences? Of course not. Browning's stellar career continued, culminating in a post as Military Secretary, while Bernard Montgomery enjoyed near-cult status and ended up serving as Deputy Supreme Allied Commander in Europe. Two fine specimens of *Homo idioticus*.

The Right to Cause Armageddon

Your life could be lawfully ended tomorrow. With the full support of the same state institutions *you* elected. Basically, you could be killed by the president of your own country, who could start a nuclear war.

As humanity, we have been playing with our own omnicide for years, ever since the invention of the thermonuclear bomb (a.k.a. the H-bomb). Contemporary H-bombs have an apocalyptic power of destruction. A single US Ohio-class submarine can carry 24 Trident II nuclear ballistic missiles, each of which can deliver eight 100-kiloton warheads. One such warhead is six times more powerful than the bomb that annihilated Hiroshima.

As a result, one submarine alone can unleash a destructive force equivalent to 1,000 Hiroshimas.[41] Never in history has a single captain of a single ship had the power to annihilate so many.

Multiple US presidents were stunned by the destructive power available to them. After a briefing on the expected power of the nuclear exchange with the Soviet Union in July 1961, John F. Kennedy left the room in shock, saying, "And we call ourselves the human race!" Dwight D. Eisenhower told his naval aide that such a presentation "frightened the devil out of me."

However, the almost godlike destructive power of a nuclear strike would be subsequently dwarfed by the secondary impact of nuclear radioactive fallout and—worst of all—nuclear winter.

Access to this apocalyptic killing machine has been managed in the past in an unbelievably irresponsible manner. Since 1945, humanity has entrusted the power of life and death to a few individuals, leaders of countries with large nuclear weapons arsenals such as the United States, the Soviet Union/Russia, France, the United Kingdom, and China. In the last three decades, the prime ministers of India, Pakistan, and Israel, as well as the dictator of North Korea, have joined this elite "Armageddon group." The ayatollah of Iran will most likely be next.

These leaders themselves would most probably survive such devastation. Those few countries with nuclear capabilities also have well-equipped nuclear bunkers with massive stores of supplies that will last for decades. You and I are unlikely to be one of the few lucky ones who will have a place inside such a bunker. This is all, then, quite a big bet on our part to give such power to a handful of other members of *Homo idioticus*. So it makes sense to take an interest in the individual who could make this call on our behalf, as well as the procedures developed to arrive at this decision from which there is no going back.

Let's take Boris Yeltsin, the president of Russia from 1991 to 1999, for example. Given his temperament and track record, we are lucky to be alive! Yeltsin was an alcoholic with periods of utter lack of control. He regularly appeared drunk in public, even at such high-stakes and high-profile events like his 1995 visit to Washington, DC, when he was found drunk in only his underwear on Pennsylvania Avenue, trying to hail a taxi to so he could get pizza. Imagine if he had made a decision about a nuclear response when he was drunk and in a bad mood. Would we be still around today?

FIGURE 7. Russia's former president Boris Yeltsin[42]
Between 1991 and 2000, this individual had the power to wipe out the human race from the earth. How does that make you feel?

As you will find out below, at least once during his presidency, he actually *was* presented with a true life-and-death decision: whether or not to launch a potentially catastrophic nuclear strike on the US. Fortunately, it appears that he was not drunk at the time.

So the first official layer of decision-makers who could initiate nuclear war does not inspire much optimism. However, let's dig deeper.

President Dwight Eisenhower, a seasoned soldier, feared that the Soviets might carry out a surprise, decapitating nuclear attack on the US, which could take out the president and vice president at the same time. In such a situation, there would be confusion regarding who could order a retaliatory strike. To prevent such a scenario, he started a practice called "subdelegation," which granted the right to initiate a nuclear strike to a designated person, such as a senior general or an admiral. (For example, the commander of the Seventh Fleet in the Pacific could start a nuclear war, thanks to Eisenhower's "subdelegation.")

At that time, such provisions might have seemed justified if observed by responsible, mature individuals with good judgment and experience. However, the power of "subdelegation" went much deeper. It is possible that such admirals, afraid of being wiped out by the first attack and having no chance to retaliate, "subdelegated" to *another* layer of lower-ranking admirals and generals. Even worse, there are some well-documented examples of realistic situations where nuclear weapons could have been launched by even middle-ranking officers.

Daniel Ellsberg was a nuclear war planner in the 1950s and 1960s, and as part of the prestigious RAND institute, he was testing the United States' "command and control" of its nuclear arsenal, looking for inconsistencies and threats of misuse. While visiting Kunsan, a small air base in South Korea, he met with the major in charge of twelve F-100 fighter-bombers stationed at the base. Each of these planes carried a Mark 28 thermonuclear weapon; the total firepower of this squadron added up to 6.5 times the total tonnage of bombs dropped by the US during World War II on the European and Pacific fronts combined. That's a lot of responsibility for a middle-ranking officer.

During Ellsberg's questioning, it transpired that this major would order his squadron to launch a nuclear attack on northeast Russia from his base if he found himself under the following scenarios: (a) sudden loss of communications with headquarters, or (b) a powerful explosion on his base.

Such scenarios seemed unlikely, but on closer examination, it turned out either could happen. Loss of communication with Pacific Command headquarters was occurring daily due to atmospheric disturbances. Additionally, the Mark 28 bombs that his planes were carrying were not "one-point safe," which meant that if two aircraft collided, or dropped a bomb accidentally, or were shot at or burned, it *could* initiate a partial nuclear explosion. There could be an explosive accident on his base while he was out of communication with his commanders.

This major's answer to Ellsberg's question on what he would do violated the explicit orders he had been given, which required him to wait for a direct, positive command from his superiors. Nonetheless, this disciplined, patriotic, and well-intentioned officer was willing to break those same orders if—in his judgment—the war had already started or his base was under attack.

It might be disturbing to know that the power to end the world as we know it was down to some middle-ranking person on a small military base that you and I have never heard of. And you might hope this was an isolated case.

Unfortunately, it wasn't.

Let's investigate the procedures that allow the use of nuclear weapons and zoom into strategic bombers and intercontinental ballistic missiles. It turns out that the strategic bombers' command-and-control procedures from the 1950s to the 1970s were very lax. The official procedure, a positive radio-code authentication order and two envelopes with matching codes, was rendered completely ineffective if a rogue pilot violated procedures and simply opened both envelopes himself. The "two-man rule" for authentication was often ignored.

Moreover, the procedures for launching silo-based land missiles were also vulnerable. After extreme pressure from civilian authorities under Secretary of Defense Robert McNamara, the military reluctantly installed an electronic lock on the missiles, which required a specific code for the launch. However, at least until the mid-1970s, the codes for the secret locks were all set to … 00000000. Yes, during most of the Cold War, the "secret unlock code" that would unleash thermonuclear apocalypse was set to 00000000! And people make fun of individuals whose password for their smartphone is 1234….

All of these examples show the vulnerability of the launch procedures to unauthorized use within the US military. These data points for America are available because of relative transparency, democratic civilian control of the military, and a free media. We can only speculate about the scale of the potential risks associated with control of the Soviet or Chinese arsenals. The US has the most competent military in the world. The risks that humanity has taken with other nuclear powers have probably been far greater.

While the general quality of the procedures among the major nuclear nations has improved significantly in the last three decades, one can be still utterly scared at the thought of what these procedures are like today in countries like Pakistan and, soon, Iran.

So now we have proof that, from an institutional, governance, and procedural point of view, we are balancing on the edge of Armageddon. What about surprises—the random, accidental, unplanned events that life always throws at us? Those are equally bad. The list of near-misses—narrowly avoided nuclear weapons disasters—is long and scary. Seems like a miracle that we have survived unscathed thus far:

- On January 24, 1961, a B-52 carrying several nuclear bombs crashed in North Carolina. One of the bombs on board came very close to exploding, with five of the six "fail-safe" mechanisms failing. If the sixth one had also failed, much of North Carolina would have been obliterated.
- In 1980, a faulty chip led to a false alarm indicating that the US was under nuclear attack and 2,200 Soviet missiles were inbound. Fortunately, the military realized this in time and did not launch a retaliatory strike.
- On September 26, 1983, the newly implemented Soviet early warning system "Oko" concluded that five US missiles were inbound. It turned out that the Oko system's satellites had interpreted the sunlight reflecting off cloud tops as "US missile launches."
- In 1995, a launch of the Norwegian science mission to study the aurora borealis was interpreted by Russian early detection systems as a nuclear attack by a US submarine, and President Boris Yeltsin was presented with a nuclear briefcase to respond. Fortunately, Russian military commanders concluded this was not a real attack. (Why would the US attack with just one missile?) President Yeltsin was probably not drunk or in a bad temper at that time, as we still are alive today.

The list above shows declassified incidents for which reports were made available to the public. In the interest of our mental health, it probably doesn't make sense to think too deeply about Soviet, Chinese, Indian, Pakistani, or North Korean nuclear mishaps....

An even scarier notion is that with the development of hypersonic missiles, the time available to react to and potentially correct a wrong interpretation will be shortened to a ridiculously small window, such as 1-10 minutes. This might put us under pressure to take humans, whose judgments have saved us from extinction in the past, out of the loop. How soon before artificial intelligence alone will decide—as it does already with investments, marketing, and logistics—whether or not we should launch back in retaliation?

POLITICAL STUPIDITY

A subcategory of our societal life is politics. The degree of stupidity here is so pronounced that it deserves to be analyzed under a separate category. Let's dive in!

Stupidly Following the Leader

Statesmen like Franklin Delano Roosevelt or Nelson Mandela and stateswomen like Margaret Thatcher or Jacinda Ardern are a rare breed. Most of the time, we choose our political leaders from among a mediocre group of individuals—sometimes, even clearly crazy individuals.

Let's take an example from Ecuador. The 1996 presidential election was won by this gentleman:

FIGURE 8. Abdalá Bucaram, President of Ecuador, 1996–97[43]

The first thing that stands out: Does he look like Hitler? Yes, he does. He also called himself, and asked others to call him, "El Loco" (the Madman). I am not sure what qualities were attributed to him by the 12 million Ecuadorians who elected him, but his performance as president was rather predictably "disappointing."

Abdalá Bucaram focused a lot on advancing his career... in singing—while in office. He started his presidency by singing a pop song, surrounded by scantily clad female dancers. During most state meetings, he liked to talk about his music and his fans' reactions to it. At an Ibero-American Summit, he distributed CDs from his own concert to fellow presidents and diplomats. He arranged for a live broadcast on nationwide television of... the waxing of his mustache. He also offered $1 million to soccer great Diego Maradona to play a soccer game with him and ordered an official presidential banquet in honor of Lorena Bobbitt, the woman who infamously cut off her husband's penis.

Bucaram was also a good family man: He took care of his 18-year-old son by appointing him as head of the Ecuadorian customs service, which gave his son the chance to rapidly enrich himself by accepting bribes. As if that was not enough, Bucaram was involved in some shady dealings with the mafia.

Fortunately for Ecuador, Abdalá Bucaram was removed from office in 1997 by the parliament on account of "mental incapacity." Well, he was also removed against the will of the people, who had given him 55% of the vote just six months earlier!

Some Western readers of this book would say that he was just a "random president of a banana republic." I want to point out, with my apologies to our Ecuadorian audience on behalf of such readers, that this phenomenon is the same for even the largest, oldest, and most powerful states in the world.

Let's zoom in on China. This country's civilization is more than 4,000 years old; its tradition of governance is probably the oldest in the world, its power and standing among nations unquestionable.

Nonetheless, Mao Zedong, the creator of the modern Chinese state, in 1958 launched a "smash sparrows campaign." This was part of the Great Leap Forward movement and turned out to be one of the worst ecological disasters known to humankind.

His logic was that the country was suffering from a shortage of food, and every little bit counted in a country as big as China. He figured that sparrows eat a lot of grains in the fields, and so killing sparrows would create more food.

A brutal fight against the sparrows ensued over the next year, when more than 600 million Chinese tried to kill as many birds as they could to show their political fervor. Sparrows died by the millions. However, the result was the opposite of what Mao expected.

The disappearance of the sparrows caused a natural disaster, as the populations of other pests (such as locusts) grew exponentially when their natural predators, the sparrows, were no longer there. This contributed to a huge famine, which led to an estimated 15–70 million *human* deaths.

To show how universal the laws of political stupidity are, let's pick another country from the heart of Europe. The people of France did not avoid the follies of following the wrong leader either. During the French Revolution of 1789–92, they fought with fervor to abolish the monarchy, guillotining their last king, Louis XVI, and his wife, Marie Antoinette. After going through the painful process of moving from monarchy to republic, in as early as 1804, the French . . . crowned Napoleon Bonaparte as their emperor! They made the whole round trip back to where they had started a decade and a half earlier.

The emperor was in essence a despot, an autocrat, clearly more powerful than the king they had executed only several years past. The ironic stupidity of this historic event is best summarized by one of the old republicans still serving in the army, who was asked by the new emperor how he was enjoying the enthronement festivities. His brave answer was to the point: "Splendid, Your Highness! I just regret that those 300,000 guys who gave their life to prevent this ceremony are not with us here today to enjoy it!"[44]

Rallying Around the Leader

The phenomenon of rallying around a leader when a country is experiencing an emergency is truly spectacular. For reasons we will discuss in the "Why?" section, we humans tend to look up to a person with authority and power. It doesn't matter that such a person might have very little, or nothing, to admire or offer. We just rally around *any* leader in place at the time, regardless of who it is.

There are well-documented examples of sophisticated, prosperous societies rallying around leaders who brought them all to misery.

A most striking example of such a phenomenon is German society's reaction to the attempted assassination of Adolf Hitler on July 20, 1944. Just to give some context, in the second half of July 1944, it was clear to the average German civilian that the war was lost. The Allies had landed in Normandy and defeated the Wehrmacht there; the Red Army in the East had just annihilated the Army Group Center, the largest fighting force on the Eastern Front; and German cities were already lying in ruins, reduced to ashes by constant bombardment by American and British air forces. Food was scarce, most of the men were serving in the military, and news of horrific losses of millions of soldiers were spreading among society.

In those circumstances, with full knowledge of who had started the war and gotten them into this whole situation, the overwhelming response to the news that Hitler had survived the assassination attempt was ... a sigh of relief. Yes, you read it right. Ordinary Germans were happy to see Hitler survive.

According to credible security service reports and censors, the prevailing mood in Germany after the failed assassination attempt was "sudden dismay, emotional shock, deep indignation and anger." Letters from ordinary soldiers confirmed the same reaction—soldiers reaffirming their "love for and loyalty toward the Führer":[45]

> Thank God he came through it again. You would not have thought such a crime possible. Among us there is the strongest indignation at this crime. Hopefully, the ringleaders will all be punished as bitterly as they deserve.
>
> *Letter home from Obergefreiter, Staff Marine-Flak-Abteilung 708*

> One is outraged by this act, which will only lead us deeper into misery.
>
> *Letter home by Richard WolffBoenish, engineer with the 116th Panzer Division*

Heinz Guderian, one of Germany's best generals, speaking freely *after* the war, reported:

> At that time, the people, the great proportion of the German people, still believed in Adolf Hitler. The people's hatred and contempt would have turned against the soldiers, who, in the midst of a struggle for national existence, had broken their

oath, murdered the head of the government, and left the storm-wracked ship of state without a captain at the helm.

So even this general, who saw Hitler destroy his country, still considered a Germany without Hitler as "a ship without a captain at the helm." Extraordinary!

Shouldn't just the opposite be true? Shouldn't the German people have been disappointed that the coup failed? Wouldn't Hitler's death have shortened the war and given German citizens a chance to end the hostilities and achieve peace faster?

Instead, their beloved leader led them through another eight pointless months of war, which cost probably around two to three million dead German citizens, several million wounded, and the complete ruin of their country.

Baffling.

So the next time you see a mediocre politician going up in the polls during a war or some other disaster, you know the real mechanism at work. Ratings always go up if you happen to be in office when your country faces an emergency. We rally around the leader and transfer onto them our hopes, pride, and dreams.

Even if this leader is terrible.

Choosing a Leader for the Wrong Reasons

One of the most interesting areas of human political stupidity is how we select our leaders. One would think that the most important qualities in a political leader would be (a) competence (ability to get stuff done), and (b) concern for others' welfare (looking after our interests).

It seems that this is not what people care about at all.

First of all, across the world, we elect people into office based on their *sales skills* rather than *management competence*. We love leaders who have charisma, charm, and likability. But somebody who is a phenomenal speaker, can connect with the room, and make everyone feel special is not necessarily a good administrator. The traits required to competently run the country include attention to detail, intellectual depth, thoroughness, domain expertise, organizational skills, and patience. Most great salespeople are not known for their attention to detail or thoroughness. For them, facts very often just get in the way of delivering a good story.

Therefore, there is an inherent flaw in how we choose our leaders: We care about the skills that are important during the six months that an election campaign lasts, rather than the skills that are important for running the country for the next four or five years. We end up being managed by "inspiring" personalities who lack the skills and knowledge to manage things efficiently.

Second, one would think that if the politician you voted for does something against your economic interest, you would no longer like them. Nonsense! We regularly vote for people who do bad things to us.

Donald Trump is an excellent illustration of both of these rules. During his first presidency, he ran the country in the most hectic, haphazard way, chaotically firing and hiring various officials, leaving ambassador positions unfilled, and failing to follow up on important topics or deal with long-term problems. However, he is a great showman. He talks with humor and swagger, has excellent punchlines, and uses simple language. He has no problem omitting facts or even outright lying if it makes a good story. And people love good stories....

On the subject of hurting your own economic interests, a big part of Trump's power base is relatively undereducated, not well-to-do, and white. This demographic would typically benefit a lot from stronger social safety net and higher taxation of the rich. However, Donald Trump defied them. He orchestrated one of the largest transfers of wealth in US history by enacting the Tax Cuts and Jobs Act in 2017, which lowered taxes for the richest people in the US by approximately $1.5 trillion. Namely, it eliminated the federal estate tax, which kicks in only on estates worth more than $5.5 million. He also eliminated the alternative minimum tax, which benefits only households with incomes of more than $200,000. He also lowered the corporate tax rate to 20%, which again overwhelmingly benefits the rich.[46] So this legislation effectively lowered the tax rate for the richest 0.1% of society by 2.5%, to 23%, versus 24.2% for the lower 50% of society.

What did Trump's voter base do? Probably 90% of Trump voters didn't directly benefit from this act, but they still applauded the legislation and loved him for it!

So Donald Trump's power base was happy when he gave tax breaks to... other people. This phenomenon is not specifically American. Countries as diverse as Turkey and Zimbabwe follow the same principle.

Playing the Rigged Game

Meet the Duck and the Earmuff. These are the nicknames for Ohio's 4th congressional district and Illinois's 4th congressional district.

These congressional districts are in two serious, important states. Don't those shapes seem highly arbitrary? Very strange, as if someone was drawing them to optimize for something other than administrative efficiency. If you think something looks fishy, your intuition is spot on! That's *exactly* what's going on here—gerrymandering at its best. When you cannot win in a district, simply change the shape of the district.

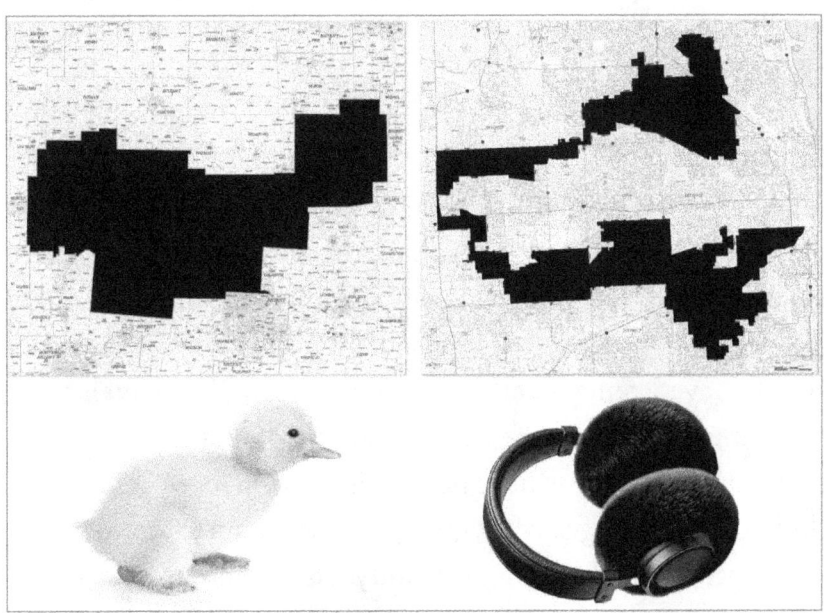

FIGURE 9. Ohio's and Illinois's 4th congressional districts[47]

Gerrymandering is defined as *"political manipulation of electoral district boundaries with the intent of creating an undue advantage for a party, group, or socioeconomic class within the constituency."*[48] The process was named after Elbridge Gerry, governor of Massachusetts, who first invented gerrymandering by creating, in 1812, a district in the shape of a deformed salamander.

The sad thing is that this trick is not a thing of the past—it is still being done today across the whole country, by both Democrats and Republicans. This is how the United States of America, the most powerful democracy in the world, operates today. Doesn't this look shameful and pathetic? Isn't the election process supposed to be an absolute pillar of a democracy? Yet the election game is unfair from the beginning.

If we play with the definition of election territories, we are undermining faith in democracy itself. Isn't it an affront to our intelligence and dignity that election districts are so ridiculous? Why are we not fixing it?

Going "Woke"

Liberalism and humanism have been the cornerstone philosophies powering our civilizational progress for centuries. Their key beliefs are that (a) we are equal and have individual rights, (b) the governed need to consent to being governed, (c) we should have agency over our own lives, and (c) the well-being of a human should be the starting point for all other judgments. These humanist ideas have helped us create a more equal world through abolishing slavery, giving voting rights to women, winning acceptance for homosexuality, advancing animal rights, and many other achievements.

However, can these well-intentioned ideologies lead to negative consequences?

It turns out humanistic vehicles of progress can be all-too-easily hijacked to bring about effects *opposite* to what is intended. It is fascinating that the *same* successful ideology that brought us so many good things can lead us toward the minefield of "woke" philosophy.

"Woke" is a catch-all phrase that incorporates the concepts of political correctness, hypersensitivity, and far-left ideals. In contemporary America, it is associated with the progressive wing of the Democratic Party. In political terms, "woke" philosophy is criticized by its opponents for preventing any meaningful public discourse, because anything that is said can be taken as offensive by this hypersensitive group. The proponents of "wokeness" point out that there is a great deal of inequality in our society, and many disadvantaged groups are overlooked, unprotected, or disrespected.

Instead of analyzing "woke" philosophy from a political perspective, which would make it very ... hmmm ... "political," let's try to distance ourselves for a moment. Let's take a step back and get a broader perspective by looking at its less political aspects.

First, let's zoom into the trend of the ESG movement, which underpins the "woke" philosophy. ESG stands for Environment, Social, and Governance (rules). These rules are meant to improve the world beyond pure financial gain, which is the primary objective of the corporate sector. ESG features prominently on the banners of "wokeism." A lot of companies have adopted such rules to prove that they are "doing something in ESG."

Unfortunately, those well-intentioned initiatives are often inspired by corporate top-down ideology and aim to maximize PR impact rather than solve real problems. Rarely do big corporations from rich countries quietly give away money to fund great, useful initiatives. They typically try to build something of their own that is related to their brand, which increases their media coverage.

Take TOMS shoes as an example. TOMS is a classic Californian "woke" company. Since 2006, it has achieved a huge following and commercial success by pioneering a model whereby for each pair of shoes purchased in a developed country, the company gives a free pair of shoes to a person in a developing country. This seems great, doesn't it?

Well, it worked very well for TOMS from a PR perspective, catapulting it to financial success with a current annual revenue of around $300 million. However, this well-intentioned initiative is actually doing more harm than good. Why? Because distribution of free shoes in developing countries is killing independent, local shoemakers. The corporate PR initiative creates unemployment and destroys the local manufacturing base. It reinforces the circle of poverty.

It doesn't mean that all ESG is "fake"—not at all, there are tons of good initiatives. But too often this term is a cushy hiding place for stupidity and ineffectiveness. In the contemporary world, it is hard to distinguish real generosity from "ESG-dressed" publicity stunts.

Let's not get discouraged, though! There are still examples of truly remarkable, deep, unconditional generosity in the style of Yvon Chouinard, the founder of clothing brand Patagonia, who donated all of his shares in the company to fight climate change. But to win broad public support, the ESG world must still cleanse itself of the "publicity stunters."

Another example of "wokeism" gone wrong is opposition to drug testing on animals. The concept of not harming animals is a natural, direct extension of a beautiful principle of humanism. The well-intentioned idea of banning cruelty to animals seems sound. However, the implementation of this approach ends up hurting the very foundation of humanism, which is ... humans.

Drug testing on animals reduces the risks of new therapies by observing how a living organism responds to treatment. This ensures that fewer people die in the drug development process.

However, there are strong organizations and strong public support advocating for banning testing of *any* pharmacological drug or medical device on animals. This means that in case of another deadly global pandemic similar to COVID-19, the bubonic plague, or Ebola, extreme animal rights activists would prefer not to test any potential medications on animals. In summary, they tacitly accept that we will lose the lives of (a) humans who will replace the proverbial guinea pig in the drug development process, and (b) humans who will not get the right medicine on time, due to delays in drug development that are caused by the prohibition on observing the effects of those drugs on mammalian organisms.

Isn't this a bit harsh and too "woke"? This is a perfect example of how hypersensitivity ends up hurting humans. Isn't it better to sacrifice a few hundred mice or guinea pigs to prevent the death of thousands of people? Well, this is not clear anymore in our world.

It is unsettling how positive, well-intentioned ideologies that have worked in the past can be turned against us over time. We need to be incredibly vigilant to maintain balance.

TECHNOLOGICAL STUPIDITY

Gene editing is a hell of a process.

In a shiny lab, you take an enzyme called Cas9, which has the ability to cut DNA. You pair it with a molecule of guide RNA, which can zero in on a specific sequence out of more than 20,000 human genes. Then you combine the two, creating a targeted pair of scissors that you can send to cut the DNA wherever you want. The guide RNA attaches itself to the target area you've chosen and then initiates the unwinding of the double helix, and Cas9 cuts the DNA at this location. Then you introduce a DNA template, which you've created beforehand, that has the characteristics you desire. Through a process called homology-directed repair, the cell repairs the break in the DNA string, including the DNA template you added. Voilà! You have just amended the DNA of a living organism!

What a feat of bioengineering! Isn't it amazing that we can do things like that? We literally redesign life! Such procedures are now performed routinely in hundreds of labs across the world by thousands of people. In 2023, you could order edited gene sequences from Chinese vendors for $0.33 a pair.[49] This means you can print yourself a DNA sequence, a precursor to life, for less than the price of chewing gum.

It seems that we've achieved scientific nirvana! We can do things of unprecedented complexity for pennies!

However, despite those marvels of technology that give us almost godlike powers, society as a whole is surprisingly stupid with technology. We do not understand it, and we do not know how to use it. Technological advancements have often gotten ahead of our savanna-optimized brains.

Technology Blind Spots

First, let's look at examples of when we have technology, but we don't use it. Besides fire, what's one of the most important inventions that humans ever made?

The wheel.

Yes, a circular thing that can be used to power transport, food processing, manufacturing, and most industrial machinery. The importance of this discovery cannot be overestimated. The wheel was invented around 4500 BCE in Mesopotamia (modern-day Iraq). However, many cultures in different areas of the world did not adopt its use until 1500 CE or later, more than 6,000 years after its invention!

Let's take the Aztecs in the 16th century. Before 1519, when Spanish conquistador Hernán Cortés invaded what is today Mexico, Aztec civilization was blooming. Their empire stretched over most of central and southern Mexico and had over 25 million inhabitants, as well as splendid cities such as Tenochtitlan. At its peak, the city had an estimated 300,000 inhabitants, double the size of Paris or five times the size of London during the same period!

The Aztec calendar was more precise than Europe's; universal education was mandatory between ages 12 and 15 (regardless of social status, which was unheard of in Europe at that time); they built aqueducts to provide fresh water to their cities and causeways up to 45 feet wide to sustain transport throughout the empire. (For comparison, European roads at that time were muddy, narrow, pathetically unimpressive, and typically unusable in bad weather.)

But the Aztecs had no wheels.

Actually, they did invent wheels, but they used them only as ... toys.

Aztec children could *play* with wheels for hours on end. But as adults, they never applied them in practice to power their transport or industry.

FIGURE 10. Aztec toy on wheels
Good for children, but nobody thought of using it at scale.

Such incredible technological blind spots are surprisingly widespread throughout history.

Did you know that the ancient Greeks and Romans were already experimenting with steam engines?

In the first century BCE, Hero of Alexandria described a simple radial steam engine, called an aeolipile, that was powered by boiling water. Pipes delivered steam to a cylindrical vessel through two nozzles facing in opposite directions, thus producing thrust and causing the vessel to spin on its axis.

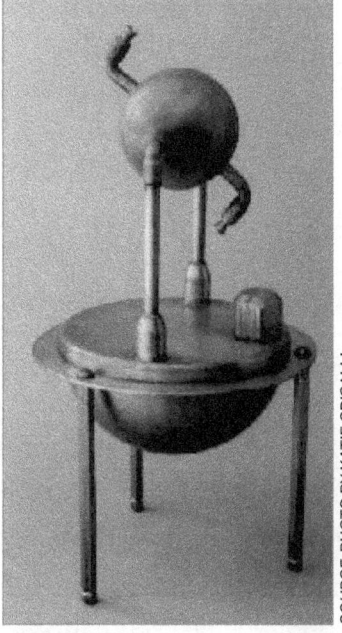

FIGURE 11. Contemporary replica of an aeolipile

Roman engineer Vitruvius described this machine in his written work called *De architectura* around the time Jesus Christ was born.

Isn't it fascinating? But for over 1,500 years, we ignored this major invention!

Imagine what our civilization today would look like if we had mastered the power of the steam engine around 0 CE rather than in the 18th century. If only there had been one determined senator or science-inclined emperor who provided sufficient funding and support! The Romans could have used this technology to power their large Mediterranean fleet and their sawmills. Maybe they could even have created steam-powered automobiles, given the impressive road network in ancient Rome! Many related discoveries that could have acted as a catalyst to enable steam engine technology were already in place by that time. For example, Romans were already mining coal to smelt iron in the second century BCE.

Stories of abandoned or underappreciated discoveries that were never put to good use on a large scale are not limited to old times. We continue to have a blind spot for technology in modern times too!

Take the example of ... the internet. It was first developed by the Advanced Research Projects Agency in 1969. However, we really deployed it only in the late 1980s and early 1990s.

Even such obvious things like rollers on baggage were only added in the 1990s! Before that, we were carrying heavy loads through airports and train stations, huffing and puffing! This was just a few decades ago, when we've had all the technology and opportunity to power such an invention for centuries.

FIGURE 12. Roller bag—a recent invention[50]

Lack of (or Too Much) Trust in Technology

We humans have an ambivalent relationship with technology. We can jump from not trusting it at all to trusting it 100% in even the most absurd circumstances!

In 1922, two brilliant engineers, Leo Young and Hoyt Taylor, invented modern naval radar. They were eager to equip the US Navy with this brilliant invention, which would allow us to detect enemy ships without line of sight, despite fog and rain, or during the night. However, the Navy ignored their proposal. In 1930, these same two men established that the same principle could be used to detect *aircraft*. They described their breakthrough discovery to the US military and requested $5,000 in funding to develop a workable field technology. The military rejected that proposal, as well, mentioning as one of the key reasons: "The time needed to see results might well exceed two to three years." As a result, the Japanese attack on Pearl Harbor in December 1941 was a complete surprise for the US Navy. Radar had not yet been fully deployed and tested in Hawaii because the Navy wasted 10 precious years not trusting a brilliant technology.[51]

On the other end of the spectrum, we sometimes put enormous trust in technology in our daily lives. Can you believe that in 2012, three Japanese tourists in Australia drove straight into the ocean because … their GPS told them to (see Figure 13)?

FIGURE 13. 100% trust in technology[52]

I would love to have been on that cruise liner to watch them do it. This is not an isolated case. Almost all of us have embarrassing stories of following GPS to a strange, completely illogical site and discovering that something is off. So let's not laugh at those three poor students who drove their rented Hyundai into Moreton Bay. We are not that different. We are all brothers and sisters in stupidity.

The Knowledge Illusion

Steven Sloman and Philip Fernbach coined the term the *knowledge illusion* to describe our unjustified perception that we understand the technology around us. The reality is that we do not. We cannot explain the simplest technological tools and processes we use every day.

In a famous experiment, the scientists asked a group of respondents whether they understood how a zipper (invented in 1893) works. Of course, everyone claimed they understood it well, but when asked to describe the process in detail, they sheepishly admitted they did not know. The same applies to most of the other technologies we use daily: the microprocessor in your laptop, your microwave, your mobile phone, air conditioning, flight, GPS, and so on.

We arrogantly believe we are the masters of technology, but in reality we have a limited understanding of it and rely almost entirely on other people who are experts in their respective fields. And even those experts do not have a full understanding of their disciplines. It takes thousands of people with extremely deep, siloed knowledge to put together complex technological products such as cars or computers.

Overuse of Technology

While on one hand, we are often skeptical about technology, when it is readily available, we also are guilty of the opposite—overusing it. Unfortunately, usually when it is completely not justified.

We look at our smartphones on average 80–150 times a day, which makes us incredibly inefficient and unproductive. Our ability to stay focused goes down because we are constantly interrupted by interesting notifications, our ability to think shrinks because we can look up everything online, our reliance on technology grows because we have to do less and less for ourselves. There are apps now that can do almost anything.

How many of us look at the weather app before leaving home instead of opening the window and seeing for ourselves? How many of us use a calculator for the simplest calculations because we are too tired to do them ourselves in our head? Here are a few real-life examples of taking the "an app for everything" culture to the extreme:

- Is it dark outside? by Dirk Malorny (4.4 stars on the Apple App Store) tells you whether it is dark outside.
- Kissing Test Booth by Damien Bernal (2.9 stars on the Apple App Store) tells you whether you are a good kisser by asking you to kiss your iPad screen.
- BeerFun by Ales Horak (4.7 stars on the Apple App Store) tell you how many beers you have drunk—if you tap your phone every time you have a beer.

These are real apps, used by real people—sometimes with good ratings and thousands of users.

Does Technology Kill Sex?

One area of human life that seems shielded from technology is our sexual life. One would think that sex is mostly about our bodies, primal instincts, and passion. Well, a shocking 2018 survey found that about 10% of Americans check their phones ... *during sex!*[53]

If that statistic has not shocked you, the graph in Figure 14 below will.

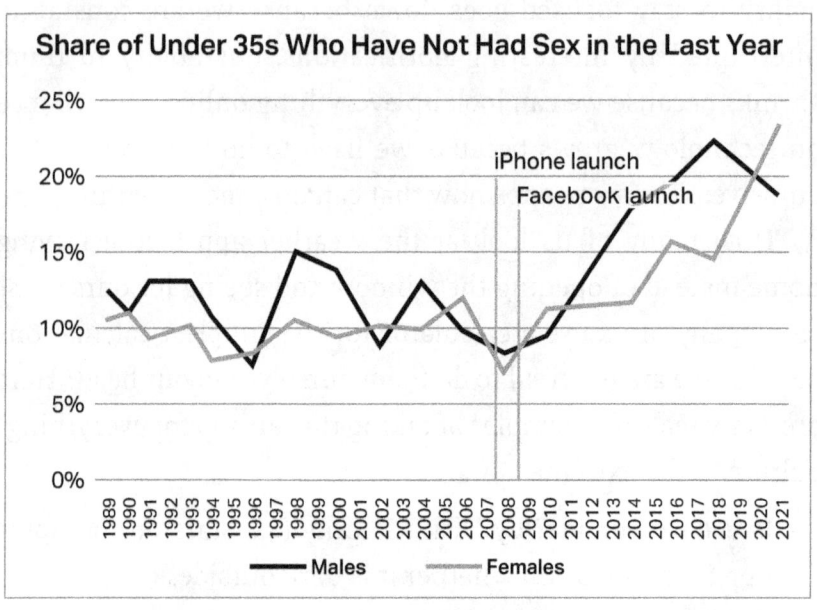

FIGURE 14. Rise in sexual abstinence[54]

It shows the percentage of people below 35 in the US who have not had sex in the last 12 months. Nearly one-fourth of men and women are going sexless! We are not talking about teenagers who have not had sex yet or senior citizens who no longer can. We are talking about people at the peak of their sexual needs.

This ratio has been climbing steadily since 2007–2008. Did anything major happen in 2007–2008? Actually, several important things happened at this time: The iPhone was launched (in June 2007) and Facebook was born (in the third quarter of 2008). Since then, we have started looking more at our smartphones than at each other.

What's more, in 2007 two dominant free porn websites were launched: Pornhub and XVideos. Pornhub pioneered revolutionary free access, with a freemium model that didn't require users to provide credit card details, thereby massively increasing reach. It became the largest pornographic website in the world—by May 2021, Pornhub had become the 8th-most-visited global website (!); in the same league as Wikipedia and Reddit and ahead of Twitter. XVideos was 12th, just behind eBay.[55]

Through technology, we made human interactions easier, safer, and less risky and eliminated the risk of rejection. You can now stay in touch with friends and be "social" from the comfort of your home via a smartphone. When nature calls for sex, it is far easier to find satisfaction and release with free porn, rather than another human being. Thus, technology has helped replace sex for a big portion of society!

Okay, there are a few other trends (such as a declining share of married people) driving this development, as well, but in my humble opinion, technology is a huge contributing factor here.

Can We Be Trusted to Handle Technology?

The unprecedented technological progress of the last century has given us powers we had never dreamed of.

Until 1945, we were able to cause destruction only in a very localized way. The most powerful weapons of the 1940s were equivalent to detonating 0.02 kilotons of TNT. This was deadly but ensured only local destruction within a few hundred meters of the blast area.

After 1945, however, we entered a completely new era. As a result of the Manhattan Project, one of the most complex, scientific, and technologically challenging projects ever completed, the US developed the atomic bomb (A-bomb), which had a thousand times more destructive power than the most potent bomb used during World War II. The magnitude of its power can be best visualized through a graphic (see Figure 15).

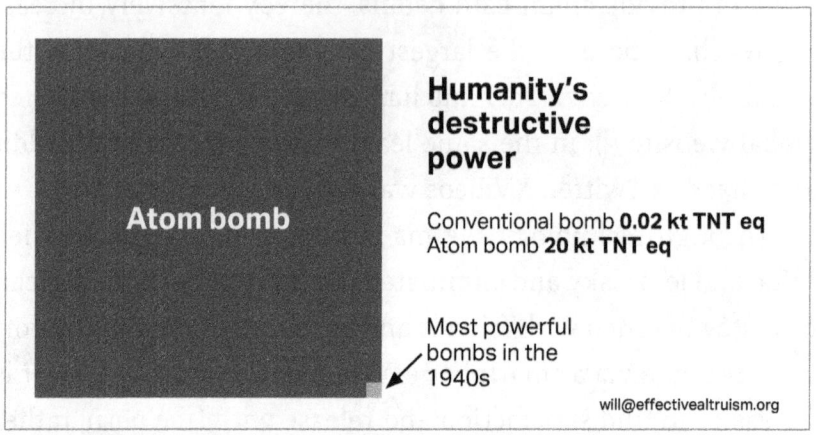

FIGURE 15. The destructive power of the atom bomb[56]

Several countries followed suit, and today nine nation-states command nuclear weapons, and several others are now working on developing them.

However, if the A-bomb gave us stunning destructive power, from 1952 we have had access to a truly godlike power of destruction. Since that time, we have mastered the technology to manufacture the *hydrogen* bomb (H-bomb, or thermonuclear bomb)—with a destructive power about a thousand times greater than the A-bomb.

The H-bomb's power is apocalyptic. It can engulf whole provinces, regions, or countries. The arsenal of H-bombs belonging to the US or Russia has the full capability to terminate the human race.

As we have such power, evaluating the risk of our extinction because of human-made, technology-derived reasons is now justified. Several academics (e.g., Toby Ord from Oxford

University) have started calculating such risks, and their numbers are ... chilling. Surprisingly, nuclear bombs are not even listed as the technology that is most likely to kill us. See the chart in Figure 17 below.

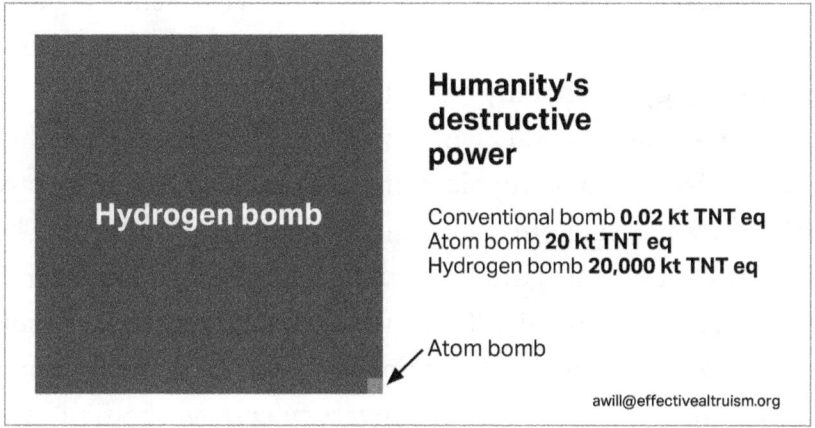

FIGURE 16. Hydrogen bomb power[57]

Existential catastrophe via	Chance within the next 100 years
Asteroid or comet impact	~ 1 in 1,000,000
Supervolcanic eruption	~ 1 in 10,000
Stellar explosion	~ 1 in 1,000,000,000
Total natural risk	**~ 1 in 10,000**
Nuclear war	~ 1 in 1,000
Climate change	~ 1 in 1,000
Other environmental damage	~ 1 in 1,000
'Naturally' arising pandemics	~ 1 in 10,000
Engineered pandemics	~ 1 in 30
Unaligned artificial intelligence	~ 1 in 10
Unforeseen anthropogenic risks	~ 1 in 30
Other anthropogenic risks	~ 1 in 50
Total anthropogenic risk	**~ 1 in 6**
Total existential risk	**~ 1 in 6**

FIGURE 17. Risk of elimination of the human race by cause[58]

Of all the potential causes for the human race going extinct in the next 100 years, the usual suspects (such as supervolcanic eruption or asteroid impact) add up to a total probability of about 0.01% (1 in 10,000).

However, the probability of *human-caused* extinction is 1 in 6, according to Professor Ord. And all those risks relate to misuse of technology. It's literally like rolling dice....

Besides nuclear war (which we've just discussed), another risk we face is catastrophic climate change, which is mostly caused by the side effects of our technological progress. The COVID-19 pandemic gave us a foretaste of what an engineered epidemic could look like. Today we have a ubiquitous technology for printing viruses ... at home. In 2002, Eckard Wimmer and his team at Stony Brook University created the first artificially synthesized virus in a lab. Ever since, that same technology has only gotten exponentially better, cheaper, and more available. It is possible to design, sequence, and create in your basement a live form that can be harmful to humans. As humanity, we do not yet have robust global procedures to prevent bad actors from creating viruses and unleashing them onto the general public.

However, the biggest danger to our existence might come from a seemingly benign cause—artificial intelligence (AI). So far, AI has been almost universally good for humanity—it powers voice recognition, huge language models such as OpenAI's GPT, AI art, autonomous driving, protein modeling, identification of cancers in imaging diagnostics, and much more. But what happens if—or *when*—we achieve so-called artificial general intelligence (AGI)? AGI is a point of singularity, a moment in time beyond which AI outpaces humans in almost all tasks and then starts improving itself by writing its own code. This means that AI will be able to upgrade itself in a very short period, decoupling from us and going to the next level. We will, in the meantime, stay in our biologically constrained, slow-changing bodies.

If at that point AI is no longer 100% aligned with humans, it might decide that we need to be exterminated. The most worrying part is that such misalignment might be completely unintentional. It might be a stupid slipup. Imagine a scenario in which AI optimizes for the well-being of the planet and decides that the human body mass creates unnecessary strain on Earth's ecosystem. If AI becomes all-powerful, running our electricity grid and nuclear power plants, overseeing food production and distribution—or worst of all, taking charge of our weapons systems—it might decide to kill us. The "science fiction" of 1984's *Terminator* might not be all that absurd today.

That's why scientists put AI causing the extinction of the human race as the highest-probability risk. Human stupidity in technology might cost us our very own existence.

ECONOMIC STUPIDITY

Misallocation of Resources

As a society, we can muster enormous resources. If every citizen of a large country contributes a small percentage of their income to a joint pool through taxation, massive resources suddenly become available. But with massive resources comes massive waste. Our societies excel at misallocating resources. Why? Because we can afford it.

If we lived in a small group of hunter-gatherers, or a family dependent on subsistence farming in a remote village, misallocation of resources would be rare, because any mistake could have grave consequences—including hunger or starvation. It would be crystal clear who is responsible for any wasted resources. Conversely, if a whole society wastes resources, the consequences are shouldered by many, and responsibility vanishes because of distance and time.

The concept of waste really annoys my economist soul. Every day, I see the suffering caused by a lack of basic resources—resources that are being squandered somewhere else. So let's start by zooming into a state and city famous for their ability to misallocate resources: California and San Francisco.

San Francisco has one of the highest concentrations of people with PhD degrees, patent holders, millionaires, and billionaires in the world. San Franciscans pay a tremendous amount of taxes to city and state coffers, much of which is wasted due to the city's and state's legendary incompetence in handling money.

The California legal system, in particular, wastes for seemingly no reason. For example, there is a special standard enacted for those who face the death penalty. Citizens sentenced to capital punishment (the death penalty) in California receive *additional* legal support, to a much higher standard and at a much greater cost than, for example, the legal support granted to those facing "only" a lifetime in prison. This seems like a rational call—it makes sense to be absolutely certain before sending someone to their death. But California has not executed any prisoners since 2006. This means that, for nearly 20 years, Californians have been paying for incremental legal costs totaling about $1 billion for their death row inmates. Those costs are completely unnecessary as, in practice, the highest level of punishment *is* a lifetime sentence, which does not incur all these double legal costs. *So why throw this money away?* Can't we better use it to help victims of crime or to prevent future crime? How many homeless people could we help get off the streets for $1 billion? Wouldn't it be more rational to formally abolish capital punishment in California and spend the saved money on fighting homelessness, which actually drives a lot of violence?

It's not only the legal system in California that's wasteful. Law enforcement suffers from the same malady. In San Francisco, I regularly see *four* police officers talking to one homeless person. Why are four people needed to respond to this situation? Perhaps several police snipers on the roof and a helicopter would be handy too.

A good example of the misallocation of resources by the San Francisco Police Department (SFPD) was a small, peaceful demonstration of Armenian people on the Golden Gate Bridge in protest against the Nagorno-Karabakh War in 2020. There were probably around 50 people demonstrating; they behaved responsibly and didn't violate any traffic laws. They were simply walking up and down, with banners calling for a stop to the hostilities, on the pavement reserved for pedestrians on the Golden Gate Bridge. Quite a normal civic action when you want to draw attention to something. The police response, though, was overwhelming. An endless line of police cars soon blocked one lane of a 1.7-mile bridge! For every protestor, there were several cops on hand.

How, and why, did the SFPD muster the resources to put more police officers on the bridge than people actually demonstrating? Why did they block an entire lane of traffic? Why weren't those police officers across the Bay in Oakland, where, on average, more than two people are killed each week? Well, because it is far easier, safer, and more newsworthy to organize a big demonstration of power on the Golden Gate Bridge than to go into the streets of Oakland and prevent crime in gang-infested areas.

The way we allocate resources for the pursuit of justice is completely ridiculous. As a society, we are incredibly selective about justice. We have a nearly medieval system of enforcing the law, even in advanced societies. We spend enormous resources on pursuing some forms of criminal activity but very few resources chasing others. Worse, those proportions are completely unrelated to the social costs of those crimes to the modern world.

Let's take robbery. In 2004, the total cost of all robberies in the United States was $525 million. Police dedicated huge resources to fighting this issue. However, in the same year, employee theft and fraud in the workplace cost around $600 billion. More than 100 times higher! Nonetheless, the police and judicial system dedicate minimal resources to finding the perpetrators of white-collar fraud and employee theft.

The US criminal system excels at prosecuting a person as a "sex offender" who, while coming back in the middle of the night from a party after a few drinks, pisses in a bush in the vicinity of a school. (A real story—this is what it takes to be a "sex offender" with a public record in the US.) It is not good, however, at chasing educated, rich dudes who do insider trading at an investment bank, steal money from their company, or refuse to pay their contractors.

Many US citizens receive several calls or messages every week from people attempting to commit fraud. Isn't it surprising that the police do not chase those criminals? It is totally possible to find the people behind those scams—you *can* follow the trail of money and arrest them at the end, even working with the police in a different country, if need be. The US government has managed to make almost every country in the world report on American citizens living there for tax purposes (through mandatory submission of a Foreign Account Tax Compliance Act form). However, the US criminal system cannot force other countries to chase known criminals who rob their population. The US government doesn't care about this problem, although it costs thousands of people every year their life savings.

Even at the street-policing level, enforcement resources are allocated completely ineffectively, pretty much across the globe. London police, for example, allocate a police officer to stand in Hyde Park to ... give tickets for riding in the wrong lane on a bike. There are multiple lanes in this glamorous park, some of them eligible for bike riding, some of them not. Is it a big deal if someone picks the wrong one for a few hundred yards, in the middle of the day, with perfect visibility and virtually no traffic? At the same time, in Hackney, gangs run the streets, walking through them with machetes, and the police do not have enough resources to intervene. Why not reallocate police officers from those low-impact, ineffective roles (monitoring wayward bicyclists and pedestrians) to places where their presence would truly make a difference—Tenderloin in San Francisco or Hackney in London, or even better, the electronic crime department?

We are an incredibly wasteful species. At every step, every moment, we devote resources carelessly because as a society we exert very poor control over them.

Two Thefts

Theft 1: In 2019, California finally figured out that, since 1996, Emma Carter-Alexander had been receiving her mother's retirement benefits, despite her mother being dead. Over 22 years, Emma cashed in about $300,000, money that was not hers. She spent it on food and medicines, as she had many chronic diseases and did not have proper medical insurance, which in other countries would have covered the cost of such medicines.

Theft 2: In 2021, Josh Smith filed a fraudulent yet very well-prepared filing for COVID relief funds available through the CARES Act. He reported multiple employees losing salaries, inflated various figures, and made up a lot of data. But given how superficial the review process was, he received a payout of $2 million in forgivable loans. Upon receipt, he left the country and never came back. Josh represents a fictitious person, of whom there were thousands who committed such fraud in 2020 and 2021, in the aftermath of the governmental COVID response. The US Department of Labor estimates that about $100 billion in funds was stolen by individuals and organized gangs in this way. Only about 1% was recovered.[59]

This was the biggest money heist in the history of humankind. But you've probably never heard of it! How is possible that we talk for weeks or months about some random jewelry store break-in, but a story about the biggest money heist in the history of humankind goes pretty much unnoticed? $100 billion is an unimaginable amount of money! Yet nobody cares; everybody seems fine with this loss.

Emma Carter-Alexander, meanwhile, was sentenced to 13 months in prison in a well-organized court process. While thousands of people like "Josh" go unpunished and live happily in the Caribbean.

This is misallocation of law enforcement resources at its best!

Killing the Economy with Society's Full Approval

Humans are known to be capable of stupidly destroying our own well-being and wealth, in full sight of everyone, in slow motion and on a massive scale. One of the Latin American countries I have lived in leads in this contest.

Argentina in 1914 was one of the 10 largest economies in the world. In the preceding 43 years, it recorded an average growth rate of 6% per annum, the highest in the world. Its income was 8% higher per capita than that of Germany, a rising European power. Buenos Aires was bustling with life, with glamorous buildings popping up, polo tournaments attracting the global elite, and tango taking over the world. While Europe was burning itself to the ground during two world wars, Argentina stood comfortably on the sidelines, living a safe, prosperous life on another continent and exporting its phenomenal beef to the hungry world.

By 1947, given the destruction of Europe, Argentina's gross domestic product (GDP) per capita stood at 209% that of Germany. Fast forward to 2002: Argentina was a bankrupt country with registered unemployment of 25%, half of society living in poverty, and GDP per capita at 35% that of Germany.[60] By 2024, 110 years after its peak, the situation in Argentina was even worse, with its income per capita at a mere 23% of Germany's and over 53% of the population living in poverty.[61]

What happened? Did Argentina have a gigantic, destructive war sometime after 1950? A horrible plague, a catastrophic earthquake? No, Argentinians simply ran their economy into the ground, in cold blood, year by year, inch by inch, with full success. Argentinian *society* made a series of terrible decisions, which put their country in a state of permanent crisis. Despite being the birthplace of several world-class economists, Argentina as a country never managed its economy rationally or logically. During the late 1940s and early 1950s, Argentinians overwhelmingly supported the government of Juan Perón, a skilled populist general, who started to destroy its economy. He was highly popular for most of his time in office, partly due to his wife, Eva Duerte, an actor better known as Evita. Perón's image was hugely boosted by Evita's popularity. She was the public face of an immense social spending program channeled through the Eva Perón Foundation, which at its peak had a budget equivalent to 1% of Argentina's GDP!

Their story is a fascinating example of how we humans cannot deal with cognitive dissonance. We struggle with understanding that someone can lift a lot of people out of poverty through social spending, big government projects, and handouts while simultaneously flirting with fascism and running the economy into the ground.

In the US, 1% of GDP was $290 billion in 2024. Imagine if Melania Trump could spend $290 billion *per year* on building schools, children's parks, and clinics, giving people home appliances, and paying for physician's visits. Wouldn't she become, overnight, the most loved person on Earth? I venture to say that anyone who gave away such amounts of money would become popular, and her husband would become popular, too, just by virtue of being her husband.

Unfortunately for Argentina, reality has an annoying tendency to catch up. By 1948, Juan Perón's policies had resulted in an astonishing evaporation of the Argentinian foreign trade surplus, the source of the country's strength. Argentina's economy was built on exports and had enjoyed tremendous tailwinds during World War II, when everyone was desperate to buy Argentinian agricultural products. Then came the bad years, with a drought in 1952, fiscal problems caused by excessive spending, and the quick exhaustion of national reserves, as well as demands from labor unions to keep increasing salaries and benefits despite economic hardship.

Perón was ousted in 1955 by a military coup, but his ideology of populism and nationalism, coupled with detachment from economics, still thrived. *Peronism*, as it became known, has produced 10 out of 14 presidents in Argentinian elections ever since. This included Isabel Perón (the *third* wife of Juan Perón), as well as Néstor Kirchner, who ran the country between 2003 and 2007.

Argentinians have a habit of electing the wives of former presidents, so in 2007 Cristina Fernández de Kirchner (wife of Néstor Kirchner) became the leader of peronism. She nationalized private pension funds as well as the country's largest energy company, fired the president of the Central Bank, heavily subsidized public services, and led her country into a sovereign debt default in 2014. But she is still rather popular.

So, while in 1914, Argentina on a per capita basis was 8% richer than Germany, by 2024 it was 77% poorer. In the meantime, Germany had two catastrophic world wars, survived the loss of its colonies in Africa and Asia, absorbed the 16 million people in the much poorer area of eastern Germany, and managed to integrate into its society millions of immigrants, who now constitute one-fifth of its population.

Argentina faced none of those headwinds, but it has continued on its path of gradual decline from economic superpower status to irrelevance. It chose to screw up its economy, year by year, by consistently electing outspoken, populist presidents who have run the country slowly but surely into ruin with bad economic decisions. Its leaders, meanwhile, enjoyed real public support and drank very good coffee. Only in 2024 did Argentinians out of desperation elect a new, libertarian president, Javier Milei, who has an ambitious program for fixing its economy.

A Modern Case of Economic Hara-Kiri

Studying Argentina as a case of economic stupidity might be uninspiring: Its decline has been long term, slow and gradual. Venezuela, however, provides a much more dramatic, time-compressed story. While it took Argentina more than 50 years to destroy its economy, Venezuela achieved it within 10 years. A truly spectacular case of economic hara-kiri.

In 1998, Venezuela was a moderately successful South American nation with a growing economy. Its oil sector was a key export-oriented industry, given that Venezuela is enormously endowed with oil deposits—it has more than any other country on Earth. In fact, Venezuela has more oil deposits than Russia, China, the US, and Iran combined. Venezuela also had a thriving non-oil sector with multiple industrial and processing players and a flourishing tourist industry.

However, in 1999, Venezuelans elected a populist president, Hugo Chávez, who quickly demolished their economy through a series of lunatic moves, with the full support of society. He started a program of massive government spending, expanding subsidies for food and energy to an absurd degree. While some of his poverty-reduction programs made sense, overall, the handouts became uncontrolled, and the economic policies destroyed any incentives for working, saving, or acting responsibly. The subsidies for basic utilities like water became ridiculous: For example, the cost of water for a three-bedroom house was about $0.03 monthly, which encouraged excessive use.[62] On top of that, despite the politically motivated decision to rapidly expand the water network to poorer areas (which in itself is a noble idea), no work was done on upgrading the underlying infrastructure. This resulted in water shortages in Caracas in 2005.

Oil, meanwhile, was sold domestically for $0.05 per gallon (1 gallon = 3.8 liters).[63] Given a very lax monetary policy, inflation grew rapidly. In order to keep control over foreign exchange, in 2003 Chávez created a compulsory currency exchange board, which required all exporters to sell their hard currency proceeds to the government. The difference between the official government rate and the actual market rate was exorbitant, often by a factor of more than 100.

Uncontrolled socialism started to hurt the real economy as Chávez intentionally weakened the private, independent sector, which he saw as "full of capitalists and profiteers." He expropriated many private businesses and gave their assets to his cronies. He took farms from a number of large, efficient food producers and distributed them among poor farmers who did not have the knowledge to maintain the same rate of production.

Within a short time, private export businesses could no longer make ends meet because they had to buy imported goods abroad at real prices based on the US dollar but could only sell them for the worthless local currency. So private enterprises started throwing in the towel. Even companies that exclusively sold domestically became the "enemies of the people" if they tried to run a rational business (i.e., where costs are lower than revenues).

One large toy manufacturer was taken over by the state, its inventory seized and distributed *for free* among citizens "because it was selling its toys at too high prices." Didn't anybody imagine that giving away toys for free one year might seem cool, but then next year, and the year after, there would be no more toys?

The economic incompetence spread throughout the country—even food distribution chains collapsed. Private supermarkets could not compete with the newly created, gigantic, government-owned supermarket chain called Mercal, which had 16,000 locations and 85,000 employees. So many private supermarkets went out of business, creating bigger queues at state-owned shops, which rarely had enough food but always had big posters of Hugo Chávez inside!

Corruption was rampant.

All of this appalling incompetence was covered, in the beginning, by a flood of easy money from oil. Chávez was a lucky guy. By coincidence, he presided over a period of an incredible oil-price bonanza. Revenues from the sale of Venezuelan oil were bringing in billions of dollars in hard currency, which he was spending hand over fist. He funded inefficient social programs, subsidies, and foreign transfers to support friendly, "revolutionary" republics such as Cuba. On top of it all, billions were stolen by his cronies.

However, deep beneath the booming economy, the first cracks started to appear. Venezuela became like a drug addict, entirely dependent on one substance—oil. The share of government revenue derived from oil increased from 51% in 2000 to 89% in 2006.[64] Government spending grew from 28% to 40% of GDP between 2000 and 2013, all funded by oil. There was nothing else to support it.

Suddenly, the music stopped. In 2014, a dramatic decline in oil prices, from $140 a barrel to $30, ended the boom. Politically, Chávez could not say "The party is over" and stop the spending spree. Instead, he chose to ... print more money! This created another epic chapter of Venezuelan hara-kiri—the death spiral of hyperinflation. Whatever economic activity still existed was suddenly wiped out by an uncontrolled increase in prices caused by the newly printed money, which did not correspond with the amount of goods in the country. The economy virtually imploded. There was no point in doing anything in the local currency because it was not worth the paper it was printed on. Salaries were devaluing within days of being paid out. Workers' salaries allowed them to buy some food at the beginning of the month, but not at the end.

Trading in the dollar was forbidden. Inflation rapidly destroyed the buying power and savings of the middle and working class. People stopped showing up to work because their salaries were worthless. For example, nominally 400 maintenance teams were responsible for taking care of the water pipes in Caracas, but only 20 of them were really functioning because of a shortage of staff and of spare parts. Food became scarce: All those farms that were expropriated from private entrepreneurs were far less efficient under new ownership, which created a massive food shortage. In 2016, 74% of Venezuelans lost on average 8.7 kilograms (15 pounds) of weight, because of lack of food. By 2017, 93% of Venezuelans said they could not afford the food they needed.[65]

Murder rates tripled under Chávez, and kidnappings had increased by 20 times by 2011. By 2007, the country had stopped releasing its own crime statistics because they were so bad. Police investigated only 7% of kidnapping cases. By 2020, the country with the richest deposits of oil in the world regularly experienced electricity blackouts, sometimes for days at a time. People were regularly killing each other in the queues for food, and bystanders did nothing. The society's humanity and dignity entirely collapsed. Under all possible metrics, Venezuela was far worse off in 2023 than it was in 1998, when Chávez took over, but his positive legend is still alive!

So, the key question is, who bears the guilt for all of that? Well, it was Hugo Chávez and his successor, Nicolas Maduro, who implemented those policies—but they did it with the full support of Venezuelans. Yes, Chávez won, credibly, four elections: in 1998 with 56% of the vote, in 2001 with 60%, in 2007 with 63%, and in 2012 with 54%. International observers would confirm that those elections were mostly fair, or at least representative of the sentiment of society. In 2013, Nicolas Maduro won with a 1.5% margin on the platform of *chavismo*—Hugo Chávez's ideology and economic doctrine.

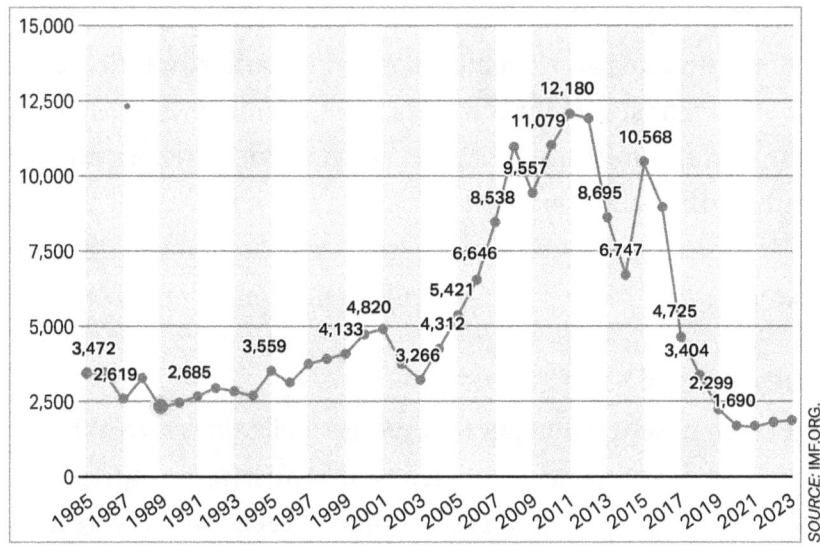

FIGURE 18. Economic hara-kiri: Venezuela's GDP per capita in US dollars

And then ... elections became irrelevant as Maduro de facto became a dictator and, ever since, has terrorized citizens into submission at gun point. So Venezuelans had five chances in the space of 15 years to stop the spread of the disease and change the course of its disastrous economic policies. But they didn't.

It is incredible how economically illiterate people can be. People will still vote you into power when you're killing the goose that's laying the golden eggs. They will still cheer you on when you put the last nibbles of this very goose on the table. Only when people miss their next meal do they realize something is wrong. Yet they still cannot make the connection between eating the goose laying the golden eggs and lack of food.

And the saddest thing? Other countries in South America look at this debacle and ... follow the same path. Chile recently elected a leftist president with an economic agenda similar to Chávez's. Colombia, Venezuela's next-door neighbor seeing a failed country from which millions of starving people are fleeing, also selected an extreme leftist with similar ambitions.

We might see in our lifetimes more examples of prosperous countries committing slow-motion hara-kiri. The economic stupidity of the people is limitless....

History clearly teaches us that people don't learn from history.

Economic Dependence

We often have the illusion that we are well taken care of by the countless institutions, agencies, and ministries of our powerful states, whose job is to protect their citizens. We devote huge resources to these sundry institutions that protect us from any potential danger: famine, disease, bad food, terrorism, intergalactic aliens. Nonetheless, these hordes of bureaucrats—who hold "very important" meetings at the highest levels of government, take home large salaries, and write long, "top-notch" memos—often have dramatic blind spots.

Even many rich and powerful countries have multiple economic "single points of failure" with the potential for catastrophic consequences. And *Homo idioticus*, predictably, is doing nothing about it. Here are some examples:

- **Russian oil.** The European Union (EU) was hopelessly dependent on Russian oil and gas. It was the war in Ukraine that unearthed this tragic dependency. Approximately 80% of Italian, 60% of German, and 90% of Hungarian gas supplies came from Russia. Many other countries were not much better off. The war in Ukraine caused a huge disruption and spike in prices, undermining whole sectors of the EU economy, such as the fertilizer and chemical industries.

- **Suez Canal.** As we found out in 2020, the Suez Canal is a massive chokepoint for the world economy. Just one simple mistake can derail global trade and lead to enormous delays in shipments, increasing costs substantially. This was highlighted in March 2021 when the *Ever Given*, a gigantic ship owned by a Taiwanese shipping company, got stuck in the canal for six days because of a human mistake. There are several other similar chokepoints, like the Panama Canal, the Bab el-Mandeb Strait, and the Strait of Malacca.
- **Taiwan Semiconductor Manufacturing Company (TSMC).** TSMC is probably the world's single most important potential point of failure. This company alone supplies more than 90% of the most advanced chips (microprocessors) that we are using everywhere in our lives, from phones and computers to cars and planes. Almost no advanced equipment can be manufactured without TSMC's chips. If there is ever a war over Taiwan, or if Taiwan is destroyed by an earthquake, the world's entire manufacturing system will come to a halt.
- **Ports on the US West Coast.** California and the western US are hopelessly dependent on the Port of Los Angeles, which processes around 60% of the sea freight coming to this part of the country from Asia. Any strike, act of sabotage, or damage due to earthquake or other reasons would create havoc for close to one-third of the US population.
- **Dependence on imported food.** Numerous countries are dramatically dependent on an external food supply. Any significant disruption of their trade links, supply routes, or port functionality could result in malnutrition or starvation of their population. Imported food as a part of overall consumption reaches a staggering 90% for small countries such

as Singapore[66], but is also uncomfortably high for vast economies such as the UK, with over 67 million people (where 42% of food is imported[67]), and even Japan, with a population of 125 million with the same dependence ratio[68]. When the logistics of international trade work smoothly, nobody thinks about food shortages, but such "once in a hundred years" shocks do happen. The UK temporarily rationed food in early 2023 because there were not enough vegetables following Brexit. Imagine what a war over Taiwan would do to Japan if China were to successfully establish a maritime blockade of the Nippon islands.

We are walking on very thin ice.

So it seems that those comfortable bureaucrats who sit in our most revered institutions, which are designed to protect us, either are not doing their jobs or are merely unable to convince people in power to deal with our strategic vulnerabilities. As a result, many countries could be severely disrupted even by a relatively minor event, such as a labor dispute or a terrorist attack. Even after regularly paying for those institutions for 50 years, they are unable to protect us against the risks they were initially created to avoid.

BEAUTIFUL STUPIDITY

At the end of this chapter, let's reflect on something different: Human stupidity can be beautiful! There's often a "human," romantic, and charming side to our willingness to act irrationally and produce suboptimal outcomes under circumstances in which rationality suggests we should behave otherwise. It is a part of who we are.

Let's start with the most dramatic, extreme version of acting illogically—or what we simply call acting "stupid." Multiple studies point to humans' innate biological resistance to killing. Even in self-defense, and even if it leads to our own death. This indeed seems to be a noble, evolutionarily useless feature. Excavations at Gettysburg, the site of the American Civil War's largest battle, reveal that 87% of the unearthed muskets were loaded; of those, 50% were loaded twice, and 25% were loaded 3–10 times. (This means that the muskets had multiple bullets in their barrels, which would prevent them from firing at all.) A staggering number of soldiers were "posturing," pretending they were firing at the enemy. In the midst of battle, where there was a lot of noise, smoke, and shouting, it was relatively easy to pretend to have fired a weapon (even simulating recoil) and then proceed again to loading the musket. That's why they were loaded more than once, but never *actually* fired.[69]

This tactic was not just due to old-fashioned 19th-century chivalry. During World War II, US Army historian S. L. A. Marshall interviewed soldiers coming from the front line and concluded that, again, only 15%–20% of them were actually firing at the enemy. Most of them fired purposefully above their enemies' heads or didn't fire at all.[70] One could say that this might be a display of American chivalry. Also, no. A similar phenomenon occurred among the ferocious fighters of Nazi Germany during World War II, exemplified by a German sniper who was taken prisoner—during the Normandy landings, he refused to shoot a British bagpiper who was going up and down the beach in full sight, playing music to rouse spirits.[71]

Doesn't it seem stupid to be in battle and refuse to use your weapon, especially when your enemy could kill you and, later perhaps, your family? It is totally irrational, but we humans are beautifully stupid about it.

From a biological and evolutionary point of view, nature favors those who prioritize their own safety over that of others. In Darwinian terms, the most rational behavior is to protect your own life and those of your offspring. Nature has optimized for it for millions of years. Our boldest, bravest, most selfless, predecessors were more likely to be eaten by lions in the savanna in our early days; or beaten to death by members of another tribe stealing your food during the early agricultural revolution; or killed by thugs in the filthy poor districts of the early industrialized world while trying to prevent the gang rape of a woman. Such fine specimens were more likely to pay the ultimate price for their bravery.

Still, humans often exhibit a completely illogical drive to help strangers, in spite of nature's brutal selection machine. From an individual point of view, it is stupid. Yet so beautiful.

On June 3, 2017, a lovely Saturday evening, London experienced a horrifying terrorist attack: a group of three radical Islamists deliberately drove into pedestrians on London Bridge, exited the car, and started a killing rampage, stabbing everyone in sight with long knives. The restaurants and pubs around London Bridge and nearby Borough Market were packed with people enjoying the start of the weekend: eating, having drinks, and laughing. The attackers descended on this unsuspecting crowd and stabbed indiscriminately while shouting "Allahu Akbar" and "This is for Allah," causing immediate chaos. Most people fled the scene screaming or barricaded themselves in pubs while victims were collapsing from their wounds and bleeding out. In only a few minutes, 56 people were injured or killed. However, the victim count would have been much higher if it hadn't been for a few heroes who stood up to the attackers, against all odds and disregarding any instincts for self-preservation.

Wayne Marques, a police officer armed only with a baton ("bobbies" in the UK do not carry firearms), saw a terrorist stabbing a woman and charged the attacker with his baton. However, the two other assailants converged on Wayne and hit him on the head. He lost vision in his right eye and now had a knife lodged in his leg. Horrified but determined, he resolved to fight as long as he could to give people time to escape until the armed police arrived.[72] An off-duty police officer, Charlie Guenigault, came to his aid and confronted the three attackers with his ... bare fists.[73] He was stabbed twice in the back and then, when he fell, three times again in the head.

Simultaneously, Ignacio Echeverría, a Spanish banker and lawyer who was skateboarding with friends at the time, noticed what was happening and attacked one of the terrorists with his skateboard to divert him from finishing off the police officers.

This bought time for a number of people to escape the scene. Ignacio bravely tried to hit another Islamist but was overwhelmed and stabbed in the back by another attacker.

Meanwhile, 28-year-old Kirsty Boden, a nurse enjoying a night out in Borough Market, seeing so many people with stab wounds, rushed to help.[74] She could have stayed out of the danger zone, as she had not been directly attacked. Instead, she ran *toward* the attackers to give first aid to the victims scattered over the area. She was assaulted and severely wounded. Several other members of the public demonstrated incredible courage confronting the terrorists, using anything they could to stop them, including a baking crate, a pole, and even a narwhal tusk from a fishmonger's wall.

The police arrived eight minutes later and shot dead all three criminals. Unfortunately, Ignacio, the brave lawyer-banker with the skateboard, and Kirsty, the courageous nurse, did not recover from their wounds. They paid the ultimate price for trying to protect others without regard to their own safety.

There are many, many similar stories, including heroic acts performed by firefighters and police officers at the World Trade Center, ordinary citizens saving strangers during major natural disasters, doctors and nurses going to Ebola-infected areas, medical staff going every day to hospitals to treat COVID patients, and on and on.

Have you ever thought about how famous human rights activists, investigative journalists, and political dissidents think? Those jobs are among the riskiest on the planet. In this role, by definition, you are going to upset someone powerful, which could lead to prosecution, legal difficulties, violence, or even death.

Yet across the world, thousands of selfless dissidents stand up to almighty states and powerful individuals in the hopeless fight for a better future. Take the example of Alexei Navalny, a Russian dissident and key domestic opponent of Vladimir Putin. Navalny, who made his name exposing corruption in the highest echelons of the Russian government, became overnight an "enemy of the state." He was thrown multiple times, with unscrupulous efficiency, into jail, where he was tortured, poisoned, beaten, and raped by inmates, with the tacit support of penitentiary personnel. He consciously endured all of that. Famously, after he'd been poisoned with the Novichok nerve agent in 2020, Navalny decided to leave the German clinic that saved him and go back to Russia. He knew what awaited him there—jail. He did it anyway. Because he felt it was the *right thing to do* and he wanted to set an example for his many other fellow Russians.

What irrational behavior! He constantly exposed himself to the ultimate risk, inviting pain and torture, making his own life a nightmare in the name of the greater good. (Navalny died in prison in February 2024, at 47, of "malnourishment.") This might not be so stupid, though, on a societal level. His sacrifice for the community, from a biological point of view, creates optionality for others in his community. Some of his followers might be inspired in the future to create a better, more democratic government that respects human rights.

This selfless instinct is not limited to a small group of elite intellectuals. Quite often whole societies exhibit this type of selfless behavior en masse. Take the example of Ukrainian men working in Poland at the time of the Russian invasion of Ukraine in 2022. Immediately after the invasion, millions of Ukrainian women and children left the country (mostly to go to Poland) in search of safety. Thousands of Ukrainian men already working in Poland went voluntarily in the opposite direction—to enlist in the army. They consciously gave up their physical safety, careers, and jobs, accepting the serious risk that they might be killed, for ideas of personal freedom and sovereignty. There are countless other such stories of silent heroes who oppose evil states and often pay the ultimate price.

Superficially, these acts of courage and kindness seem stupid. From a biological and Darwinian point of view—the *Homo economicus* perspective—it is totally irrational to follow in the path of these individuals. Their actions are not good for them or their families. But they make sense in the context of a group. Their actions are what change the world. These heroic people provide leadership and are inspirational examples to others.

Humans are a fascinating, illogical species.... Ultimately, we are not *Homo economicus*; we are *Homo idioticus*, which sometimes manifests itself in a most noble, beautiful form.

Trust in the (False) Story of Money

Another beautiful stupidity that characterizes *Homo idioticus* is trust in a handful of good stories that are abstract and objectively false. However, believing them makes us all better off. This is an incredible paradox: If we all believe in a certain story that is not really true, we can achieve more.

The most powerful of those stories is the story of money.

Money (banknotes, coins, gold, or your bank account number) in its physical form is not worth anything. You cannot eat it; it will not protect you from the cold or rain. Any person that has been in a disaster zone can confirm that people will not sell you water after an earthquake, or food during an armed conflict, or a pontoon when the city is flooding and the water level is nearing your roof, not even for a million dollars. If you get shipwrecked on an island with $100 million in your coffers, this will not help you survive either.

Money is a theoretical, abstract concept that lives only in our minds. Money is nothing more than an *account of a favor*. Let's discuss this concept in detail.

In the animal kingdom, there are a lot of examples of returning favors. This is how successful group-based species thrive. Apes help each other remove insects, red-winged blackbirds protect the nests of their neighbors in a tit-for-tat manner, even rats spend more time grooming other rats that have groomed them in the past. The reciprocity principle is deeply wired into many mammalian brains.

From the early stages of civilization, humans have been used to returning simple favors, such as sharing food with someone who has fed you before, taking care of the children of other adults who have taken care of your own children, or arming yourself and presenting a formidable front to aid your neighbor who once helped you repel thieves from your field. These were simple favors that created basic trust and bonds in society.

However, keeping a record of those favors proved exceedingly difficult: Is donating a chicken a fair return for a pair of warm woolen pants? How many times did my neighbor take care of my children last year? What about favors done for my son, which I haven't noticed? What if somebody who received a lot of favors died without paying them back? Should the deceased's family be responsible for that "favor debt," and who would know how much was due and to whom? Additionally, exchanging favors with each other created a barter problem.

Imagine that you are an exceptionally talented smith in the idyllic Celtic Gaul before the arrival of the Romans, and you make great horseshoes and excellent swords. You are organizing a wedding for your daughter and want some honey to impress the party guests. You go to Getafix, the local beekeeper, but he is an older chap with pacifist beliefs, so he does not need your sword, nor does he need horseshoes (as he annoyingly walks everywhere). What do you do then? Well, you have a huge headache. You go to Ambiorix, who makes great buckets, and beg him to give you some of his buckets, because you know that Boudica needs them to color the shoes that she makes. And your cunning plan is to exchange 10 horseshoes for 2 buckets in the hope that Getafix needs shoes, so that when you show up with a pair, he will give you some honey....

This takes a huge amount of time to arrange! What if, instead of walking around and trying to find out who will exchange what, you could merely exchange your horseshoes for anything you want? This is where the brilliant story of money started.

At some point, people agreed that there should be a unit of measurement for all the favors or work done for each other, and it should be something easy to count and store. Over the millennia, shells, pieces of metal, coins, and (later) paper have been used to fulfill that role. Now I have some physical objects, such as shells or coins, to show as proof of the favors I have done for my neighbors, elders, or other people in my community. And the more I do, the more objects I can expect in the future. Money, in other words, codified and accounted for favors that need to be returned.

In the past, I had to be nice to other people to get them to do things for me, as they would act only to reciprocate favors. Now I can walk into an ice cream shop and a total stranger will give me a vanilla cone with a smile, although I have never done anything nice for him. This is because I give that person a few dollars as a transferable "favor" from me. Then he can use this to pay rent or buy whatever he wants.

Believing the story that objects such as shells, coins, and banknotes have value is one of the greatest inventions of humankind. We invented a way of storing "favors" that could be redeemed in the future, regardless of the identity of the person we did the favor for, or their financial situation, or the weather. This greatly accelerated the development of civilizations, as humanity was able to waste less time on barter and know for sure who owed what to whom, resulting in more time and incentive to specialize. If I make even better swords, you make excellent buckets, and the chill Druid brings his delicious honey, I no longer have to be a jack-of-all-trades and waste two hours every day walking from one person to another to barter.

This is why those societies that were the earliest to adopt money advanced the quickest from a civilizational point of view. This is one of the reasons why eastern Europe's economic development fell behind that of western Europe during the late 18th century. It was slow to adopt money. Instead, it relied much longer on mandatory free farm work by peasants to take care of landlords' fields. Literally, quite an ancient way of exchanging favors. In western Europe, serfdom died out much earlier, replaced by landlords collecting rent in cash. This accelerated specialization saved people time, brought people to cities, and gave a further boost to the rise of industry.

That is all great—except that the money story is inherently fake, and from time to time, a war, a natural disaster, or an idiotic politician calls that story's bluff. On September 1, 1939, when Germany invaded Poland and started World War II, a lot of wealthy Polish citizens held government bonds, which they considered rock-solid assets. Four weeks later, those bonds were worthless, as the Polish independent state had been crushed by Nazi Germany and the Soviet Union. After the war, the best use of those pieces of paper ("the safest investment ever!") was probably as a wrap for sandwiches. The bonds were never bought back. "Favors" were not returned.

In 1923, Germany set an example of how fake the story of money can be. After its defeat in World War I, the country's economy was in shambles. The government figured out that by printing small amounts of extra money, it might cover a bit more of the urgent needs that crippled the so-called Weimar Republic. Before they knew it, the "small amounts" had transformed into a huge stream of printed Papiermarks. The result was dramatic—the currency's value dropped by up to 30% *a day*. People did not want to sell anything. Children were playing in the streets with huge stacks of money as toys. Suddenly, nobody believed that the money was worth anything, and everyone wanted to own real assets, from real estate to bikes, pigs, and cognac.

Even the most powerful economy of the 20th century had a major hiccup in the validity of *its* money story. On August 15, 1973, Nixon's government gave in to decades of financial pressure and announced that the US's celebrated dollar-to-gold parity would no longer be honored. This finished the illusion that the US dollar was backed up by gold bars. The dollar tumbled against other currencies by about 30%, and gold shot up from $284 per ounce in August 1973 to $974 in 1974 and to $2,367 in January 1980.

This story repeats itself again and again, with Hungry and Greece going through similar problems in the 1940s, Zimbabwe in the 2000s, Venezuela and Argentina in the 2010s, and so on.

The conclusion from these examples is that the story of money works only if *everyone* believes in it. In other words, there has to be trust in the system. Banknotes, coins, or digital bank account numbers will translate into sausage, a vacation, a car, or a house, when, and only when, I decide it does. Trust is critical in maintaining this valuable myth.

Therefore, the most successful countries have been nursing this trust story for ages, assuring incessantly that "such-and-such national bank" and "such-and-such currency" is strong and stable. And guess what? It worked.

It is not surprising that it has worked best in the countries with the highest levels of general trust. The story is so useful in governing human economic life that rich, developed countries bet their future on it, throwing the whole weight of institutions and personalities behind it. This, in turn, creates a positive feedback loop in the form of sustained economic growth. Note Figure 19 below, which shows the correlation between the wealth of nations (measured by GDP per capita) and the level of trust.

There is a strong positive correlation between the richest countries and the highest level of trust. The abstract story of money as a way of storing and accounting for future favors works.

Now, imagine what would happen if somebody with a magic wand created "favors" that nobody has performed yet and convinced people that they are real. Suddenly, these newly created favors would translate into people working extra hours, new building construction, additional roads, new workshops or factories. It is basically economic growth.

That is what central banks do. They "create" money, which means that—out of thin air—they create a fake set of favors that is then printed as US dollars or lent to the government. Then these imaginary dollars make real people do real things to get this newly printed paper. Brilliant, isn't it?

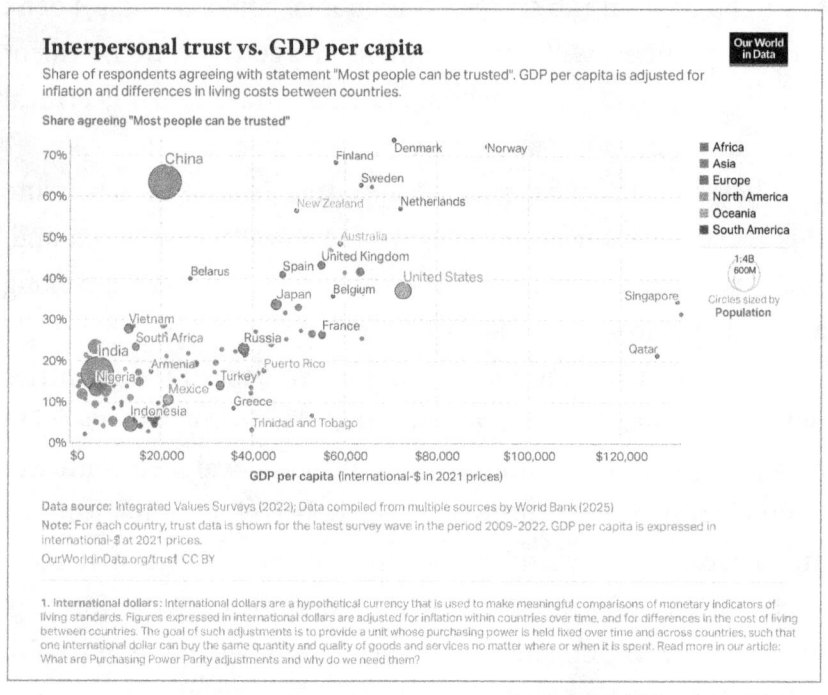

FIGURE 19. Trust v. GDP per capita[75]

This is exactly what happened during the COVID-19 pandemic. The US's central bank created an extra approximately $5 trillion, which allowed real favors to be done in America, such as giving benefits to unemployed people and stimulus checks to the general public. You could then take those favors and exchange them for pasta, alcohol, flour, and toilet paper (sometimes!). This artificial creation of goodwill between people prevented a severe recession.

As mentioned, this magic of creating money works only when everyone thinks the system is stable and reliable—that you will be able to exchange money for goods at roughly the same ratio as before. If governments are too greedy and start printing money too fast, inflation comes and eats the benefits of such actions or even makes things worse. However, if you do it very slowly, in a predictable way, wrapped in the complex terminology of institutions such as a central bank, everybody is happy. Regular citizens do not understand concepts such as seigniorage, M1 and M2 money supply, reverse repo rate, and mandatory deposit rate. All they see is the central bankers, old men with gray hair in perfectly cut suits, serious and professional, whom everyone else celebrates. This makes them feel safe. If, in recent memory, those men have not created a major shock (such as hyperinflation), the public, trusting the system, will assume they should go about their business as usual.

In human history, there are many examples of this mechanism being put to spectacular positive use. In the US, the expansionary policy of Franklin Delano Roosevelt in the 1930s managed to kick-start the American economy after the deepest recession in history by spending more money than the state was collecting. Essentially, he was creating favors to be repaid in the future. The public enthusiastically agreed, and the country started growing again.

Even more powerful is the story of China in the late 20th and early 21st centuries. Between 1990 and 2020, the Chinese economy grew from 15th to 2nd in the world, achieving a staggering 10% annual growth rate. Such a high, sustained growth rate is unheard of in the history of humankind. There were several reasons for this growth, but one of the major drivers was a massive expansion of public and private debt that financed a huge investment program. It was generally relatively productive: The extra favors and goodwill went to building roads, railroads, power plants, new factories, new apartments, and the like. Debt levels soared from 30% of GDP to 250% of GDP, and absolute debt levels increased from $50 billion to $3.5 trillion between 1990 and 2020. This was probably the best executed "myth of money" project in the history of the world. Trust in the system, which is exceedingly high in Chinese culture, helped a lot.

You might ask, then, *Why haven't other countries done it in such a spectacular way?* Well, some have, partially and not as well. For example, the US has played this trick to some extent from the 1930s to the 1960s, but most of Europe (and the US, at least partially) has spent the benefits of creating money on the least productive goal of all—war. The UK, the country that has the best historical data over an extended period of time, is a good example. The graph in Figure 20 below shows total government debt as a percentage of gross domestic product (GDP).

The national debt fluctuated from virtually nothing in the early 17th century to over 250% of GDP after World War II. The big spikes coincide with multiyear military conflicts: the Napoleonic Wars, World War I, and World War II. The same applies to most other European countries and partially to the US. Europe and the US have created the same tremendous amounts of money as China, but they wasted this incredible opportunity on ... fighting each other. Huge stockpiles of bombs, tanks, and machine guns do not contribute to economic growth *after* they are produced. Roads, dams, factories, bridges, skyscrapers, and power plants do.

During World War I, the UK spent about 1.5 years' worth of gross domestic product to equip about 9 million soldiers and sent 900,000 of them to death in battle. That was a disastrous use of the money that was created. On the other end, China used its newly created debt to build up its country on an unprecedented scale. In just three years (2011–13), China produced more cement than the US did during the entire 20th century. In 2019, one single city in China (Shenzhen) built more skyscrapers (15) than the whole of the United States (14).[76]

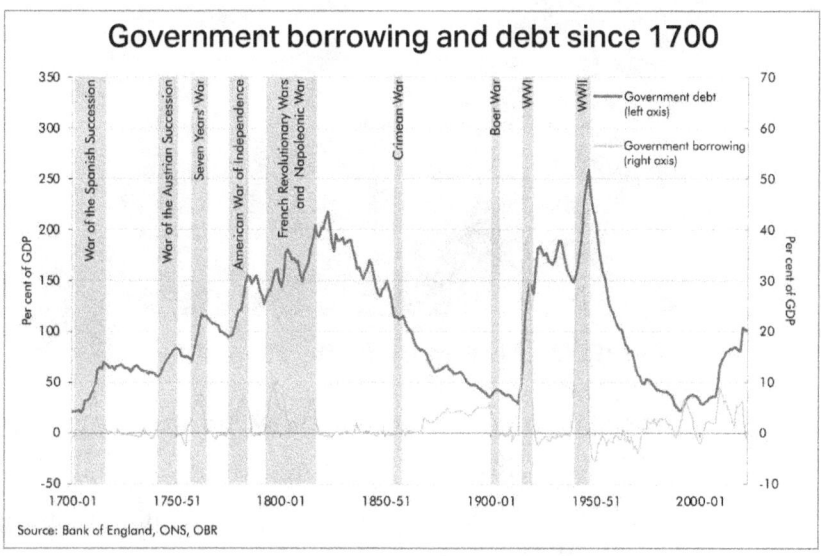

FIGURE 20. UK national debt as percentage of GDP[77]

So how does it look in aggregate? That's very interesting too. The world, as a whole, owes in total about 180% of its GDP. And who does the world owe this money to?

Martians? Aliens? No, all humans on Earth have collectively agreed on a fiction that in the future, they will be paid favors worth almost twice what they produce in a year.

This is how our belief in illusory stories can accelerate the growth of civilization. And this is yet another example of the beautiful and productive stupidity of *Homo idioticus*.

Art

Have a look at Figure 21, a photo of a famous art installation presented in the Tate Gallery in 1999 as one of the short-listed works for the prestigious Turner Prize.

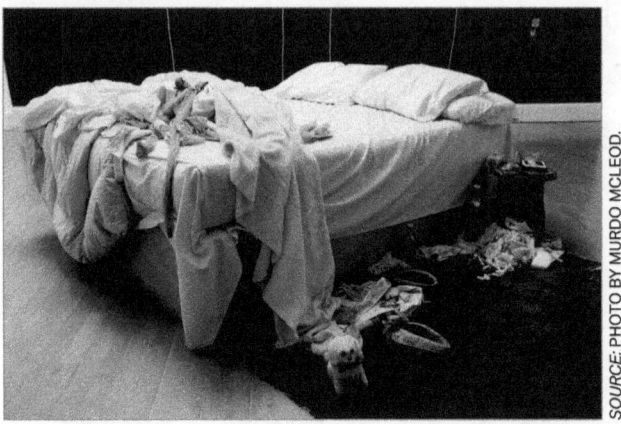

FIGURE 21. My Bed, by Tracey Emin, 1998

This is the bed of Tracey Emin, an artist who spent four days in her bed without eating, and drinking nothing but alcohol. Then she decided to expose the result in all its detail, including dirty bed sheets with bodily secretions, stained underwear, and used condoms. The installation stirred a huge controversy but became incredibly famous. *My Bed* was bought first by Charles Saatchi for £150,000 and then auctioned in 2014 for £2,546,500. Yes, you read it right—a dirty bed was sold for over £2.5 million!

Art is often completely absurd and illogical, which meets our definition of stupidity. If the picture above is a bit too much, you may better appreciate another classic example of irrationality encapsulated by art.

The flagship surrealist painting in Figure 22 takes us right into a dreamlike universe where soft and hard objects coexist, fooling our eyes, discrediting the world of reality. By any measure, this piece is completely illogical. Yet, it's given many of us a pause and generated deep, reflective thoughts. Isn't it beautiful, then?

Indeed, a big portion of art of all types can be considered stupid by everyday standards. Isn't it silly to spend months or even years and millions of dollars to prepare a production of an opera that is only performed six times? Isn't it crazy that Cirque du Soleil artists risk their lives every time they perform? Isn't it foolish that some artists spend months, or even years, perfecting one piece of music, one sculpture, or one painting before showing it to the public?

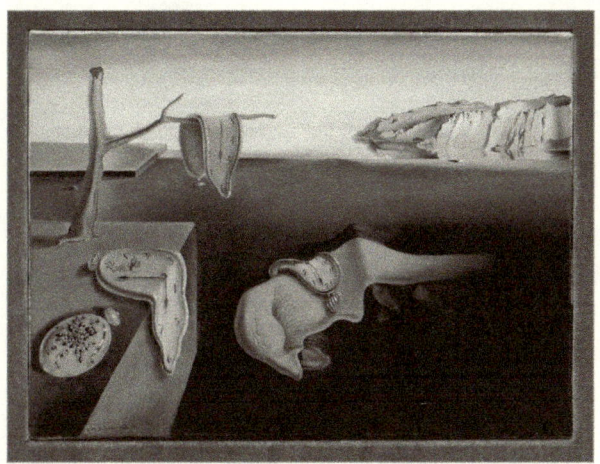

FIGURE 22. Salvador Dali, *The Persistence of Memory***, 1931** [78]

Art can indeed be irrational, but that is also part of its appeal. It challenges and expands our perceptions and understanding of the world around us and is one of the few idiocies we should keep.

As to the rest, if there is to be any hope, our first step is to understand where—psychologically, physiologically, biologically—all this silliness really comes from.

It's time for us to explore the WHY of human folly.

WHY?

"We are not logical, we are biological."
Barbara Oakley

BIOLOGY

Genetics

A quick statistic that will promptly make us feel biologically excused for being stupid: Our DNA is 99% the same as that of chimpanzees and bonobos.[1] This startling fact was confirmed in 2005 by a team of researchers from the Max Planck Institute, who established without doubt that chimpanzees (*Pan troglodytes*) and bonobos (*Pan paniscus*) are our closest relatives. We shared common ancestors about four to seven million years ago. (Gorillas are a close-second relative with 98% shared DNA.)

Our DNA defines how we look, how we behave, and even how we interact with the environment. This remarkable proximity to apes should make us feel humbled. Biology has a big sense of humor, as it sees us as similarly linked to all other earthlings:

Did you know that we also share 98% of our DNA with ... pigs? And 65% with chickens—and 60% *with bananas*!

Nature, it seems, writes very efficient code.

So the next time someone calls you a "pig" in a heated discussion, perhaps instead of responding with another profanity, it would be better to say "Well, you are actually 98% correct!"

Overall, the 1% difference in DNA between us and chimpanzees is still quite huge. It is fair to say that we are the best version of ourselves, refined by hundreds of thousands of years of natural selection and cultural coevolution (society's learned behaviors).

We are all a product of what is called the *Baldwin effect*, which stipulates that those organisms who survive are the most adaptable. In our darkest hour, about 75,000 years ago, when the climate changed very rapidly, causing havoc in our environment and food system, *Homo sapiens* was down to just a few hundred individuals. From this tiny troop, we came back. Those who survived were the smartest, most flexible, and most adaptable. And we are their proud grandchildren.

However, we also inherited some biological mechanisms that, in the modern world, are no longer beneficial human traits. They are simply redundant or maladaptive.

The Amygdala

Mother Nature is responsible for a lot of our shortcomings. Our bodies and minds have been built to be optimized for where we as humans originate from: the warm African savanna.

One of those fundamental optimizations is reliance on the amygdala, a part of our brain resembling two small almonds on either side of the brain's temporal lobe. Its role—cuing the fight-or-flight response—is critical to survival. The amygdala is a hypervigilant early warning system that is our first line of defense in case of danger. It sifts through the deluge of information we gather every second and decides what's critical and what's casual. A mistake in this process might be lethal. That is why the amygdala is somewhat "alarmist" and prioritizes "alarmist" information.

The amygdala is the reason why, in a split second, we can decide whether to fight or flee, get scared by an "ugly" face, choose whether or not to approach someone, and so on.

HOMO IDIOTICUS 125

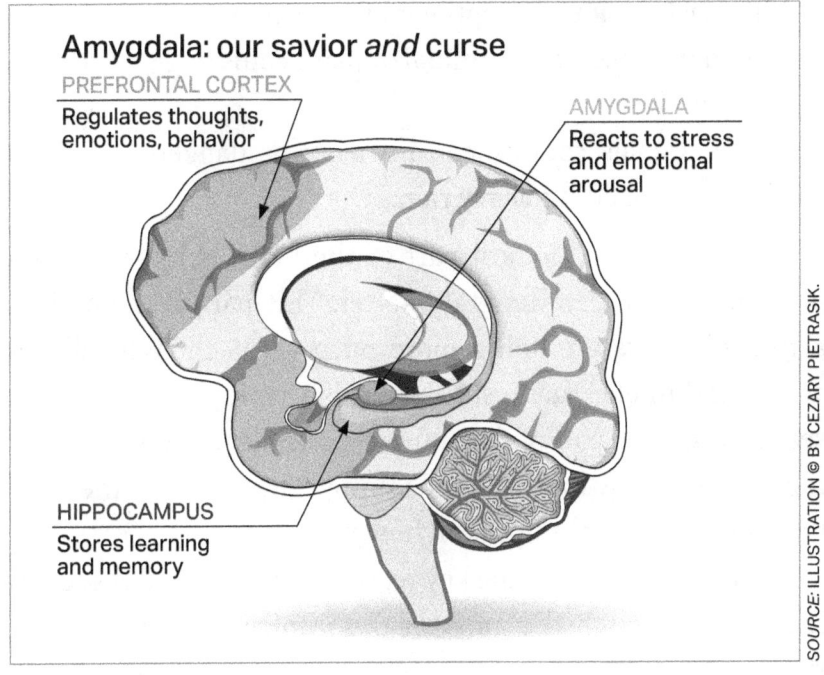

FIGURE 23. The amygdala: our savior and curse

This organ was perfected through the process of evolution over hundreds of thousands of years. Our hunter-gatherer ancestors were constantly on the lookout for potential risks—eating the wrong plant could result in poisoning, hunting an animal that is too strong could result in injury, an unwelcome confrontation with another tribe could end up in homicide. Basically, every step our forebears took could have had tragic consequences. That's where the amygdala comes in, with its ultrafast, intuitive processing and prioritization of information. It favors the unexpected, the moving, the colorful and flashy, and the potentially dangerous. Why? Because it was critical to our survival:

- Rapid movement somewhere in your peripheral vision might mean risk of an attack (e.g., a lion in the bush).

- The flashy color of a reptile might mean it is poisonous.
- An unknown, strange animal or plant could suggest possible danger.
- Noise signals could mean intrusion, a dangerous animal, fire, or impending heavy rain.

The "reflective," logical part of the brain is located in the prefrontal cortex, in the gray matter. This part of the brain is active when we are doing more purposeful, thoughtful, proactive, and intellectual tasks. Here, also, is the hippocampus: a seahorse-shaped part of the brain responsible for housing learning and memory. Interactions among these parts of the brain have a fundamental impact on how we behave.

In a nutshell, one of the key reasons we are stupid is because the brain (through the amygdala) optimizes for speed rather than accuracy. It has a tendency to err on the side of caution. In a crisis moment, it reacts immediately, using heuristics and shortcuts to save those valuable milliseconds, instead of relying on more rational, processed information supplied later by the prefrontal cortex. In the old days, in the savanna, this was often what made the difference between life and death. That's why we've made it to today!

Unfortunately, in the present day, the amygdala opens up a hacking vulnerability in our "modern" brains.

How? Well, the same mechanism that causes us to prioritize flashy, moving, colorful, negative information is used today—by politicians and the media—to *manipulate us*.

Did you ever wonder why you see on TV yet *another* story of "this guy shot that guy"? There are more than 40 murders a day in the US. Why would we show the same story again and again? Exactly due to the vulnerability of the amygdala—it is primed for negative information. Our brains filter and pick up the negative information first, scanning for potential risk to ourselves. That's a hack!

The media and politicians use it to improve viewership ratings.

Why aren't there more stories on your evening news about "such-and-such woman overcoming a disease" or "elderly parents receiving a beautiful gift from their grown children?" Well, because our brains do not register stories like that as critical information. They will largely be ignored.

Why are weather newscasters dressed so nicely, and often sexily, for the mundane job of talking about precipitation and the temperature? Because a sexy red dress with cleavage or a nicely cut suit attracts far more attention than some plainly clothed person. It plays on our primal instinct to identify a mating partner.

Why are the most effective ads in your Instagram feed animated? Because they're moving—and your eyes immediately prioritize it over a stationary object. (Remember the "lion in the bush" movement priming?)

Why does a loud voice, song, or announcement attract so much attention? Because it is coded into our DNA that loud signals indicate potential danger, so our attention is easily hijacked by this simple trick.

All those things we blame the younger generations for—online eyeballing, a preference for loud audio, flashiness, movement, color, and negative images and stories—are actually genetically programmed. Those behaviors are universally governed by our amygdala, the part of our brain responsible for rapid processing and immediate, "intuitive" decisions.

Testosterone

Stupidity can in large part be explained by a hormone secreted by our bodies that is associated with masculinity and high libido: testosterone. Given that men have far more of it in their bodies than women, this brings up a valid question: Are men fundamentally more stupid than women? The negative side of testosterone—higher aggression and in-the-moment irrationality—makes men far more susceptible to acts of violence and recklessness, which we included in our definition of stupidity.

Take primitive societies before the onset of civilization. Among the Jivaro Indians of Ecuador, approximately 60% (!) of their males historically died because of violence. Among the well-studied Brazilian Yanomami, this ratio is at nearly 40%.[2] Aggressive, warlike cultures contribute a lot to this phenomenon—but women in these same groups are nowhere near as likely to die due to violence as men.

You might think this is a matter relegated to the past. Not at all! In the contemporary urban world, testosterone still haunts our male populations.

Take the US phenomenon of gun violence. From 1982 to September 2024, there were 151 mass shooting incidents, of which 145 were committed by males. An astounding 96% of these mass shootings were committed by boys.

We all know, or have even witnessed, men who have gotten into potentially lethal fights over the most trivial reasons—such as someone accidentally spilling a drink on them, looking directly into their eyes, or simply unintentionally touching them. In psychology, this is called a *character contest*.

A shocking example comes from Aberdeen, Scotland, where in 2015, two boys got into a fight at school because one boy refused to give the other an additional biscuit and then called his

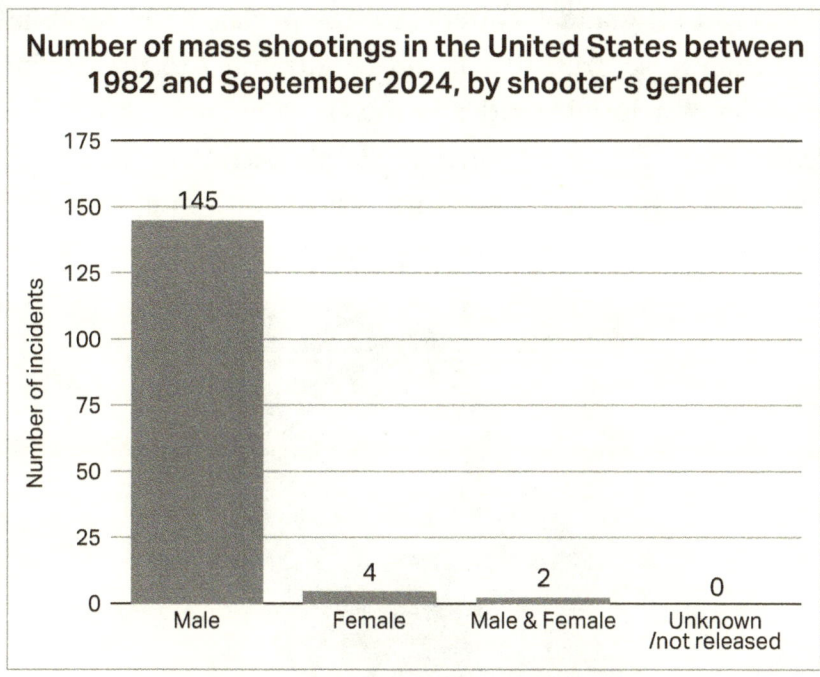

FIGURE 24. Mass shootings in the US, 1982–September 2024, by shooter's gender[3]

mom a "fat c*nt." The 16-year-old boy, Daniel Stroud, feeling utterly offended, pulled out a small knife and stabbed his classmate, Bailey Gwynne, in the heart. Daniel regretted his murderous action shortly afterward, during the trial and likely during his nine-year sentence, which ruined his life. However, in that moment, he felt obliged to "be a man" and defend his mother's honor. Stupid, isn't it? (Also, for some reason, men get tremendously offended if someone says bad things about their mother. This rule travels across cultures and continents—it's worth a separate research study to find out why).

Such acts are not isolated cases. Unnecessary violence by men is a statistically relevant, well-known phenomenon. It is men in their 20s who typically create the most trouble in the world. This is the age when testosterone levels are the highest;

they taper off gradually afterward. The prevalence of this phenomenon is so grim that it can be attributed to the decline in violence across big cities in the US (e.g., famously in New York City in the 1990s), where a simple decline in the size of this demographic (20-something, testosterone-pumped males) brought relative peace to the neighborhoods.

FIGURE 25. The 16-year-old rage killer, Daniel Stroud

Even men in their 40s, 50s, and 60s have much higher levels of irrationality, irresponsibility, and aggression compared to women of the same age. Although for every 100 baby girls born globally, there are about 105 boys born, around the age of 50, their numbers equalize, and by age 60 to 70, women are significantly overrepresented in the demographic pyramid. This trend is so stark in some male-dominated countries that demographers are shocked by its magnitude. In Russia, for every man aged 70–74, there are almost *two* women of the same age![4] This is mostly because men more often die earlier due to traffic accidents, violence, alcoholism, smoking, reckless behaviors, and so on. Their high testosterone levels make them do stupid things such as chain smoking cigarettes, eating unhealthy food in male company, betting on who can drink more vodka or climb from one balcony to another, or refusing to consult mental health experts because it is "not manly."

Beyond irrational aggression and reckless behavior, men have also demonstrated inferior self-care. A 2009 study showed that, in the US, 69% of men do not wash their hands after visiting a public bathroom (compared to 35% of women).[5] Visiting a public bathroom exposes you to a lot of germs, and it is common knowledge that frequent handwashing reduces this risk. Clearly, two-thirds of men do not agree.

The difference is even more pronounced when it comes to *preventive* health. Women are twice as disciplined as men at maintaining a schedule of preventive screenings and are 33% more likely to see a doctor.[6] Basically, men are more likely to ignore the opportunity to catch diseases early.

Being a man seems to be a serious evolutionary disadvantage, so maybe this is why nature produces more males from the get-go.

Reckless Cat Owners?

Would you believe cat owners, on average, are more susceptible to unreasonable risk-taking and careless behaviors?

The common perception is that cats make us calmer and friendlier. However, a very interesting twist relating to cats was documented by researchers at the highly respected Karolinska Institutet in Sweden.

Cats regularly suffer from the *Toxoplasma gondii* parasite. Unfortunately, this parasite can transfer relatively easily to humans through contact with a cat's feces. It is estimated that today 30%–50% of the human population is infected!

After infecting an organism, the parasite causes toxoplasmosis, which, after initial light flu symptoms, typically enters a dormant, chronic phase—one that was considered symptom-free until recently.[7] However, in 2012, researchers proved that toxoplasmosis causes ... irrational behaviors! For example, infected rats become *unafraid of cats* (which typically ends badly for the rats but is good for the parasite, because it then infects the bodies of the cats).

Among people, infection results in the secretion of a signal substance called GABA that—shockingly like in the infected rats—*inhibits the sensation of fear and anxiety*. This results in humans exhibiting more extroverted, more aggressive, and riskier behavior.

These findings were serious enough that pregnant women were warned to avoid contact with cat-litter trays. Toxoplasmosis can be fatal for fetuses.

So much for those "mellow" cat owners. Hard science proves cats are contributing to the biological reasons for human stupidity—in this case, by manifesting more aggressive behavior and increasing irrational risk-taking.

But I still like cats!

Lead Pollution

What is the connection between aggressive Romans in 1 CE and widespread violence in the US from the 1960s to the 1980s?

Lead.

Romans were famed architects who used a complex system of aqueducts to carry water from the mountains to the cities via ... lead pipes. Lead is one of the easiest-to-process metals; it is malleable, easy to shape, insulates water well, and was, and still is, broadly available. Ancient people mastered the technique of using it quite early. Unfortunately, they didn't know what we know today—that lead both causes aggression and lowers IQ.

According to multiple studies—studies that were delayed, belittled, and fought against for decades by the chemical industry lobby—lead is highly poisonous for human infants, even at very low levels. It inhibits development of the anterior cingulate cortex and prefrontal cortex, which are responsible for managing behavior and mood. It was observed that this effect is stronger for boys than girls. As a result, people who were exposed to lead in childhood suffer as adults from increased attention deficit disorder, aggression, and impulsiveness.[8]

Lead found its way into human bodies mostly because it was added to gasoline from the 1930s to the 1990s. Once burned in combustion engines, it can easily be inhaled. Particles of lead are then absorbed by blood vessels and the brain.

The second pathway for poisoning was through wall paints. From the second half of the 19th century until 1978, lead was used extensively as a paint additive.[9] As a result of those two trends, children in America were exposed to huge amounts of this toxic substance, both through cars and the painted walls of their own homes.

This fueled an unparalleled increase in violence. The correlation between levels of lead and violent crimes in the US is nothing short of spectacular. Please note Figure 26 below, which shows the relationship between crime rates and lead levels about 23 years earlier (to account for the lag between exposure during infancy and when those kids reached adulthood and started doing bad things).

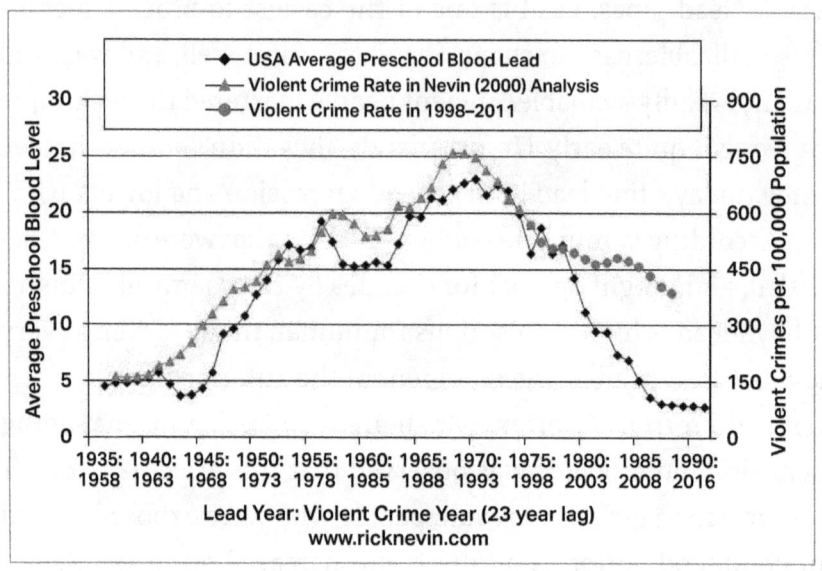

FIGURE 26. Lead levels and crime rates 23 years later[10]

The high correlation between violence and lead can be analyzed even on a neighborhood level. A 1986 study estimated that 18% of White children and 52% of Black children in the US have lead levels of more than 20 milligrams per deciliter in their blood. Basically, Black children were more likely to live in old, unrenovated houses with lead paint peeling off the walls and alongside busy roads with lots of exhaust gases.[11] As a result, Black neighborhoods suffered from particularly high levels of violence two decades later.

Many scientists attribute half (!) of the decline in violence in the 1990s to the phaseout of leaded gasoline.[12] Forget Rudy Giuliani, forget rock-star police bosses who took credit for such success. Forbidding lead in gasoline alone did half the job.

Other Pollutants

We suffer from many other similar effects due to environmental pollution. Our brains' productivity and IQ are hampered by many other substances such as polychlorinated biphenyls (PCBs), organophosphates (used in pesticides), methyl, mercury, and others.

Even common dust or smoke from road traffic, chimneys, and burning coal has a tremendously negative impact on us. An Iowa State University study estimated that in China, areas with high air pollution have visibly lower results on standard student exams: 2.2% to 2.5% lower for literature and a staggering 2.8% to 5.3% lower for math.[13] Studies in Israel confirmed the level of pollution on the day of an exam has a visible impact on academic outcomes. Based on a study of 56,000 students across 415,000 exams between 2002 and 2003, low air quality (air quality index greater than 75) on the date of an exam was associated with a 2.25% decline in scores.[14]

Air pollution has also been linked to worse memory, lower attention, and poorer vocabulary.[15] In other words, if you live in an industrial area with high levels of pollution, your intellectual capability is lower than it could be if you lived in a cleaner place.

Environmental pollution is part of the reason why we are stupider than we need to be.

Bad Food or Not Enough Food

Biological determination is merciless. The better the quality and quantity of food we consume, the better cognitive performance we achieve. The reverse is true as well. Science provides overwhelming evidence that bad food or lack of food leads to lower IQ. The drivers are diametrically different in rich and poor countries, but the result is the same—depressed cognitive ability.

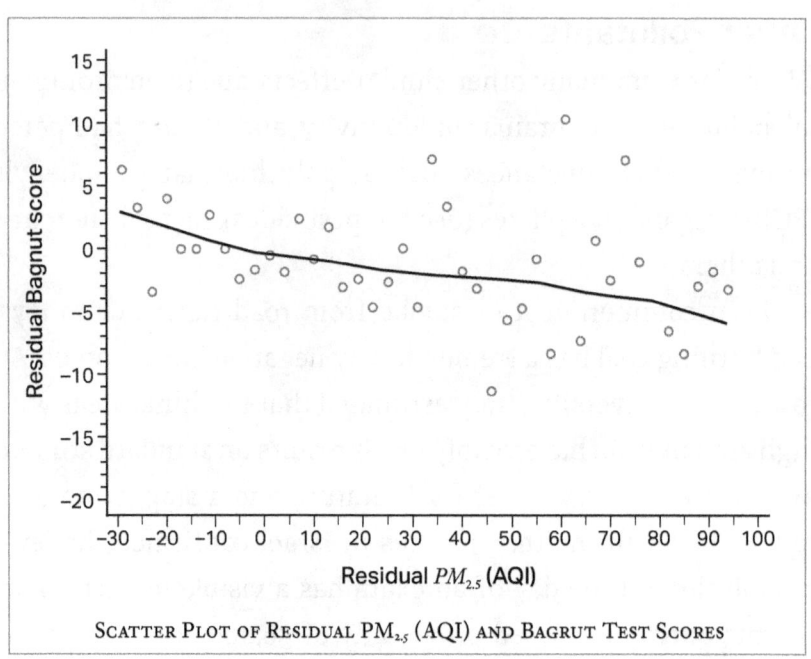

FIGURE 27. Correlation between air quality index (AQI) and test results[16]

A study performed on a group of more than 1,500 malnourished children from Mauritius found a deficit of 15.3 IQ points at age 11 due to lack of quality food at age 3.[17]

On the opposite end, a study by researchers at Ohio State University observed almost 12,000 American 8th graders who were split into groups that ate fast food either 1–3 times a week, 4–6 times a week, every day, or not at all. The study showed that test results for the group that ate fast food most frequently were about 20% lower than for the group that ate no fast food.[18]

The disruptive impact of lack of food can be observed also on a microscale, in intraday actions. We tend to be harsher and more ruthless when hungry. A controversial 2012 study in Israel pointed out that judges delivered significantly harsher verdicts when they were hungry—they denied 35% of parole cases right after breakfast, but that number climbed steeply to 85% right before lunch.[19] While the study has some critics, the magnitude of this difference is telling.

"Food" for thought: Your eating habits have an impact on not only your silhouette but also your intellectual capability and behavior. Also, if you ever land in court, make sure the judge reviews your case *after* lunch.

Alcohol

We typically assume that a glass of wine (or two) is not harmful. However, alcohol consumption indeed damages our brains and makes us stupider. Reliable research shows that alcohol kills our neurons and that people who consume excessive amounts have visible changes in their prefrontal cortex that impair their cognitive abilities. Nonetheless, we do it with gusto!

Alcoholism in the Soviet Union and the whole Soviet bloc reached shocking levels in the 1980s, devastating society. It was also responsible for an unnaturally high mortality rate for men beyond age 40. But this is not a modern phenomenon. Economic historians have analyzed alcohol consumption over time and reached a jaw-dropping conclusion—in Europe, we have been walking tipsy for hundreds of years! A typical Englishman around 1450 consumed 34% of his daily calories through ... alcohol! This compares to only 1.3% of Englishmen in 1790[20] and 3% in the modern US.[21]

Wondering if there was any correlation between the start of the "age of reason" in the 18th century and a decline in alcohol consumption? Wonder no longer.

Stress

Stress is not a theoretical, ephemeral, emotional state of our mind. It is a hard biological process that can be measured in molecules, secreted hormones, and the speed of our internal processes. Stress causes the *bandwidth effect*, which essentially means the crowding out of your brainpower and, in short bursts, the lowering of your IQ.

A 2013 study measured the impact of unexpected stress on a group of participants. After being told they would need to pay an unexpected $3,000 car repair bill, participants' IQ test scores were 10-12 points lower. Stunningly, IQ scores did not drop much at all when the subjects were told that the repair bill was only $300. The sheer difference in financial obligation made a huge difference in how they performed on the IQ test. Basically, while the group could (with minor difficulty) handle a $300 bill, $3,000 was often beyond their financial means and therefore caused significant stress—which led to poor IQ test results.[22]

Similar results were achieved in a big sample study in 1983 by researchers at the University of Georgetown. They concluded that emotional or physical stress had a 13-point negative impact on the IQ test performance of seven-year-olds.[23]

The effect of stress on IQ reinforces the cycle of poverty—the stress of not being able to meet everyday obligations results in poorer cognitive performance, which in turn results in fewer well-paying jobs, which creates *more* financial stress.

Temperature

Did you know that you are more likely to act stupid in warmer temperatures than in ambient temperatures? This is one impact of global warming that you probably have never heard of!

There is rapidly growing evidence that higher temperatures lead to increased crime, due to their impact on our psychological judgment. Basically, they cause heightened aggression, loss of control, and greater willingness to engage in unethical or violent acts. Put simply, we become stupider when it is hot.

It starts innocently. In higher-temperature environments, we are more likely to swear (per the 2015 study of a billion tweets[24]). We are also more likely to honk at each other: An experiment in Phoenix, Arizona, tested how likely drivers were to honk at other cars that didn't move fast enough when the light at an intersection turned green. The higher the temperature, the more honking there was.

It gets much darker from here. In a higher-temperature environment, we are more likely to perceive the same situation as more dangerous and respond with an incommensurate level of aggression.

Let's take the example of an experiment done during a training session for the Dutch police force. Officers were split into two groups doing the same exercise, which involved confronting a burglar inside a training building. For one group, the indoor temperature was 70°F (21°C), while for the other, it was 81°F (27°C). The scenario was designed so that the appropriate response, according to the Dutch code, was not to shoot the suspect, as he didn't pose an immediate threat to a police officer. When the temperature was 70°F, officers opened fire on the simulated suspect in 45% of cases. This percentage increased to 62%, however, when the temperature was 81°F. So a temperature increase of 11°F increased the rate of this most aggressive response by 38%!

The evidence for higher temperatures leading to higher aggression is undeniable. This thesis is confirmed not only by theoretical experiments but by longitudinal studies of actual crime statistics. Let's take, as an example, a large-scale study by Matthew Ranson that spanned 49 US states over a 30-year period, from 1980 to 2009. This study looked at temperatures and violent crimes such as murder, manslaughter, or rape, with the data broken down by month. The results (see Figure 28) were astounding.

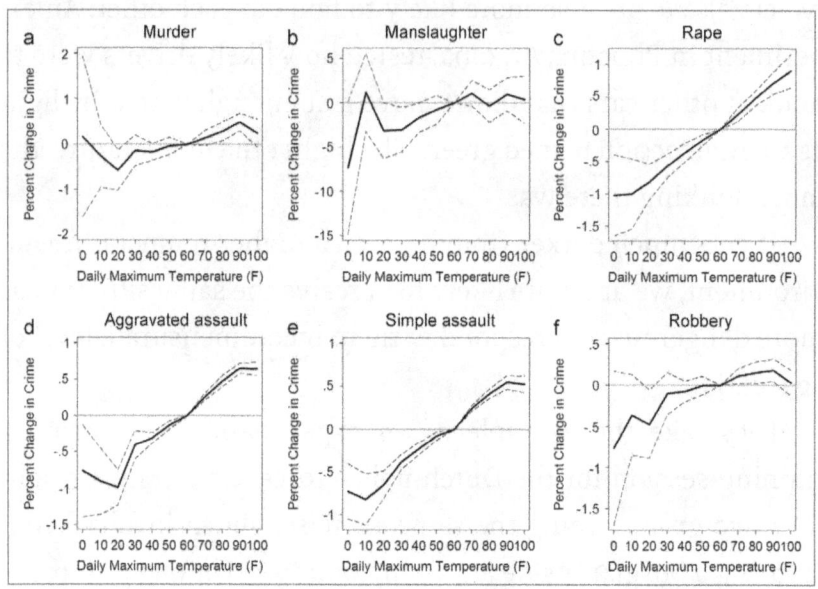

FIGURE 28. Correlation between various categories of violent crime and temperature[25]

Another study by Hsiang, Burke, and Miguel from 2013 based on 60 primary studies confirmed that higher temperature leads to higher violence on a group (societal) level (see Figure 29 below).

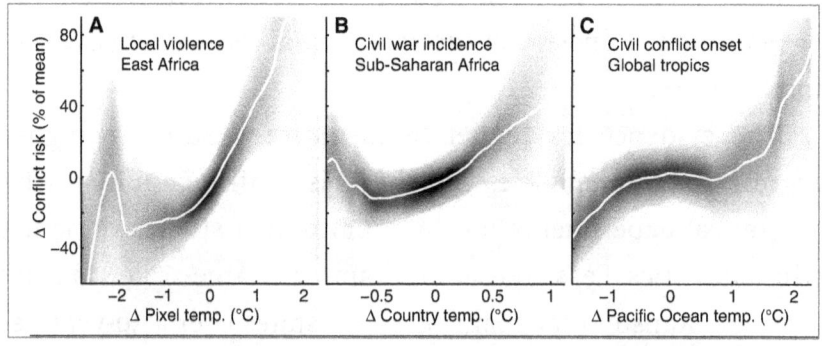

FIGURE 29. Societal-level violence and temperature[26]

This is huge! Most scientists expect that by 2050, temperatures will increase by two to four standard deviations, which projects a dramatic increase in societal conflict!

Higher temperatures also have an adverse effect on our productivity. Singapore's founding father, Lee Kuan Yew, who transformed this once-destitute, marginal breakout province of Malaysia to an independent economic superpower, famously said:

> Air conditioning was a most important invention for us, perhaps one of the signal inventions of history. It changed the nature of civilization by making development possible in the tropics. Without air conditioning, you can work only in the cool early-morning hours or at dusk. The first thing I did upon becoming prime minister was to install air conditioners in buildings where the civil service worked. This was key to public efficiency.

Indeed, there is a lot of research that links moderate temperatures to high productivity.

According to a 2015 study by Burke, Hsiang, and Miguel, temperature has a profound impact on economic productivity.[27] They even calculated the optimal average temperature for economic development throughout a year: 13°C (55.4°F). The US, as a country, has a yearly average temperature of 56.1°F, very close to the optimum, while San Francisco, its most productive city, sits pretty much *exactly* at 55.4°F.

Figure 30 shows that only a tiny percentage of the world's GDP is created in countries with an annual average temperature above 15°C (59°F). Our brains simply do not work well when they are overheated—just like computer processors. The impact of the environment on our biology is profound.

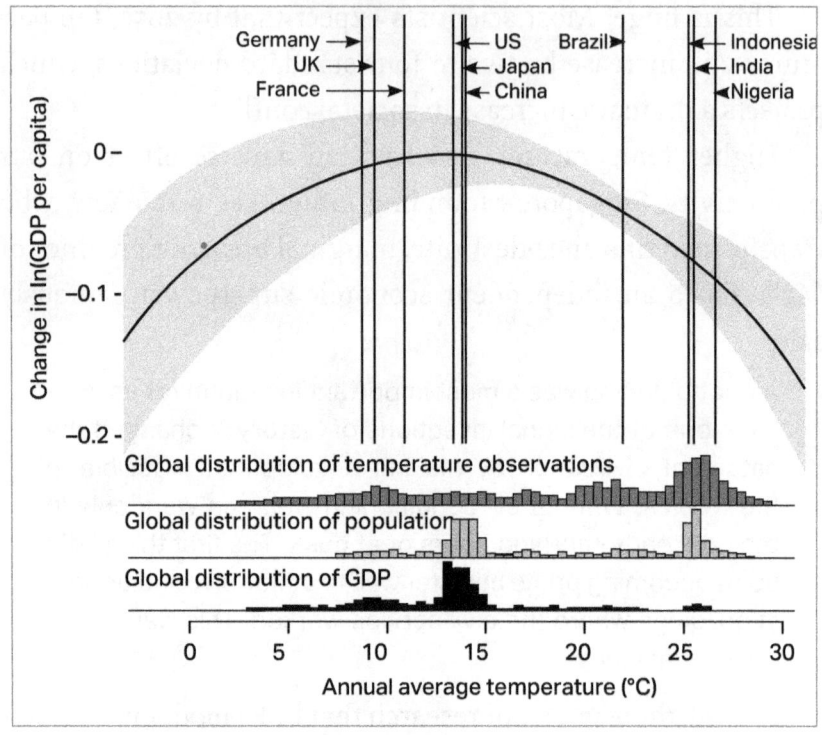

FIGURE 30. Temperature v. GDP: hot is bad[28]

To summarize, high temperature has a strong negative biological impact on our behavior and productivity. It encourages us to act irrationally and aggressively or simply makes us slower at work. Climate change is very unwelcome news for the world—it will make us less mentally stable and less industrious.

Lack of Sex

Can lack of sex make us stupid? Serious research confirms this thesis, if we treat unnecessary aggression as part of our definition of stupidity.

Multiple studies point to the fact that societies with gender imbalance suffer from more violence. Typically, it means a surplus of men over women, which reduces the chances of single men having sex. This creates frustration and leads to aggression.

Imagine you are a young man in your 20s, overflowing with testosterone, who cannot find a sexual partner. You spend more and more time with other single male friends, which is often a recipe for disaster, as you come up with all those crazy ideas to entertain and prove your manliness. On top of it all, frustration builds up and surfaces unexpectedly in any situation involving conflict.

A 2018 study of six Asian countries with or without significant gender imbalance found that a mere 0.1% increase in the ratio of men to women led to men being more likely to commit violence with a weapon, with the odds ratio increasing to 1.59 (when no gender imbalance exists, the odds ratio is 1.00), and more likely to rape a woman, with the odds ratio increasing to 1.80.[29]

This does not bode well for India and China, two countries with the largest surplus of men. Due to a strong cultural preference for male heirs and mass-scale abortions of female fetuses, there are approximately 71 million more men than women in those countries.[30] This is abnormal compared to the rest of the world: In 2020, India had 108 males per 100 women and China had 105, whereas the US had 97 and Poland had 94. More than 70% of those excess males in India and China are below age 20. This is a recipe for serious trouble ahead.

So if you want to make world a better place, make sure you find yourself a romantic partner!

PSYCHOLOGY

To survive in the savanna, *Homo sapiens*'s first habitat, evolution gave us a helpful tool: minimization of the brain's workload.

Our brain is a very "expensive" organ to maintain—while constituting only 2% of our mass, it devours approximately 20% of our oxygen supply. Scientists think we receive roughly 11 million bits of information per second, but we can consciously process only about 40–50 bits per second.[31] This creates a deluge of information, which we need to triage somehow.

The bottom line: We need shortcuts.

Well, we create those shortcuts every minute. Let's zoom in on a trivial situation: You're at a house party and you grab an apple from a basket. You typically don't meticulously inspect the fruit to evaluate its safety and nutritional value. You could definitely spend a lot of time asking the host a lot of questions about the source of the apple, whether it was grown using herbicides, whether it has been washed, and so on. But using this level of analysis to make every single small decision would be too expensive a process. And if you conducted such a detailed interrogation, the guests at the party might consider you a psychopath.

We need to make a lot of simple decisions very fast, almost automatically, with a minimal but helpful dose of analysis. That's why we developed *heuristics*, which in essence are mental shortcuts that allow us to act faster. A heuristic kicks in when you take an apple: As long as it looks relatively healthy, not rotten, you subconsciously decide it is acceptable to put it in your mouth. However, when your eyes spot a rotten part or an insect wriggling inside, you automatically pause.

This is how we developed a whole range of *biases* that govern our daily lives today and often contribute to our stupidity. We formed simplified ways of thinking to arrive at decisions more quickly. We still maintain the capability of thinking more slowly and making more thoughtful decisions—but we exercise this mode sparingly.

Heuristics lead to biases, which govern most of our everyday decision-making.

Biases

There are 175 biases that have been catalogued. Let's dive into a few of the most powerful and interesting ones.

Confirmation bias

We humans often interpret information in a way that confirms already-held beliefs or values. For example, if my previous interactions with Anna have led me to perceive her negatively, when there is a conflict between Anna and John, I will most likely pay little attention to facts supporting Anna's case. I will take John's side and construe all data as favorable to him.

This is a serious flaw in our psychology. Unfortunately, this bias leads to a lot of bad decisions.

Imagine a detective who "doesn't like Mexicans." In a murder investigation, that detective might jump prematurely to the conclusion that a Mexican suspect killed the victim, even if there was no obvious evidence and an unbiased detective would prioritize a different hypothesis. Alternatively, imagine that someone strongly supports a political party whose leader behaves obnoxiously and makes irrational decisions. Such a person will be less likely to criticize the leader and will back their initiatives, regardless of their individual merit.

Confirmation bias is one of the key reasons behind the growing polarization of American politics. Basically, more and more voters blindly follow their party's guidance without evaluating it for themselves. Their shortcut heuristic is "Well, I am a Republican, so if a particular piece of legislation is coming from the Republican Party, then it must be good."

This is a terrible process, as it leads to increasing animosity between Republicans and Democrats and the isolation of huge swaths of society. It reduces the amount of constructive legislation that in normal circumstances would be approved by both parties.

Availability bias

This bias makes us interpret the world incorrectly because, all too often, the only data immediately available to us are on one side of an argument, but not the other. For example, imagine that your neighbor is a successful entrepreneur who quit his corporate job, started a company, and now makes millions. When asked about the probability of building a successful business, you will naturally be predisposed to overestimate it, purely based on one successful outcome—your neighbor, who might be floating in his new infinity pool in front of your eyes each day when you get home from work. The reality is that around 80%–90% of start-ups fail.

Availability bias often destroys our ability to rationally weigh relative pros and cons. Imagine that Ante lives in Finland,

and in 1996, his friend's child receives a measles-mumps-rubella (MMR) vaccination and develops a serious complication. Ante is likely to turn into an anti-vaxxer because he personally observed an isolated case of a negative reaction. He had information readily available on one side of the argument. However, what he didn't have access to was the study, finalized in the same year, based on 14 years of observations of 1.8 million individuals in Finland who were immunized with the MMR vaccine between 1982 and 1996. If he had, he would have read that serious negative reactions were observed in only 173 cases and only one person died as a result.[32] The mortality rate for measles is typically 1–2 per 1,000,[33] which means the immunization program indeed caused the death of one person but saved approximately 1,800–3,600 lives. Had Ante lived in the country, where he would have observed people dying from measles daily, he would likely have been totally in favor of a vaccination program and would consider one death a completely rational price to pay for saving thousands.

One form of availability bias is something called the *priming effect*.

Would you believe that the words we are exposed to can make us walk faster or slower? This is exactly what happens!

In a famous experiment conducted at New York University, psychologist John Bargh asked students ages 18–22 to put together four-word sentences from a range of displayed vocabulary. For one of the groups, half the words had a discreet association with the elderly (e.g., gray, bald, forgetful, wrinkle, Florida, etc.). After the participants created the sentences, they were sent to another building to do, allegedly, another experiment. Here was the whole point of the exercise: Bargh's collaborators measured the speed at which they walked between the buildings. Subjects in the group that had words associated with the elderly walked considerably slower.[34]

Astonishing!

The word *old* was never used in any of the scrambles! When presented with the results, none of the students had noticed a theme for the vocabulary they were playing with. They were also adamant that they hadn't walked any slower than usual. Well, precise external measurements showed something else!

We are subconsciously primed to act differently depending on the visual clues we are surrounded by. It turns out that we act more honestly and generously in the presence of a poster with an image of eyes looking at us. This was confirmed by an experiment in which scientists measured the amount of donations deposited in an "honesty box," which was meant to help pay for coffee. They ran the experiment for 10 days; on 5 of those days, various images of flowers were placed above the box, and on the other 5 days, various images of eyes. On the "eye days," the donations were on average three times higher (!) than on "flower days." Shocking!

Priming is, therefore, a phenomenon in which the mere exposure to a certain stimulus (visual, textual, situational, olfactory, etc.) unconsciously influences our response to another stimulus.

Some more practical examples of priming? Rap music (I will lose a lot of readers here!) is typically full of aggression, vulgarity, and violence. Per a 2005 University of Pittsburgh School of Medicine study, 77% of the top rap songs for teens in that year mentioned alcohol and drugs. As a result, people who listen to rap music are more likely to swear and be more aggressive and violent.[35] Researchers at Emory University looked at teens ages 14–18 who listened to rap music about 14 hours per week.

Compared with the control group, the kids who listened to rap were 2.5 times more likely to get themselves arrested and 1.5 times more likely to do illegal activities like drugs or underage drinking.[36]

So, if you can, listen to Mozart instead. It has a confirmed positive impact on your cognitive abilities after about 10–12 minutes of listening.[37]

Equalizing bias

Our brains have another well-known malfunction: the tendency to equalize the importance of arguments in our decision-making. Basically, our minds are abysmal at assigning differentiated weights and instead give each argument a similar level of importance.[38]

When facing big decisions, many of us make a list of pros and cons on a sheet of paper. It is believed to be a valuable exercise to help us make good decisions, thanks to its perceived analytical rigor and transparency.

However, if we do not ascribe a weight to each argument, this practice might even be counterproductive. Subconsciously, our mind will think that the three points in favor of something are weaker than the five on the other side of the page, even if the three are far more powerful.

Chief manipulators know this trick well and take advantage of it.

For example, Donald Trump's team used this equalizing bias to deflect the weight of various charges relating to his alleged sexual assaults on women by bringing one (very weak) case against Joe Biden. Donald Trump had about 26 women accuse him of unwanted sexual advances, from groping to rape.[39] The allegations against Biden included making comments about a woman's appearance and putting his hand on her shoulder. That's a big difference in the severity of allegations. But by highlighting these Biden moments, Trump's team was playing on the equalization bias: "Well, both candidates have some issues with unwanted sexual advances." Despite a massive difference in the numbers and gravity of the allegations, in many people's minds, the issue ended as an equalized problem for both politicians.

Framing bias

We are psychologically susceptible to another well-known bias called the *framing effect*. This cognitive heuristic causes us to make different decisions based on *how* the information is presented, rather than the information itself.

So, for example, people will typically choose a product that is "95% sugar-free" instead of "only 5% sugar!" Whether you say something is 5% sugar or 95% sugar-free, the meaning is exactly the same; however, our reaction to each is vastly different.

We all prefer to hear that we have a 10% chance of winning something than a 90% chance of losing. We want to hear that the detergent is 99% effective in killing germs rather than 1% ineffective.

Shrewd politicians play this trick on us all the time!

During the George W. Bush administration, Republicans used a framing effect in their campaign to abolish the US inheritance tax. An inheritance tax is levied on the estate of a deceased person above a certain tax-free limit. Taxing transfers of large fortunes between generations typically helps fund social programs such as education, allowing more people to get on the path to financial independence, rather than fortifying the existing wealth structure. Republican experts under the Bush administration found a way to win public support for abolishing this tax by ... framing the narrative differently. They started calling it a "death tax" instead of an inheritance tax. This had a persuasive effect on society. Everybody thinks death is a bad thing and no one should penalize death. They forgot about the lofty ideals of an equal, harmonious society and sympathized with the visceral instinct to not penalize death!

How brilliant!

The bigger concept behind the framing effect is something called *prospect theory*. It shows that we evaluate losses and gains asymmetrically: We are more influenced by the possibility of loss than the prospect of gain.[40]

So how you frame what you say has a substantial impact on how it is perceived by your audience.

An interesting fact is that the framing effect is weaker if we use a foreign language. Our decision-making is less biased when we evaluate the same information while *not* speaking our mother tongue. It seems that such situations require us to "use more brain," and we pay more attention to the actual content of the information, rather than the form of communication—and, therefore, are less likely to be biased.

I attribute part of the success of my relationship with my life partner, Mercedes (a Spaniard), to the fact that we speak to each other in English, which is not our mother tongue. Basically, because of the extra half second needed to verbalize and translate our thoughts into a foreign language, we probably select words more carefully and accurately and are less likely to say something irresponsible.

So funny that speaking in a foreign language can make your conversation more rational and fact based!

The psychology of numbers

Don't you find it annoying when prices aren't quoted in whole numbers? For example, $0.99 instead of $1.00, or $2.99 instead of $3.00. Isn't it awful? Why use two decimal places if something really costs a dollar? Why make adding the numbers so complicated, why carry this $0.01 of change in your pocket, why bother? Dear store marketing manager, do you think I am so stupid that I will not know you are trying to manipulate me?

Well, it turns out—thanks to the framing effect—that we indeed *are* that stupid. We allow ourselves to be manipulated even after being told that we will be manipulated!

In Figure 31 below, we see data from Gumroad, an e-commerce platform that enables creators to sell directly to consumers, showing what percentage of customers buy products at various prices.

price	conversion rate	price	conversion rate
.99	3.06%	1.99	5.2%
1	1.88%	2	2.39%
2.99	3.44%	3.99	3.21%
3	2.11%	4	2.39%
4.99	4.67%	5.99	1.56%
5	3.84%	6	1.42%

FIGURE 31. The power of prices ending with .99[41]

If you change the price from $1 to $0.99, 63% more people will buy your product. Instead of a sales conversion of 1.88%, you will achieve a whopping 3.06%. In other words, our reaction to a 1% price change is 63 times greater than it should be—we are fooled 63-fold! The larger the amount, the smaller the impact (which is intuitive), but the magnitude of change, particularly with small numbers such as $1 or $2, is astounding!

Isn't it telling that such a cheap, vulgar, well-known trick still gets us so often?

Who still thinks we are not stupid?

Omission bias

We are psychologically wired to make irrational decisions when it comes to harmful actions or inactions. Basically, we have a natural, unjustified tendency to tolerate *inaction* that will lead to a bad result. At the same time, we are much harsher in judging *action* that would lead to the same outcome.

To explain the omission bias, let's take the famous "trolley dilemma." Imagine you are faced with this situation:

A runaway trolley car is going down the railroad tracks. You happen to be next to the lever that can redirect the trolley onto another set of tracks. If it continues on the current track, it will kill five people. If you switch the trolley to the other track, it will kill one person. Would you move the lever and choose to kill this one person?[42]

From a mathematical, rational perspective, it is obviously better to reduce the number of people killed by activating the lever. However, it requires you to *take action*. This creates a direct relationship between your *action* and someone's death, whereas not touching the lever leaves you as a bystander. In reality, your inaction results in a much higher price being paid, but you are not *directly* involved.

This scenario was tested in real life with an experiment involving subjects who had to decide whether to kill five mice or one mouse. One-third of the people declared they would not act.[43] When faced with the actual setup, with the exercise happening live and five mice ready to be killed in front of them, 84%

of people chose to save the five mice and sacrifice one. (For the animal lovers: The mice ultimately were never killed.)

FIGURE 32. The trolley problem[44]

This implies that a huge percentage of society, at least 16% would likely allow five *people* to be killed instead of one, by failing to interfere in the situation. In other words, they believe that inaction absolves them of guilt.

You would think this is a highly theoretical, improbable problem with no practical application. However, this bias plays out in our society all the time!

A lot of glamorous old buildings in many grand cities around the world decay and eventually collapse because city councils or the cities' chief architects do not allow them to be renovated. Those institutions or individuals typically demand irrationally high standards of construction, move very slowly with approvals (which extends the project timeline immensely), and create a ton of demands that are incredibly difficult to fulfill. I have seen so many such glamorous buildings in the best cities in the world, often in the most prestigious locations!

Many real estate developers give up on such prospects and deal with easier, simpler, safer projects. The city planners are fine with leaving a historic building in terrible shape for years and risking its collapse—all to avoid taking action! Taking action means doing work, taking responsibility, weighing the arguments for preserving historic style versus making it affordable to renovate. Instead, far more typically, city architects decline reasonable renovation proposals, tacitly acknowledging the option of collapse. But then they claim it is not their fault! The building collapsed because of old age, not their *inaction*!

Omission bias is also evident in administrative red tape. A ton of human energy is spent on wasteful processes that do not allow things to move ahead. Setting up new charities, granting rights to do creative things in public spaces, allowing someone to use existing public assets, trying new policies, implementing new solutions—all those actions require a "yes" from some bureaucrat, which typically is not forthcoming because it is safer for them not to act than to act.

Another example is the approval of new drugs. It is easy for a bureaucrat sitting on a drug safety committee not to approve a drug that causes 1 death per 1,000 patients in a clinical trial. This person can claim that the drug is not safe enough, effectively preventing it, through their inaction, from coming to the market.

However, what if such a drug saves 100 (different) people for each death? Shouldn't we allow it anyway? There are a multitude of drugs that have a high positive impact (e.g., ketamine), but also have potentially dangerous side effects. However, is it moral to allow *thousands* of anonymous people to die from a certain disease in order to avoid pointing to *one* specific death?

In 1995, during the civil war in Yugoslavia, omission bias resulted in a particularly deadly outcome. A group of 370 Dutch soldiers was part of a peace-keeping mission that was supposed to protect civilians in the town of Srebrenica, which had been declared a "safe zone" by the United Nations. However, the Serbian forces of Ratko Mladić descended on the town and started killing men and boys. The Dutch had to choose whether to act or not. Inaction was safer—avoiding armed confrontation with the Serbian army carried little risk. Choosing to act, on the other hand, would have risked a gun fight. The Dutch soldiers chose inaction—they chose omission. The price the civilian population paid was horrendous. More than 8,000 Bosnian men and boys were killed in organized and spontaneous executions, and hundreds, if not thousands, of the town's women were raped.

We prefer not to act because we consider the consequences of our inaction not to be our fault. Utterly stupid!

Cognitive Dissonance

Our brains are not good at dealing with conflicting information. We have a hard time absorbing evidence that undermines a belief we have held true to date. Seeing negative information about something we considered positive (and vice versa) makes us feel uncomfortable.

In such a situation, we cope by simply ignoring the information, rationalizing it, or avoiding the very receipt of that information. Our standard operating procedure is often to *reject* data that is both true and useful. Incredible!

A great example of this is the reaction of Russian civilians to the atrocities committed by their armed forces in the war in Ukraine since 2022. There are many heartbreaking scenes of independent journalists on the streets of Moscow or St. Petersburg asking random people what they think about the bombings of hospitals, shootings of Ukrainian civilians, and other horrors. The typical reaction of a Russian citizen is to turn around and try to avoid contact, typically murmuring "I support Putin" or "That's not true!" Their body language so clearly indicates that they reject this information and do not want to hear any more about it!

The same phenomenon applies to smokers who, when told about the detrimental effects of cigarettes on their health, typically claim to be the lucky exception to the rule.[45]

We do not like being told the truth if it goes against our beliefs.

Reciprocity

We humans have a deeply rooted need for reciprocity. Our psychology predisposes us to practicing the game of favors, which from an evolutionary point of view is highly successful. During prehistoric times, our ancestors exchanged food and other favors (such as grooming, insect removal, or childcare) to get through hard times. This mechanism is widespread in the animal kingdom, as well, and has been particularly well-studied among our closest common ancestors: chimpanzees.

Chimp studies have proved there is a high level of reciprocity in sharing food among these primates. If chimpanzee A shares food with chimpanzee B, then chimpanzee B is much more likely to later share food with chimpanzee A in return.

Those few apes that are reluctant to share encounter a higher probability of aggression when approaching others for food.[46]

This psychological rule creates a shortcut in our brains that makes us susceptible to manipulation. The political game is mostly about doing favors for your voters and then expecting votes in return. Think lower taxes, more social spending for certain demographic groups, pushing such-and-such law through parliament, and so on.

A brilliant example of this is Belarus, which is ruled by Alexander Lukashenko, the "last dictator" of Europe. Lukashenko, a former collective farm worker, perfected the manipulation technique of ordering a state agency responsible for pension payments to include a specific line item called "Presidential bonus." By associating a small amount of pension with himself, Lukashenko created a unique relationship with pensioners, invisibly calling: "You see, I do something for you and hope you will do something for me."

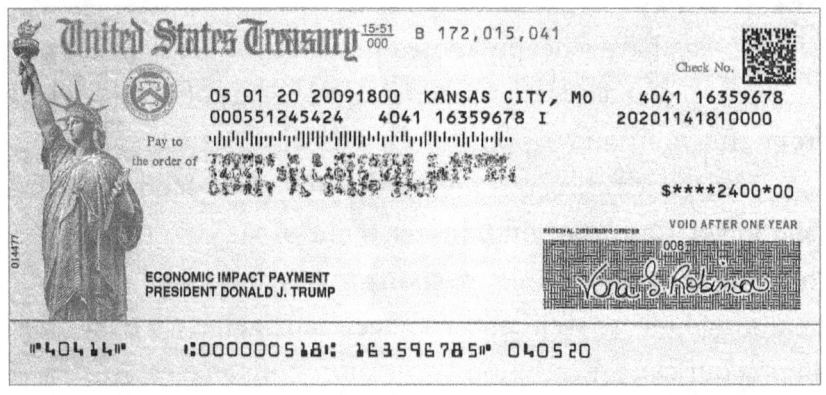

FIGURE 33. American stimulus check from 2020[47]
Donald Trump wanted to maximize political dividends for himself by including his name in bold on stimulus checks—a brilliant move.

Donald Trump did the same thing when stimulus checks were distributed during the 2020–21 pandemic, insisting on including his name and signature in bold on the stimulus documentation. The underlying message: "This is from me! Now it's your turn to help me out!"

So next time you receive something "for free," watch out for the expected manipulation.

SOCIOLOGY

While biology and psychology are partly to blame for our idiocy, we really cannot blame anybody but ourselves for creating societies that *promote* stupidity.

Since *Homo sapiens* first started roaming Africa, advanced cooperation between individuals was the key component of our success. That's how "society" was born. We outsmarted and ultimately exterminated other hominoid species, such as Neanderthals, who had inferior social skills.

Homo sapiens was better able to mobilize and manage bigger groups of individuals around common goals. Those big groups were very effective at accomplishing complex tasks that individual hunter-gatherers could never do: building barns, halls, and mines; processing metals; doing abstract thinking, which resulted in poetry, mathematics, and philosophy. Over time, society started allocating more resources to selected individuals, enabling them to concentrate only on intellectual work. They didn't have to do traditional jobs such as farming or hunting and could focus on thinking, theorizing, studying, or practicing religion. Do you think Socrates would have been able to come up with his philosophy if he'd had to labor in some field for 12 hours every day? Probably not.

As a species, we were able to foster the growth of civilization through the invention of a set of complex societal rules called a positive code of conduct:

- Mutual aid (reciprocity), which encouraged cooperation
- Self-sacrifice in the interest of the group as a whole
- Control of immediate instincts and emotions for the greater good (e.g., eating after others, sexual restraint)
- Division of labor and specialization, which over time produced better tools and technologies

The Primacy of Society

Society became the secret weapon of *Homo sapiens*—it was the critical innovation that put us on the path to world domination. Society has been so crucial to our success that we subconsciously and blindly believe in it, without much control or critique. Throughout history—and still today—we continue acting utterly stupid as long as our behavior is consistent with *societal rules*. We use conformity to societal rules as a blanket excuse for various irrational, absurd, behaviors.

Why is this so? It's our innate gratitude for and awe of society that has elevated us to where we are today. We don't even think about how the plumbing system that brings clean water into our homes works, or why we can get electricity through our power outlets. We just flush the toilet and plug our phones in to charge. We believe that "society," as a whole, figured out how to provide those things to us in a safe and reliable way. We normally don't check every time whether there is water in the tap or the power outlet has electricity—we assume *someone* in society is watching over it all. We just assume that it works. That society works. Therefore, we are subconsciously immensely grateful for and respectful of it.

We also believe that society is inherently good—it brings order and curbs violence. This is a valid assumption. There is very good evidence for it on an individual level. Let's zoom in to this aggression-reduction paradigm. In general, we can divide aggression into:

- Reactive, spontaneous ("hot") aggression, such as losing one's temper or lashing out
- Proactive, planned ("cold") aggression, which is carried out deliberately[48]

An example of reactive aggression is shouting at someone who cuts into your lane on a highway or getting into a fight in a bar after someone accidentally spills beer on you. Proactive aggression, on the other hand, is when someone spends days meticulously planning an assassination.

Throughout the last several thousand years, humans—through the process of self-domestication—have dramatically reduced the level of spontaneous aggression. When we compare ourselves to primitive tribes, a very low proportion of contemporary people die from direct violence. The world, on average, has a homicide rate below 1 per 100,000 people per year. This is 10–100 times lower than the last primitive, isolated societies that were studied between the 1880s and the 1960s.

The self-domestication of humans took hundreds and thousands of generations and resulted in the genetic evolution of *Homo sapiens* as a whole. How? Well, the most aggressive, violent individuals were simply eliminated over millennia by society, which gradually shrank the genetic pool of aggressive individuals and propagated the DNA of more docile persons. This process of elimination took many forms: primitive killings of dangerous members of prehistoric societies; wars, which typically eliminate the most ferocious individuals; years of a brutal legal system with capital punishment and long prison sentences that limited procreational opportunities.

Society is a ruthless arbiter, and no one person, not even the greatest warrior, can stand up to its power. The fundamental rule is: If you, as an individual, pick a fight with society, you die. Three stories from completely different parts of the world illustrate this universal law.

One of the hottest places on Earth, in the Kalahari Desert, is inhabited by a famously peaceful hunter-gatherer group, the !Kung San, which was studied by anthropologist Richard Lee in the 1960s. When a surprisingly aggressive member of the !Kung killed three other men without reason—a highly unusual act in that community—the whole village ambushed him with poisonous arrows in full daylight. As a show of community solidarity, every man wanted to participate in this ritual; so after a few moments, his body looked like a porcupine due to the multitude of arrows sticking out of it. What's more, when he was dead, each member of the community stabbed him again in a cathartic moment of collective justice.[49]

At the other end of the world, in the snows of Arctica, one of the coldest places on Earth, a primitive society of Inuit practices the same rules. In an 1888 book, traveler Franz Boas described a man named Padlu who ran off with another's man's wife. When the husband started searching for his wife, Padlu killed him and, subsequently, also the husband's brother and a friend who was helping in the search. Upon learning these facts, the whole society decided to kill Padlu. They did so by shooting him in the back during a hunt.

Today, the modern judiciary system serves the policing role that was enforced *directly* by those native communities. However, if the system is perceived to be ineffective, the same primitive methods of collective *direct* justice kick in. Conformity to society's rules is the ultimate law.

A chilling story from Poland is a great example of such a mechanism. Poland is one of the safest countries on the planet, with a homicide rate of 0.8 per 100,000 (versus 1.1 in rich and stable Sweden, 5.3 in the US, and 62 in Honduras).[50] Poles normally do not own weapons; gun ownership is among the lowest in the world (2 per 100 inhabitants versus 20 in Germany and France, 23 in Sweden, and 120 in the US).[51] By and large, the criminal law system was working relatively well in the early 2000s, with most serious crimes being detected and punished. However, on certain occasions, the police did not follow up on repeated calls about regularly problematic individuals. This breach of a fundamental social contract resulted in spectacular and horrifying consequences in a small rural community in northeast Poland, illustrating how brutal, universal, and basic the laws of society are.

In June 2005, the village of Włodowo in the Warmia region was terrorized by the arrival of Józef Ciechanowicz, a serial offender who, between 1963 and 2004, was sentenced no less than 13 times (!) for various grave atrocities and spent a total of 27 years in prison. He committed multiple crimes: physical assault, theft, bullying, attacking police officers.

On June 29, 2005, he assaulted his ex-girlfriend, who sought refuge at the house of her friend's family. Ciechanowicz entered their private property in search of her and, with an axe, badly injured a man who tried to stop him. The scared villagers reported the matter to the police, who did not intervene, claiming they were too busy. Villagers reported it again and asked three times for intervention, in vain. To their absolute terror, Ciechanowicz came back the same evening, even more aggressive, waving a large cleaver. He vowed to kill a few individuals, including children playing in the courtyard.

This was the last straw. The primal societal rule about protecting children was invoked, and ancient instincts kicked in—there was no return from this point. A group of six men grabbed any random tools of combat they could find around them, including a spade, hammer, crowbar, and car suspension spring, and attacked Ciechanowicz. Faced with unfavorable odds, he decided to withdraw, but the group pressed on, finally feeling they had an advantage. The absence of police after repeated calls emboldened the group to take things into their own hands.

The showdown happened in a nearby ravine, where a primitive, horrific melee ensued between the villagers and Ciechanowicz. The long-standing criminal finally succumbed to numerical superiority, and his skull was smashed open with a spade, while his neck and chest were brutally clubbed and crushed with other random tools. Multiple members of the community came later and did the same thing that was done to the !Kung San man in the Kalahari Desert—dishonored the body, beating it with sticks or whatever else they could find. In 2005, in a relatively rich, well-educated country in the middle of Europe.

Three of the individuals who participated in this lynching were convicted of murder and sentenced to prison. However, the president of Poland granted clemency, absolving all villagers of any consequences. He felt (similarly to a large chunk of society) that the formal legal verdict did not reflect an inherent sense of justice: that the villagers *had the right* to take Ciechanowicz's life.

The ancient rule of societal justice prevailed again.

Social rules apply even in some of the most dysfunctional, extreme circumstances, where society does not seem to work.

For example, in Auschwitz, a Nazi German concentration camp, prisoners living and dying in extreme, inhumane conditions spontaneously developed informal "bread laws." These laws basically instituted a death penalty for anyone who stole food from other inmates. In concentration camps, death by starvation was an everyday possibility. Although the location of any scraps was known to all—overcrowding in the barracks prevented inmates from having secret hiding places to store saved food—stealing bread from each other was rare, because the death penalty would have been imposed collectively by all other inmates.

These examples illustrate that the rules of society haven't changed much over millennia. They follow the same effective, primitive concept: You disobey the societal norms—you die. Those laws are universal geographically (from the Kalahari Desert to Arctica) and work across the wealth spectrum (from rich to poor countries), and even in the most absurd, extreme circumstances, under which society is far from elevating itself (e.g., in gulags or concentration camps).

The absolute power that society commands over our lives has imprinted in our minds the need for conformity. We obey because we either (a) admire society for elevating *Homo sapiens* to where it is today, or (b) fear being punished for being different.

This fear of rejection by society—in other words, the need for conformity—is the mother of all societal stupidities.

The Need for Conformity

Societal conformity reached absolutely irrational levels after our victory over Neanderthals about 50,000 years ago. It is surprising how much individualism and independence we give up every day for the sake of looking similar to other members of our group.

Take innocent choices such as our clothing and makeup styles. Across the globe, each subculture or geographic region has a distinct and strict dress code, from the sari dresses of Calcutta to the dark suits of London's financial district and the baggy skateboard clothes in New York City's Harlem. Anyone who looks different attracts attention and potential ostracism.

This rule seems benign, but it only underlines the small blocks of obedience on which society is built. Take a few steps forward using the same blocks, and you land in a very dark place.

Let's take Pakistan, for example. Most of its society adheres to a draconian, conservative code of how women should behave. If you break this code, even in a seemingly innocent way, you risk the ultimate price—death. Qandeel Baloch was a model and celebrity in Pakistan in the 2010s. She became highly popular after a Pakistani version of the *American Idol* competition kick-started her social media celebrity status. She continued posting various pictures that, although they did not show full nudity or explicit sexual content, were very forward for conservative Pakistan. Her most famous stunt was promising to strip dance if Pakistan won a cricket match against India. This was too much for her own brother, who in July 2016 strangled her to death and later stated in court that his sister "was bringing disrepute to our family's honor."

A divergence from the prevailing social model, however mild, ended in the death of the experimenting individual. This is not an isolated case. The UN estimates that every year, about 5,000 women die from "honor killings" similar to that of Qandeel Baloch's.[52]

The mechanism that underlies desire for conformity has deep roots in our social life and biology. Neurobiologically, our brains consider difference as wrong by default, and only then do the cognitive work needed to change this opinion. It takes only 200 milliseconds to notice that a group has picked a different answer than ours. Our brains are biased toward going along with the group.[53]

On top of this comes the constant societal conditioning that results from social learning. This mechanism is so ancient, so universal, that we can see profound similarities to human behavior in, once again, primates. For example, a chimp is more likely to copy an action after seeing three other individuals do it than after seeing one individual do it three times. Often, when the young chimp sees all adult chimps conforming, it will not even try to break the rule.

The power of conformity is so strong that it literally obscures our basic sensory capabilities.

Look at the four lines in Figure 34. Can you say whether lines A, B, and C are shorter or longer than the target line?

The answer is easy and unequivocal: A is shorter, B is longer, C is the same length. However, in a famous experiment in 1951, 32% of study participants gave wrong answers to this question.[54] The context was important, though: Participants had to give their answers aloud after six other people had answered before them. Those six were accomplices who were told to purposely answer incorrectly by the study designer, who wanted to see if the accomplices' wrong answers would influence others. The exercise was run for multiple rounds (12 trials), and scientists measured how many times participants conformed with the majority view (32%). However, an even more stunning statistic is that 75% of participants conformed with a clearly incorrect view at least one time! In the control group (with no one purposely shouting wrong answers), only 1% gave wrong answers.

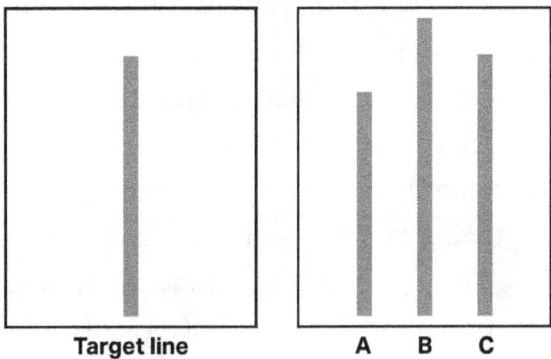

FIGURE 34. Longer or shorter than the target line?[55]

Can you believe how many times over our lifetimes we go along with obviously incorrect statements and support the wrong side, merely because the majority of the people around us do so?

And life overall is much more ambiguous than those four lines above!

This illustrates how susceptible we are to the need for conformity. A 1955 study by Morton Deutsch and Harold B. Gerard found that we do so because we want to fit in with the group (normative influence) or believe that the group is better informed than we are (informational influence).

Absolution by Social Acceptance

Out of conformity with social rules comes another absurd paradox: the belief that society's acceptance can absolve us from wicked acts. In other words, while each of us individually might avoid doing bad things, we do them without guilt when we have society's blessing.

A perfect example is killing civilians in a war. Most *individual* humans would consider it morally unacceptable to purposely kill civilians during wartime. However, there are many examples in recent history in which the same individuals—good humans—gladly participate in such murders and do not feel guilty at all because society absolves them.

The Nazis committed so many crimes during World War II that studying their example would be too obvious. Let's study the Allies, the good guys in this war. In 1943, the Allies launched a campaign of unlimited bombing in Germany. The focus was initially on the armaments industry and vital infrastructure such as railway junctions, bridges, and dams. Gradually, however, the focus turned to big cities, which were far easier targets and presented an easy way of terrorizing the population to break morale and reduce the willingness to fight. American and British war strategists started planning missions to bomb Hamburg, Berlin, and other major German cities with the explicit purpose of ... killing as many civilians as possible.

Yes, the good guys in this war were optimizing for killing noncombatants, women, and children. Sophisticated techniques were developed just for that purpose. First, a small number of fast, nimble Mosquitos from pathfinder teams would drop magnesium parachute flares on heavily populated, dense areas of a town, marking the targets. Then the main formations of B-17, B-24, or Lancaster bombers would arrive and methodically wipe out whole quarters of the cities, aiming at the flares but with the blissful comfort of knowing that missing by half a mile or two would not matter that much—their bombs would still be on target, because the target was the whole city.

The most vicious example of such an attack was Dresden in February 1945. At that time, the city did not present a target of military significance and was filled with internal refugees. The war was already practically won, with Soviet forces preparing to take Berlin and Allied forces deep into German territory. Against that backdrop, almost 800 British and 1,300 American bombers attacked the city on February 13–15, practically wiping it out and killing approximately 25,000 people, almost entirely civilians. Margaret Freyer, a German survivor, remembers the night of the attack:

> To my left I suddenly see a woman. I can see her to this day and shall never forget it. She carries a bundle in her arms. It is a baby. She runs, she falls, and the child flies in an arc into the fire. Suddenly, I saw people again, right in front of me. They scream and gesticulate with their hands, and then—to my utter horror and amazement—I see how one after the other they simply seem to let themselves drop to the ground. (Today I know that these unfortunate people were the victims of lack of oxygen.) They fainted and then burnt to cinders.

I am sure that if the crews of those B-17 bombers had been presented with the option of shooting this woman and her baby with a pistol, they would have resolutely refused. Most of them would have even disobeyed a direct order to shoot a civilian, knowing they would be court-martialed. However, as a group, they all participated in this danse macabre, throwing bombs at defenseless civilians.

Isn't it shocking? These planes were crewed by ordinary, good men, who often showed extraordinary sacrifice to save their comrades. They were good sons and husbands—caring, loving, empathetic. But they were turned into a ruthless killing machine *as a group*. Each individual man would refuse to shoot point-blank at one person, but together they would drop two tons of bombs, each of which would kill 12 people on average. How irrational....

Society's absolution is not limited only to such dramatic actions as wartime killing. Just the opposite—every day, a lot of well-intentioned, hardworking people participate in activities that cause harm in everyday lives.

Take coal mining and coal-fired power plants in Poland as an example. Poland produces about 76% of its electricity from coal-fired power plants.[56] Burning coal in stoves in individual houses and at industrial power plants is a key contributor to air pollution. As a result, the country had the worst air quality in the European Union (EU).[57] (The situation is improving recently, though.)

That air pollution causes cardiovascular diseases is not well known to society at large. The mechanism of transmission is surprising: Burning coal pollutes the air with very small particles (PM2.5) that are absorbed into our bloodstream and create blood clots, which results in a higher incidence of cardiovascular diseases. Scientists and doctors estimate that every year, around 44,000 excessive deaths in Poland are caused by air pollution. For a country of 38 million people, that is a staggering number.

Despite these figures, the coal-mining and coal power-generation industries are untouchable. They enjoy full societal absolution. There are two reasons for that. First, the coal industry has extremely strong labor unions that wield significant political power. Second, coal mining is presented as a patriotic activity to protect the country's energy independence from Russia.

Polish citizens bear a huge economic cost for its coal-based economy: Poland's carbon emissions tax (charged per megawatt hour of produced energy), is on average three times higher than that paid by the average EU country, making its electricity one of the most expensive in the world.[58] The highest price, though, is paid in lives—Poland sacrifices 44,000 people every year for the sake of keeping fewer than 80,000 coal miners at work.[59]

Isn't that too high a price? Would you do a job that requires someone to die every second year for you to keep the job? However, if you were told that your work is critical to keeping your country's energy independence (a very valid point for Poland), that you are a true patriot, wouldn't your perception change? This is the power of social acceptance.

The hardworking, well-meaning individuals who are employed in coal mines do not understand or acknowledge that their work creates harm. They trust people of high social status, such as government officials or labor union leaders, who tell them that they are the soul of the country and their job is critical to sustaining its economy and sovereignty.

The choice is not between Polish energy independence and letting thousands of people die. It is between choosing coal-fired power plants or nuclear power plants, wind turbines, and photovoltaics.

However, the societal narrative uses patriotic fervor (which Poles never lack) to justify a complacent, incompetent government hiding the real cause of the problem—lack of investment in clean electricity generation.

Group Behavior

Psychologists a long time ago discovered a phenomenon called *group behavior*, which explains how individual actions are different in group settings versus individual settings. It is a fascinating topic.

Basically, while in a group, we are far more likely to show abnormally aggressive, irrational, and extremist behavior. A lot of the usual safety switches go silent, and we do things we would never have done on our own.

We are dangerous when we are in a group, as we are inclined to undertake far more radical steps because of the intoxicating support of the crowd and our sense of safety, invincibility, and impunity. (Your dear author was at several football games where he chanted things that would not win the approval of the editor of this book. You, dear reader, were probably in large gatherings where you did things you normally wouldn't do either.)

Hooliganism at sporting events, where individuals completely lose themselves in a group, is a perfect example. They very quickly start acting violently without provocation—even if there are no major differences between the clashing groups, even if they share the same nationality, ethnicity, religion, and language or live in the same area. Take the example of football teams (European football is called soccer in the US) from the same country. There are many documented examples of highly aggressive clashes of fans, such as the massive riot in February 2012 between fans of the Masry and Ahly football clubs in Egypt, who started fighting each other because of the exhilaration of being part of a crowd. In this famous riot, 73 football fans died and more than 500 were injured.[60]

One could say that football riots are caused by a small group of chronically aggressive individuals. Well, then let's study examples in which normal, "good" citizens fall into the trap of groupthink. Or even better, let's start with the people who are supposed to be keeping the world in order.

The police are state agencies meant to protect citizens and ensure physical safety. However, sometimes these seemingly highly trusted organizations lose themselves in group behavior as well. In 2017, the police force in the city of Vitória in Brazil (just north of Rio de Janeiro) announced a strike over pay. They refused to patrol the streets for 10 consecutive days. This brought mayhem to the city. Thousands of bad actors suddenly appeared on the streets, looting everything from shops to banks, stealing cars, and murdering people. Public transport stopped operating, shops closed, citizens barricaded themselves in their houses. A total of 215 murders happened during the strike.[61]

Didn't it occur to those police officers that they were there to protect the people? That refusing to patrol the streets would encourage plunder and violence? Nonetheless, the officers were so stubborn and determined in their group thinking that they continued to strike, even when people were being slain in front of their eyes at a rate never seen before. If any individual was told that their inaction would cause 215 to die, they would typically feel guilty and do the right thing—in particular, when it is their job to prevent such things from happening.

But not when we are in a group. Group resolve, fear of "failing" the group and being considered the "weak" element, makes us so callous and ruthless that we will even accept loss of life.

There are some reports of another illuminating fact concerning the same incident. Apparently, a lot of middle-class citizens joined the plunder of shops when they saw everyone else doing it. Their moral norms were vanquished within hours when they felt that "others in the group" were doing the same and there was "permission" to do so. The middle class went amok and turned into a mob because of groupthink....

Where does this all fundamentally come from? Hogg, Adelman, and Wagoner postulated that:

> People are motivated to reduce self-uncertainty, specifically feelings of uncertainty about their life, their future, and uncertainty about their self and identity. One way to solve this problem of self-uncertainty is group identification. Individuals use the groups that they are part of to define their self-concept. Social groups are represented as prototypes, sets of attributes, values, beliefs, feelings, behaviors that define the group and its members and distinguish it from others. Therefore, by prescribing prototypes, groups provide people identity and reduce uncertainty regarding who they are, how to behave, and what to think, and who others are and how they might behave, think. When self-uncertainty becomes chronic, pervasive, or acute, people are strongly attracted to extremist groups, because they prescribe a clear prototype for how one should behave, think, and feel in all situations, and how to behave toward out-group members. Self-uncertainty drives people toward distinct and clear groups, motivates them to defend their in-group against out-groups who are perceived as a threat to their group's values and beliefs.[62]

Per psychologist Henri Tajfel's social identity theory, the concept of who we are is heavily shaped by social context—which groups we are a member of and which groups we are not. Imitating someone's actions activates the mesolimbic dopamine system, which gives us a "high," as if we were on drugs. It also numbs our discomfort when we make wrong choices, interfering with our ability to make the right calls.

We are following in the footsteps of the monkeys—primates that aggressively target an individual only because another primate is already doing so.[63] Marmosets (cute little monkeys) become more aggressive if a neighboring group vocalizes aggression.

FIGURE 35. Marmosets: our distant cousins
These cuties succumb to group mentality as well....

Similarly, whole societies can lose their minds for years or even decades and project grand aggression because of group behavior.

In 1930s Japan, most of the local elites—intellectuals, journalists, economists, business and military leaders, and even some philosophers—resolved that Japan could enjoy long-term economic success only by subjugating Manchuria, Korea, and China. Through years of group debate, they concluded that access to these countries' resources was the only way to prosperity, given that Japan itself is not endowed with many natural resources. As a result, Japan's elites launched a terrible war against China in 1931 and then against the British Empire, Australia, and the US in 1941.

It turned out they were entirely wrong! Not only did their policy bring death and destruction to Japan itself, when it was bombed into submission by the US Air Force, but the postwar period *also* proved their thinking was completely flawed. After World War II, Japan *prospered* in a spectacular way, *despite* the lack of natural resources. It built industries and services based on skills and knowledge, rather than access to minerals. It created world-class manufacturing, building ships, cars, and electronics, and then shifting to pharmaceuticals, robotics, and financial services—none of which were based on local natural resources. Japan imported the key raw materials and components, added huge value locally through processing, knowledge, and intellectual property, and then consumed the products internally or sold them abroad.

Even democratic, resource-rich, prosperous countries can be turned into aggressive war machines through the groupthink spiral. Take the US after the September 11, 2001, terrorist attacks. Everyone empathized with the US's desire to find and punish the perpetrators. However, the American political elites (led by George W. Bush, Dick Cheney, and Donald Rumsfeld) decided this was a good opportunity to overthrow the rulers of several countries that were not friendly to the US. Ten days after September 11, Wesley Clark, the commander of NATO in Europe, went to the Pentagon to see Secretary of Defense Rumsfeld and Deputy Secretary of Defense Wolfowitz. He recollects meeting one of the generals who were privy to their plans and having this conversation:

> He [the friendly general] says, "We've made the decision we're going to war with Iraq." This was on or about the 20th of September. I [Wesley Clark] said, "We're going to war with Iraq? Why?" He said, "I don't know." He said, "I guess they don't know what else to do." So I said, "Well, did they find some information connecting Saddam to Al-Qaeda?" He said, "No, no." He says, "There's nothing new that way. They just made the decision to go to war with Iraq." He said, "I guess it's like we don't know what to do about terrorists, but we've got a good military and we can take down governments." And he said, "I guess if the only tool you have is

a hammer, every problem has to look like a nail." So I came back to see him a few weeks later, and by that time we were bombing in Afghanistan. I said, "Are we still going to war with Iraq?" And he said, "Oh, it's worse than that." He reached over to his desk. He picked up a piece of paper. And he said, "I just got this down from upstairs"—meaning the Secretary of Defense's office—"today." And he said, "This is a memo that describes how we're going to take out seven countries in five years, starting with Iraq, and then Syria, Lebanon, Libya, Somalia, Sudan and, finishing off, Iran."[64]

This group, and hundreds of other American leaders, deluded themselves into thinking that aggressing against those countries was the only way forward. With this groupthink fervor, they co-opted many other rational leaders to support that outrageous idea.

What did it have to do with the September 11 attacks? Very little or nothing. Of the terrorists who flew planes into the World Trade Center and the Pentagon, 15 out of 19 were Saudi Arabian citizens, 2 were from the United Arab Emirates, 1 was from Egypt, and 1 from Lebanon. However, none of these countries were among those that George Bush and his acolytes chose to invade. Instead, they decided to invade *several other countries that were more advantageous targets*.

Nonetheless, the American elites, fueled by patriotic fervor, succumbed to groupthink and convinced themselves in the space of just a few months that the US should invade Iraq, Libya, Somalia, Sudan, and Iran. And they started executing this plan, beginning with Iraq.

In a famous briefing to the United Nations (UN), Secretary of State Colin Powell presented "evidence" that Iraq had weapons of mass destruction (which was a lie) and therefore the UN should sanction an invasion of Iraq. Powell was personally not in favor of attacking Iraq but finally yielded to the pressure of groupthink and lent his authority to support this illogical case. Before 9/11 and until the invasion of Iraq in March 2003, most of the world loved America, wanted to be like America, and wanted to help America. Within two years of the invasion, the US lost all its moral high ground and became an object of antipathy or hatred around the world (see Figure 36).

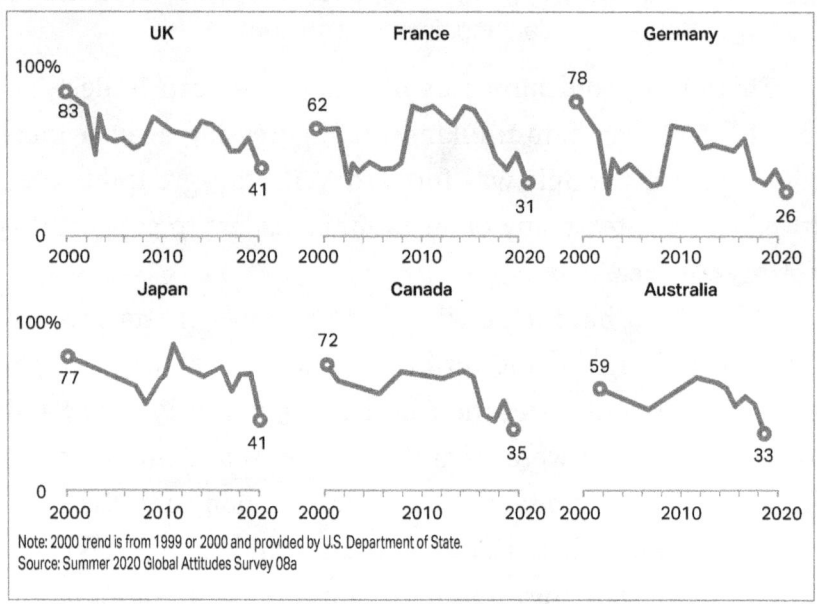

FIGURE 36. Favorable views of the US globally[65]

From top to bottom, in just a few years. How sad.

The mania of groupthink and group righteousness went so absurdly far that a campaign was even started to rename *french fries* to *freedom fries* to "punish" France for not joining the US in its ill-conceived invasion of Iraq.

Let's play out a scenario: What would have happened if US leaders at that time had *not* succumbed to groupthink mentality? For convenience, let's hypothesize that Al Gore had been president, rather than George W. Bush. (By the way, this is not a hard scenario to imagine, as Al Gore actually won the general vote in the 2000 election by approximately half a million votes, and the only reason he did not become president was because of the brilliant legal game of George Bush's campaign staff). And let's assume he would have been less susceptible to being swayed by the group.

Under Al Gore, the US would have probably *still* supported the overthrow of the Taliban regime in Afghanistan to find and punish Al-Qaeda there. This was actually achieved by the George W. Bush administration within months of the 9/11 attacks, at minimal cost, through support provided to the Northern Alliance, the competing Afghani faction.

But then, with punishment meted out to the organizers of the attacks, the US could have returned to the path of peaceful development, beloved by the free world, enjoying tremendous empathy as the victim of an unprovoked attack. It could have continued extracting the peace dividend of a benevolent giant, leading the free world morally, economically, and politically. Its international reputation and standing could have remained extremely high, while its values, such as democracy, an independent judiciary, and human rights, would have continued to radiate and inspire many nations.

Also, the US would have been much wealthier now. Instead of spending approximately $2 trillion on the Iraq War alone[66] (and an estimated $6 trillion on the whole War on Terror[67]), it could have invested in new industries and upgraded its infrastructure.

Let's assume that out of that total $6 trillion war bill, $2 trillion had been spent by Gore on the War on Terror to provide limited support to overthrow the regime in Afghanistan and increase internal security spending at home.

Imagine what would have happened if the US in the early 2000s had invested the remaining $4 trillion into infrastructure and renewable technologies such as batteries, solar, wind, and nuclear? Today, the US would be the most advanced country in these sectors, and China would probably never have become dominant in those industries. Today, the US would have a world-class infrastructure, cheap electricity, and a modern manufacturing base. What's more, it would have inspired the whole world to start following suit.

This is how the world could have looked today if American elites had been less prone to groupthink.

Society-Sponsored Violence

While on an individual level, *Homo sapiens* has become less and less violent over the centuries, as a group we are still vulnerable to being manipulated into extreme brutality. Look at Figure 37—see how individual violence has plummeted in western Europe over the last 700 years?

That's great news! Individually, we are becoming more docile and peaceful! However, on a societal level, when it comes to organized violence, it is a completely different story (see Figure 38).

This shows that, as a society, we have maintained our murderous inclinations over time. So it is society that keeps us more violent than we would have been as individuals. It cancels thousands of years of progress on an individual level! What a spectacular illustration of the negative power of society!

Even well-developed, relatively prosperous countries with high levels of literacy and education fall easily into group-led violence traps. Europe, one of the richest regions in the world, is a stunning example. In the first half of the 20th century, it was

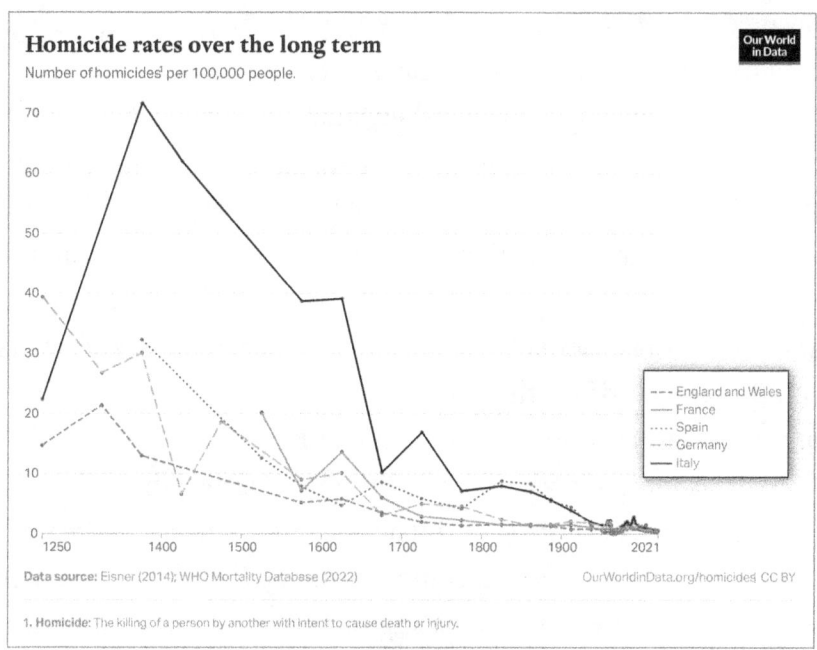

FIGURE 37. Long-term homicide rates since 1300[68]

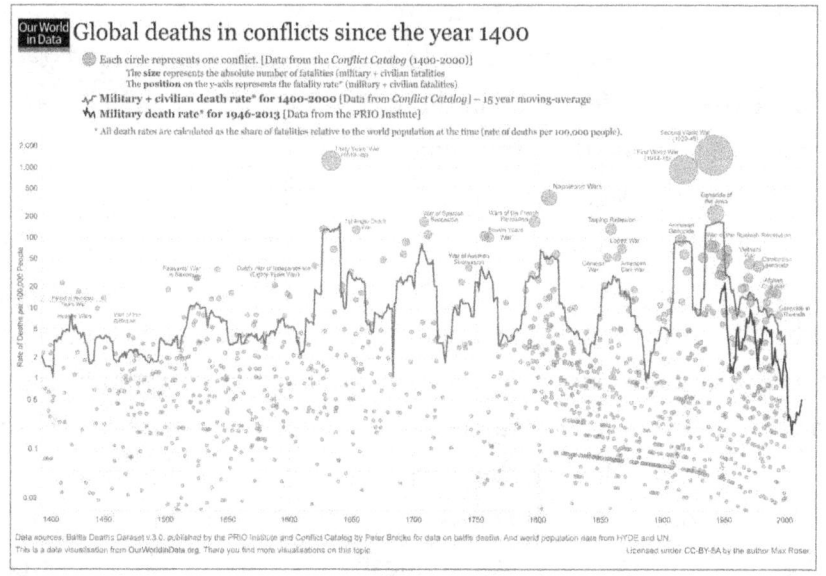

FIGURE 38. Global deaths in conflicts since 1400[69]

ravaged by two world wars, started by Germany, which butchered its societies across the social strata.

World War I was a watershed moment for the UK. In the early days of the war, there was a true eruption of joy on both sides. The propaganda machine in countries around the world was spectacularly effective at drumming up support for the war. Everyone was manipulated into believing that going to war and killing the other side's soldiers was a most noble, righteous act. Society glorified the upcoming conflict—there were huge prowar demonstrations in London and Berlin.

British men of both lower and higher classes joined the military with overwhelming enthusiasm. They viewed it as a great sporting event, where you could prove your valor and advance your social status by participating in a truly gentlemanly sport: war. Trains carrying German troops to the front lines displayed "Trip to Paris" plaques. The streets were covered with flowers that had been showered by a euphoric population on the thousands of volunteers who joined the army, war bonds issued to finance the war effort sold on the spot, and young men lied about their age and health so they could enlist.

Nobody expected it to be an industrialized killing spree that would last over four years. It shook society to the bone. At the end of the war, close to a million British men had fallen in battle, a bewildering 2.2% of its population.[70] An additional 1.6 million were wounded. One in 20 citizens of the UK had personally paid a price in blood for the war. For some cohorts, in particular those who volunteered early, the price was even more shocking—33% of the Oxford University class of 1912 didn't make it to the end of the war.[71] In previous wars, typically the poor and uneducated gave their lives for the glory of the UK. But the Great War of

1914–18 "democratized" this sacrifice and ripped through the elites as well.

If you were born male in the Soviet Union in 1923, it was probably the least auspicious time you could choose to be alive in Europe in the 20th century. When this cohort was 18 years old, Hitler launched Operation Barbarossa, and these young men were fed hurriedly into an ailing, chaotic Soviet war machine. They paid a horrendous price in life. About two-thirds of them didn't make it to the end of World War II, when they would have been 23 years old.[72]

So in 20th-century Europe, on a seemingly civilized, wealthy, industrialized continent with automobiles, phones, and radio, violent deaths at some points were comparable to or exceeded those of primitive bushmen tribes from thousands of years ago. Shocking!

All due to the blessing of society.

We can observe the same mechanism of organized violence across the world and across eras. Some societies were built around this principle. For example, the rapid spread of Islam was achieved through brilliant military exploits rather than peaceful missionary efforts. Islam glorified military prowess and demanded the spread of the faith with sword in hand. Just 30 years (!) after the prophet Muhammad's death in 632 CE, his early followers had expanded the empire westward to modern-day Tunisia and eastward to modern-day Afghanistan. Muslims conquered this vast territory mostly thanks to a phenomenal cavalry, which was incredibly combat-effective, determined, and fast.

Isn't it stunning how powerful society-sponsored violence can become? All our natural security valves, "handbrakes," and stop-loss mechanisms, which work well on an individual level, fail miserably under the influence of society-endorsed aggression.

Even institutions associated with peace, piety, and restraint can be hijacked and turned into group-led destructive forces that act against their key principles.

Let's take the Catholic Church. Christianity was founded on the principles of selflessness, generosity, and nonviolence. Jesus Christ famously commanded:

> Love your enemies, do good to those who hate you, bless those who curse you, pray for those who abuse you. To one who strikes you on the cheek, offer the other also, and to one who takes away your cloak do not withhold your tunic either. Give to everyone who begs from you, and from one who takes away your goods do not demand them back. And as you wish that others would do to you, do so to them (Luke 6:27–31, English Standard Version).

Despite this pacifist foundation, during the Middle Ages, the Catholic Church was transformed into a formidable fighting force almost overnight by Pope Urban II, who initiated the Crusades. After a famous rousing speech at the Council of Clermont in 1095, he blessed war against the Muslim world and encouraged it by promising to pardon the sins of all Christians who took up arms to reclaim the Holy Land. This encouragement was enthusiastically received throughout Europe, and within a year, *four* Christian armies descended on the Middle East with the goal of capturing Jerusalem. The religious fervor created elite military units such as the Knights Templar and Knights Hospitaller, which had monastic ideals, took religious vows, and were highly disciplined and phenomenally effective in combat.

Thus, a religion based on ideals of peace gained a highly capable military arm. Like the Muslims almost 500 years earlier,

Christians created formidable, religiously inspired cavalry units, ruthless and deadly effective. (What is it about cavalry and religious fervor?)

Simply by receiving society's approval, we humans turn into violent beasts, often despite our own beliefs or even against earlier societal norms.

The Power of Incentives

In 1946, three Bedouin boys were grazing their goats near Qumran when they made an incredible discovery: a full library of manuscripts in Hebrew, Aramaic, and Greek from the third century BCE to the first century CE. The scrolls, which included biblical, apocryphal, and sectarian texts, had enormous archaeological value, allowing scientists to study those ancient languages and cultures and their religious discourse. After the initial discovery, the euphoric scientists announced bounties for any person who brought them more similar manuscripts, hoping that more scrolls would be excavated from nearby caves. They were right! Over a period of 10 years, numerous further discoveries were made and a total of 11 caves were identified in the same area, about a mile from the shore of the Dead Sea. However, never again were so many *fully well-preserved* scrolls identified. All subsequent discoveries were coming in smaller and smaller pieces.

Roland de Vaux, one of the archaeologists, rationally asked the right question: Why? After some deliberation, he figured out that because the Bedouins were remunerated for each piece of manuscript, they were breaking the newly found scriptures into smaller parts to earn a higher bounty. Shocked by this discovery, de Vaux changed the remuneration system and started paying per square centimeter rather than per piece.

What a shame, isn't it? The archaeologists discovered not only the ancient scriptures but also the eternal law of wrong incentives. We have perhaps lost forever scriptures that didn't survive the primitive process of splitting into parts.

The tendency to strictly obey the rules of incentives, rather than following their spirit, is an incredibly powerful phenomenon. Throughout history, we have seen remarkable examples of this inclination at work.

In the Soviet Union, after the 1917 Bolshevik Revolution, agriculture was forcibly nationalized in the form of *kolkhoz* (collectively owned farms) and *sovkhoz* (state-owned farms). The former peasants were forced to work for those huge organizations without any recognition of their individual performance. So if you plowed 10 acres of land a day, while your peers did only 5, you would not get twice as much food or salary. You would instead enjoy the same terrible lunch as your less productive colleagues because of the Soviet ideological obsession with equality. This resulted in unmotivated workers and a massive decline of productivity, which contributed to the great famine of 1930–33, when more than five million perished.

Perhaps learning from this catastrophic mistake, Stalin in 1935 approved a new initiative, allocating small plots of land (only 2% of the total area) to be managed directly by the individual *kolkhoz* and *sovkhoz* workers. Most importantly, the workers themselves were allowed to fully consume or sell the produce from these plots. Suddenly, the productivity in those areas exploded! By 1973, this paltry 2% of the land was responsible for 25% of the Soviet Union's entire agricultural production! This equates to a stunning 16 times higher productivity rate per acre!⁷³ Basically, this small change stimulated entrepreneurship and hard work across the country.

Since then, Soviet citizens have been working with dedication on the land they were allowed to retain, while still performing lousy jobs on their official, state-owned estates. This is a truly amazing example of a productivity boost on an unprecedented scale, which helped make the difference between famine and food security. Changing incentives unleashed a dramatic improvement of the system, even helping the Soviet Union to temporarily become a food exporter.

The share of C-section births in the US grew from 21% in 1996 to 32% in 2020.⁷⁴ Vaginal, natural birth is generally safer for the mother and better for the baby: less blood loss, lower risk of complications and infections, faster recovery, stronger support for the baby's immune system. In certain situations, a C-section is necessary medically, but typically this does not exceed 10%–15% of all cases. Nonetheless, the rate of C-sections is increasing year by year in America and varies dramatically between hospitals: 7% in some and even 70% in others!⁷⁵ That clearly cannot be explained by medical necessity alone! Moreover, "emergency" cesarean births typically decline around lunchtime and at the end of the day (when doctors leave the hospital).

Can you hypothesize what is at play here? Obviously, the system of incentives! Doctors are paid significantly more for C-section births than for vaginal births, and C-sections can be scheduled and planned, unlike unpredictable vaginal births that require expensive labor rooms with 24/7 staff. In short, they are more remunerative and easier to manage.

So the phenomenon of C-section births is growing like a weed in the US, fueled by a wrong system of incentives. Interestingly, physician-patients (female doctors who have given birth themselves) are 10% less likely to choose a C-section than other doctors.... This should give you food for thought.

Finally, have you ever walked into the men's bathroom at an airport? This is typically a scene of carnage, a true Rambo-like battlefield! "Spillage" all around the walls and on the floor, toilet paper everywhere, as if a typhoon with very bad aim had visited the bathroom. Even in the first-class lounge, the state of the men's lavatory is often pathetic. Do you think the wealthy gentlemen traveling on intercontinental flights for $10,000 a trip have worse aim than men who stay at home and do not travel? I don't think so. It is really about incentives. At home, masculine aim seems to be superbly better than at the airport.

This is because men at the airport don't care about where they piss—someone else will clean up after them, and they will not get criticized by their partner at home.

Okay, let's end this painful section on a positive note: Serious research proves that merely printing a fly next to the urinal's drain reduces "spillage" by 80%![76]

Give a man a purpose and he will win the day!

Bureaucracy's Innocent Beginnings

One of the most ridiculous aspects of societal acceptance is bureaucracy. It calls for unconditional adherence to strict rules, often brutal and primitive, that do not typically stand up to a rationality test. But we respect them, regardless—because society has blessed them.

It starts innocently, such as by naming things ... awkwardly.

For example, when communicating with average citizens, US bureaucracy uses the following terms: Medicare Part D,

K9, 401(k), 8802. For non-American readers of this book, these mean, respectively: prescription drug insurance, a police dog, a pension plan, and confirmation of tax residency.

People visiting from other countries do not know that American police dogs are called K9s, so when I first saw a sign at the airport that read "K9s operate in this area!" I wondered what to expect. A James Bond type of agent? A self-driving vehicle? Maybe an elite counterterrorist police unit? What a stupid name to call a dog at an airport—a place that has a ton of foreigners who do not know your jargon. In airports, things should be identified as simply and universally as possible.

The term *401(k)* is now so commonly used by Americans that they do not even realize how awkward it is to refer this way to their pension plan. Think about it! It is your pension plan, the source of your income in your old age! So why do we define it as a three-digit number, as if it doesn't even make our top 100 list? Isn't it important enough to deserve just one or two digits? And why *k*? Is it not important enough to be *a*, *b*, or *c*? It is just some nonsensical bureaucratic jargon.

That's a classic start to bad beginnings—once we acquiesce to small, strange bureaucratic customs, the floodgates open. Once we accept, as a society, the use of K9 or 401(k), why are we surprised the next time bureaucracy talks to us about filing our 83(b) or exercising our *Miranda v. Arizona* rights?[77] They are the same custom, the same language.

We allow it once—we suffer forever.

Try to read this excerpt from an insightful, yet jargon-filled scientific article by Lukas Schwingshackl and others:[78]

> Results: With increasing intake (for each daily serving) of whole grains (RR: 0.92; 95% CI: 0.89, 0.95), vegetables (RR: 0.96; 95% CI: 0.95, 0.98), fruits (RR: 0.94; 95% CI: 0.92, 0.97),

nuts (RR: 0.76; 95% CI: 0.69, 0.84), and fish (RR: 0.93; 95% CI: 0.88, 0.98), the risk of all-cause mortality decreased; higher intake of red meat (RR: 1.10; 95% CI: 1.04, 1.18) and processed meat (RR: 1.23; 95% CI: 1.12, 1.36) was associated with an increased risk of all-cause mortality in a linear dose-response meta-analysis. A clear indication of nonlinearity was seen for the relations between vegetables, fruits, nuts, and dairy and all-cause mortality.

Nuts: Sixteen studies with 80,204 mortality cases were included in the high- compared with the low intake meta-analysis (overall intake range: 0252 g/d). A strong inverse association was observed for the highest compared with the lowest nut intake category (RR: 0.80; 95% CI: 0.74, 0.86; I 2 = 84%; P-heterogeneity, 0.001) (Supplemental Figure 12), and for each additional daily 28 g (RR: 0.76; 95% CI: 0.69, 0.84; I 2 = 82%; P-heterogeneity, 0.001; n = 16) (Supplemental Figure 13).

Did you understand any of it? Probably not. How about if I translate it for you in more human language:

The results show, with 95% confidence, that mortality is reduced for people who eat diets high in the following nutrients: whole grains (by 8%), vegetables (by 4%), fruits (by 6%), fish (by 7%), and nuts (by a stunning 24%), while all-cause mortality increases by 10% for people who eat diets high in red meat and by 23% for diets high in processed meat. The analysis of nuts, which used data from 16 studies in which 80,204 people died, measured the impact of an incremental daily intake of 28 grams of nuts. It was found that people who ate the most nuts had the lowest mortality rate.

Isn't that better? It is half the length, and you can actually understand what it says.

This article has phenomenally important insights. Processed meat is a killer—it increases mortality by 23%, whereas consumption of nuts is the most potent game changer for your health! Its impact is a whopping 24% reduction in mortality, 4–6 times higher than for eating a diet high in the celebrated and well-known fruits and vegetables!

But you probably haven't heard that amazing news. Almost nobody has heard of it—the knowledge is buried in unbearable jargon in some obscure papers known only to researchers and insiders!

Scientific language—jargon—makes science unavailable for the masses, alienates the general populace, and reduces interest in science and the number of people who choose to study it. But jargon also makes scientists look serious and competent. Why not satisfy both purposes at the same time? Adding a simple paragraph with more understandable language would extend the article's length by less than 1%, while probably increasing its impact by 10–100 times.

Scientists use a lot of shortcuts and abbreviations, such as RR (relative risk) and CI (confidence interval), but it costs so little to explain the term once at the beginning or provide a layperson's summary at the end.

Tolerance of unfamiliar names and abbreviations—a seemingly small annoyance—is growing larger and larger. But all too suddenly, you may find yourself in an absurd circumstance caused by those strict rules of bureaucracy.

Bureaucracy in Full Swing

Take the example of an entrepreneur who starts a new business. The number of bureaucratic rules and regulations you have to comply with is overwhelming. In my opinion (having gone through the process of building two companies in the US from scratch), it is extremely difficult to follow all the rules if you are a solo or small business founder. You need a whole army of lawyers, tax advisors, privacy law experts, and security and employment advisors to submit so many forms and filings. If you were to do it yourself, you would have no time to run the actual business. This, again, skews the system to favor large corporations and rich people. In many countries, the rules for setting up a business are so complicated that it takes from two months (in Liechtenstein) to *five months* (in Cambodia) just to ... open a business.[79]

If you give powers to an official, they will try to expand their team and authority so they can feel as important as possible. Regardless of whether this is important for society or not.

Let's look at the modus operandi of the US Federal Drug Administration (FDA) until 2025. This agency oversees the approval of new pharmaceuticals for the US market. It was created to protect the public from harmful substances by verifying which drugs are safe and which are not. However, over time, it got corrupted by its own power, demanding more and more resources and complicating approval processes to an absurd degree. The FDA now requires so many bureaucratic and expensive studies, reviews, and procedures that the cost of getting a new drug to the market in the first half of the 2020s averaged around $2 billion, and could go as high as $5–$10 billion.[80]

A huge percentage of this figure is the cost of complying with bureaucratic procedures—not the physical process of actually inventing a drug. So often, the cost of innovation does not lie in paying for those smart PhDs in white uniforms who diligently test one hypothesis after another but, rather, paying the sad bureaucrats in gray suits who point out problems and raise objections for every solution. Consequently, if an arcane approval process alone costs a few billion, pharmaceutical companies impose sky-high prices for the drugs to recoup their investment. The result? Drugs that are unaffordable for normal people. (My cousin has a rare musculoskeletal condition, and a new-generation, promising drug that took about 10 years to approve costs ... $2.1 million per treatment. He cannot afford that. Who could? He might have to stick to his wheelchair because the bureaucratic approval process is so inefficient.) This is the real, tangible cost of bureaucratic stupidity.

Astronomical hidden cost of a bureaucracy that we do not reflect enough on is the amount of time it wastes. Time is the most precious resource we have in life, regardless of our financial or societal status.

However, we all accept that bureaucracy can take up a huge part of our lifetimes, and we accept the stupidest requests because they are coming "from the government." Take a look at selected questions from the application for a US green card, Form I-485 (these questions are taken from the 2017 version of the form, which is 18 pages long):

Excerpts from Form I-485 (Part 8. General Eligibility and Inadmissibility Grounds)

32. Have you EVER illicitly (illegally) trafficked or benefited from trafficking of any controlled substances, such as chemicals, illegal drugs, or narcotics?

36. Have you EVER directly or indirectly procured (or attempted to procure) or imported prostitutes or persons for the purpose of prostitution?

46.c. Do you intend to engage in any activity whose purpose includes opposing, controlling, or overthrowing the US Government by force, violence, or other unlawful means while in the United States?

56. Have you EVER been a member of, or in any way affiliated with, the Communist Party or any other totalitarian party (in the United States or abroad)?

57. During the period from March 23, 1933 to May 8, 1945 did you ever order, incite, assist, or otherwise participate in the persecution of any person because of race, religion, national origin, or political opinion, in association with either the Nazi government of Germany of any organization of government associated or allied with the Nazi government of Germany?

58.a. Have you EVER ordered, incited, called for, committed, assisted, helped with, or otherwise participated in … acts involving torture or genocide?

Isn't this form silly? First of all, this whole section is titled "Inadmissibility Grounds," which suggests that if you answer "Yes" to any of these questions, your application to enter the US will be rejected.

So if your intention is to blow up the US government, why would you tell the government in advance, in a clear, mannerly statement via question 46.c on Form I-485, that you are planning to do so? Is this the smart method the US government uses to screen for potential terrorists? Do we think people will self-identify as terrorists on a government form? Really?

Why does this form ask all those detailed, awkward questions but not ask others? Who created this section and selected these questions but didn't include others? For example, why not ask questions about whether you want to fly a plane into a high-rise building (for which there is historical evidence—the 9/11 attacks—whereas there is no evidence of immigrants successfully overthrowing the US government)?

I would love to see the statistics on how many people answered those questions positively and how many human traffickers, terrorists, and rebels the US government has caught in this way.

If you plan to ask stupid questions, then at least ask them logically! Why is the question about helping the Nazi regime restricted to between March 23, 1933, and May 8, 1945? Hitler came to power on January 30, 1933, about two months before the start of this government-picked range. Also, World War II ended on the Eastern Front on May 9, not May 8 (Germany signed two separate unconditional surrender protocols, one to the Western Allies and one to the Soviets). So if you helped in the genocide of the Jews on May 10, 1945, or on March 15, 1933, should you be off the hook? And why is prosecution only on the grounds of race, religion, and political affiliation mentioned? What if you helped killing gay people under the Nazi regime (which systemically eliminated this social group)? How stupid!

The question about membership in the Communist Party seems to have been there since McCarthy's commission in the 1950s. Why hasn't anybody updated this question in the last 70 years? There are several communist parties in the world today that are not world threatening, such as those in France (where it is fashionable among certain intellectuals to be a communist), Vietnam (where it is the only party of a country that is actually friendly to the US), and China (where practically all elites are members of this party). However, should the US government treat a French guy with a Dali-esque mustache who joined a communist party because he thought it was chic, as a threat to its existence? If not, why collect this data and waste people's time?

This form is so toothless—full of omissions, inconsistencies, and stupidities—that it offends the prestige of the United States as a sovereign state, as well as of the people who apply for green cards. People who come to the US and see this form surely must think that the government is run by idiots, judging by its work product. Moreover, not only does it take a long time to fill out this form, but it also takes a ton of unnecessary time for all the people whose job it is to read it. What if we redirected those people to work on forms in, say, healthcare? How many lives could we save instead?

It is shocking how much we accept bureaucratic negligence and the status quo "because it has always been that way." I remember my despair when my mom fell from a bike at age 71 and broke the head of her femur bone. She was rushed to the hospital by an ambulance, everything moving fast, and then … *nothing*. Nothing happened for two days, because she was unlucky enough to be admitted to the hospital at the beginning of a weekend. She ended up lying on painkillers in some hospital bed, stabilized but not operated on. In terrible pain, knowing that she would receive no real help or treatment for the next 48 hours. Why? Because the standard across most hospitals in the world is that operations that are not super urgent are typically not performed during weekends.

Let's analyze this in more detail with a cool head. Hospitals have typically only skeletal staffing on weekends as most of the team enjoy their free time. Isn't that stupid? There is overwhelming evidence that a delay in trauma surgery, including for a broken femur, substantially increases the risk of complications and death. Per a 2016 article in the *Journal of the American Medical Association*, the mortality rate of patients who underwent surgery for a hip fracture within 48 hours of admission was 12.6%, while for those who had surgery *after* 48 hours, it was 20.2%.[81] Waiting over a weekend almost doubles mortality! My mom has never returned to the level of mobility she enjoyed before the accident. But she survived, at least; many people don't.

In aggregate, according to a study published in *Lancet* (a leading medical journal), the mortality of people admitted to hospitals on a weekend is on average 10% higher than those admitted on a weekday. A US study of stroke admissions from 2008 to 2009 shows a 26% higher mortality rate for those admitted during weekends.[82] How irresponsible and cruel it is for us humans to tell a person admitted to the hospital on Sunday: "Sorry, dude, your chances of recovery are much lower than this guy who was admitted two days ago. On weekends, we play golf."

So many other, much less crucial industries have full teams of people during weekends: restaurants, bars, hotels, amusement parks, ice cream shops. But bureaucratic choice dictates that you can have a fresh pizza on Saturday night, but not surgery on your broken femur. How idiotic.

The cost of changing this absurd situation would not even be that high. A British National Health Service study from 2018 estimates that the cost would be a mere £1.1–£1.4 billion each year, with a potential benefit of 29,000–36,000 quality-adjusted life years per year.[83] In other words, if there was full weekend service, Britain would give 3,000 people 10 more years of life per year. This doesn't require straining the same doctors and nurses with more work. We simply have to educate and hire more of them. It is a money problem, not an insurmountable challenge.

When your wife, husband, or baby is in pain, you don't really care whether it is Saturday or Tuesday. You want them to get competent help as soon as possible. But this is not how we have built our society. The bureaucratic rule accepts the "Sorry, closed for operations!" sign on hospital doors because … it is a weekend.

So, the next time you have an accident, make sure it is on a Monday through Thursday. Or fight stupidity and start demanding full-week hospital service from your politicians.

***

After all the stress of thinking about having an accident over the weekend, you would think that we could at least drown our sorrows over bureaucratic stupidity in a glass of wine or a beer. Well, bureaucracy might prevent you from doing that in the US as well.

Most supermarkets (including Safeway, one of the largest chains in the country) and most bars enforce a strict age-verification procedure, regardless of your age. This means that a 50-year-old has to show their ID to buy a bottle of red wine. Yes, you read it right. A man or woman who physically appears two or three times as old as a 21-year-old (the legal age for alcohol consumption) has to present a driver's license or passport to buy a bottle of wine in the United States of America.

Let's reflect on this for a moment. It is not only an annoyance—it is a crime against human intelligence. Asking for an ID even if a person has completely gray hair, is using a walking stick, and has the aura of a good grandma requires zero judgment. When we consistently apply this low bar to ourselves and follow such primitive rules, it makes us stupider. It wastes our time. It makes us less differentiated from machines. So in an area where humans still have an advantage over machines, why are we giving up on our humanity?

Another example of the stupidity of bureaucracy: Which of these two guns requires a license to be purchased in North Carolina?

FIGURE 39. Two firearms[84]

North Carolina's bureaucratic apparatus requires you to get a license to buy the handgun on the right but *does not* require you to have a license to buy the one on the left.[85] Yes, you read it right. This big gun on the left—an AR-15 with a 30- to 100-bullet magazine—does not require a license, while a small pistol with 6 rounds does.

Isn't this idiocy?

This is the power of the social acceptance of bureaucracy. Bureaucracy thinks that handguns (like this pistol) are easier to conceal, so they should require more oversight than a rifle or long gun such as an AR-15. It makes sense that the bigger gun with lethal power should have tougher purchase requirements than the small one, but bureaucracy thinks differently. AR-15s were used in half of the biggest mass shootings in US history, including the infamous Las Vegas tragedy on October 1, 2017, when a 64-year-old auditor opened fire from the 32nd floor of the Mandalay Bay Hotel on the participants of a music festival, killing 60 people and wounding 411.[86] He would not have been able to inflict so much death with a pistol with 6 bullets.

However, it is bureaucracy that sets the rules, not rational thinking or common sense.

Bureaucracy is a self-serving beast

Bureaucracy's first priority is to preserve itself. This is far more important than addressing the problems it was created to solve.

We humans regularly create organizations that turn themselves into self-serving and arrogant entities.

The founder and CEO of Watch Duty learned it the hard way. Watch Duty is a charitable organization in California, created by ex-tech entrepreneurs to help save people from wildfires. The bureaucratic rules mandate that the responsibility of informing people about potential evacuations due to wildfires belongs to sheriffs, who work closely with public information officers (communication officers) for CAL FIRE (the California Department of Forestry and Fire Protection). However, this process is typically inefficient and slow, which delays the dissemination of information and hence results in higher casualties. A typical fire in California spreads at 10 miles per hour, so acting quickly is of the essence. However, because of its bureaucratic nature, CAL FIRE takes a long time to share information about potential evacuations. Before sending an evacuation order, you need to call this guy or that guy, make sure you inform everybody up your chain of command, perhaps even inform some bureaucratic big fish. And even then, such an order is classically announced in bureaucratic jargon such as "Everybody needs to evacuate zone 0650." Who the heck knows where zone 0650 is? Also, CAL FIRE does not say in which direction people should evacuate. South, north, or maybe east or west? Where is the fire coming from, and how fast? How do I make sure I don't evacuate *toward* the fire?

Bureaucracy does not like when people ask questions or when they have independent information from elsewhere. Still, Watch Duty built a network of dedicated volunteers who listen to fire engine radios, compare the data with live video and satellite, radar, or other imagery, and use this information to inform people of the situation. So, for example, they can report that a fire has broken out 30 minutes earlier than an official communication, as well as *where* it is headed and *at what speed*. On this basis, people can make judgments and flee the area, knowing where to go. In fact, the service is so good that the actual firefighters (not the bureaucrats, but the brave men and women who fight the fires) use the Watch Duty information service. However, they sometimes are afraid to use it on their work phones because it would displease their bosses.

So Watch Duty volunteers do a brilliant job, for free, while CAL FIRE spends millions of taxpayer dollars every year! You'd think that CAL FIRE would love them. Just the opposite. CAL FIRE's senior officials have very negative perceptions of Watch Duty because it "moves a lot of people without authorization" and it "prevented many times CAL FIRE from receiving extra grants from FEMA." Basically, Watch Duty has helped save more people and taxpayer money. But this has reduced the financial power and standing of a bureaucratic organization.

Similarly, I also have a hunch that if tomorrow San Francisco's homeless problem were miraculously solved with one wave of a magic wand, the next day there would be a lot of very unhappy people there. Several departments that support the homeless—the bureaucrats who disburse the money; the mid- and high-level officials that have safe jobs, enjoy high prestige, and have lots of people reporting to them, making them feel important and powerful—would lose their fiefdoms *and their budgets*.

Bureaucracy cares much more about sustaining itself than solving the problems it was originally created to address. Frankly, there is good support for the claim that most organizations, without reforms and the occasional purge, turn into wasteful beasts that serve only their own self-interest.

Compartmentalization

In order to live with each other as a group, we have developed a lot of coping mechanisms. This is where compartmentalizing comes in.

Let's look at the home of one of the richest men in India, Mukesh Ambani.

Ambani built a 27-story residence in Mumbai called Antilia at an estimated cost of $1.2 billion. It is truly spectacular: indoor pools, spas, a theatre, a grand ballroom, and hanging gardens. But there is just one family who lives there.[87] As you can see from the photo, the rest of Mumbai is not that prosperous. In fact, the backdrop of his incredible house is ... a slum. In this city of more than 20 million people, half the population lives in slums without running water, and a third goes to bed hungry. Therefore, Antilia is essentially an island in a sea of poverty.

FIGURE 40. Antilia, the residence of Mukesh Ambani

Doesn't seeing it create cognitive dissonance? It might feel a bit inappropriate to enjoy such luxury, when everybody around you is poor and miserable and you literally can see it all from your balcony. Well, compartmentalization is here to help. We simply cut out references to the external world and look inside our bubble, disregarding any bothersome external inputs. This coping mechanism is employed not only by Ambani. You and I are very likely using this technique as well. There is always someone you could help tremendously by reducing your current consumption levels: not buying the new iPhone, not spending $150 on this dinner out, not going for that holiday, and so on. If, instead, you donated the money you would have spent on such luxuries, that could be life-changing in the poorest countries of the world, whose citizens have an annual income of just $400. But we don't do it. We compartmentalize.

Somebody is eating your lunch

Another compartmentalization statistic that always shocks me is the discrepancy between the salaries of the CEOs and average employees of the largest companies in the US.

In the 1970s and 1980s, a CEO of a successful public company earned a salary 20–60 times higher than that of their average employee.[88] This sounds like a lot, but still seems reasonable given the need for high qualifications and experience, the more stressful nature of the job, and the greater risk of being fired. However, somewhere around the mid-1990s, the compensation for CEOs of large companies took off and completely lost touch with reality.

By 2020, the total remuneration of listed companies' CEOs reached 351 times that of an average employee, with an average salary of $24 million![89]

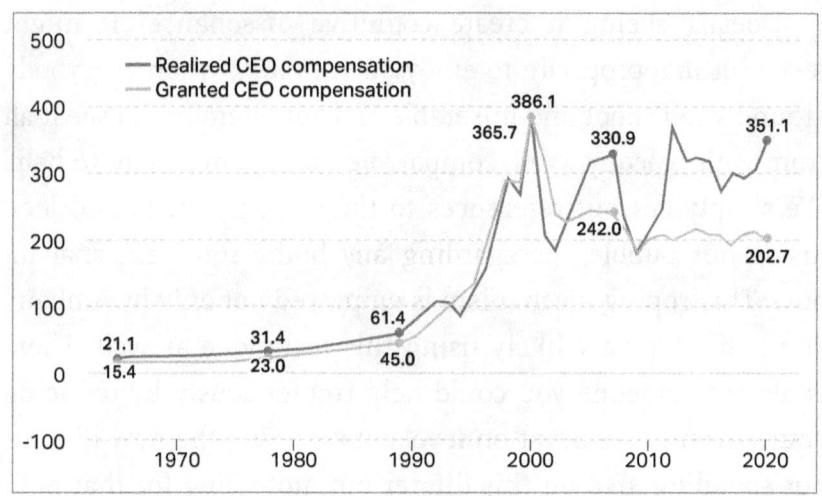

FIGURE 41. CEO-to-worker compensation ratio, 1965–2020[90]

Isn't this stupid? Don't you think we could find a lot of competent people, with great experience, who would lead those companies for, say, $12 million, $8 million, or even $5 million a year?

Aren't we terrible at calibrating here? It seems that in 1995, a (mostly) boys' club of CEOs decided to push their boards for more money, and the boards started comparing their companies to others with top-paid CEOs, which initiated an arms race in executive compensation. One board trampled over another to race for "the best talent," which blew things completely out of proportion.

This created such distortions that today millions of employees of S&P 500 companies are not able to support their families while working a 40-hour week, and they never get a free lunch at work. Meanwhile, their CEOs earn—in one day—more than the average employee earns in a year, and they get lunch paid for by the company! This is what a lot of iconic companies in America do today—and we buy our stuff daily from them!

In our heads, we have put bosses who earn ridiculous amounts of money into one box, rationalizing that they literally need a free lunch, whereas we have created a different box for line workers, accepting with resignation that they should pay for their own lunch and sometimes will need another weekend gig to put bread on the table for their family when they finally get home.

Extreme compartmentalization

Look at the picture in Figure 42.

Seems like a group of joyful men and women from the armed forces, having a great time — singing, joking, laughing. If not for the uniforms and the photo being in black and white, this would look like a perfect party picture from Instagram today.

FIGURE 42. Almost Instagram-like[91]

The key difference is that this picture depicts the staff of the Auschwitz concentration camp on July 22, 1942, on a short retreat in Solahütte, just 18 miles from the camp. These are members of the Nazi SS who managed the extermination of thousands of people and regularly sent hundreds of innocent men, women, and children to the gas chambers.

Unbelievable how "normal," almost friendly, these people look in this picture. They seem to be a fun bunch who respected and were kind to each other. But they didn't show any humanity to non-SS members. In their minds, they had a clear compartment for their own group members (Germans, Nazis, SS staff) and an entirely different one for everyone else (Jews, Poles, Russians, Hungarians, etc.). They could be caring friends, fathers, and mothers to their own kind, but at the same time could be beasts to everyone else.

On the same day the photograph was taken, about 150 new prisoners arrived at Auschwitz, just a few miles away, where the SS selected 33 captives for work and killed the rest in the gas chambers.[92]

This is extreme compartmentalization, which illustrates that educated, mentally healthy humans can switch swiftly and dramatically between different sets of social norms. One moment they can embrace a colleague with compassion, and the next moment they can beat an innocent prisoner to death.

With the full blessing of society.

Love of Strength and Authority

We humans admire strength and authority! This trait explains so many of our failings as a society. We typically follow strong leaders, those who project authority and decisiveness—and are often aggressive and ruthless. This is surprising given that, on a personal level, we mostly value the opposite traits: compassion and sensitivity.

Why is that so?

There are a few mechanisms at work here. As always, history plays a big part. From an evolutionary perspective, for 98% of the time that *Homo sapiens* has been around, we have been roaming the world in small groups, in search of food and shelter, *without* the benefit of civilization. Throughout most of our history, our survival was dependent on the swift actions of the leaders of such groups, who would alert the rest about any risks and provide the first line of defense. The same principles apply to other mammals, such as a pack of wolves, a troop of monkeys, or a herd of musk ox.

The origin of leadership is defense against enemies—the strongest, tallest, most aggressive, and valiant to the front!

Our ancestors perceived the strength and aggressiveness of their leaders as an asset. These powerful individuals exhibited

FIGURE 43. Musk ox defensive formation
When defending against predators, the usual tactic of musk ox is to form a defensive circle, with the strongest and bravest animals on the outside and the weak, old, and young protected inside the circle. How romantic and noble! Similar concepts applied to early humans.

courage, muscle, and determination in opposing various enemies. Typically, they were the most adept or experienced at using weapons and were able—in a world that was much more violent than today's—to take the right actions. We rationally chose those people to lead us, then, because we expected they would fight for us when the need arose.

However, things have changed. In the last 4,000 to 5,000 years (less than 2% of the time our species has existed), most of humanity abandoned their nomadic lifestyle and started living in permanent settlements, freeing themselves from being at the mercy of animals and bad weather. Living in today's New York or even in ancient Babylon required completely different skills for survival than living on the savanna. Our well-being and safety are no longer tied to an ability to project raw aggression. It is more—or *should* be—about good governance, a sophisticated game of social interactions and organization. However, our brains still haven't fully absorbed this. Our natural instinct remains to still follow "strong" people, because they decisively and aggressively solve problems with simple, fast, ruthless ideas such as "build a wall."

Is it only a coincidence that in 67% of US presidential elections from 1789 to 2012, a bigger (taller) candidate won the popular vote?[93]

Recent history provides a vast amount of evidence for this faulty love of authority. Some of the worst villains are still idolized today. And some ineffective and callous politicians in our societies are still cherished, despite their huge shortcomings, because they came across as "strong."

A few examples:

Joseph Stalin was responsible for around 20 million deaths in the Soviet Union and abroad. There is irrefutable evidence attributing the deaths of millions of people to this leader's specific actions, such as his insistence on forced collectivization of farming (around 6–12 million deaths), building the gulag system (around 1.5 million deaths),[94] or targeting specific minorities or even individuals with tailored execution orders (more than a million Poles and thousands of Lithuanians, Latvians, Estonians, Chechens, officers in the 1937 purge, etc.).[95] Despite these facts, Joseph Stalin was truly loved by many Soviet Union citizens. At his funeral, crowds were so desperate to pay him a last tribute that they trampled over each other, killing hundreds of people.[96] Even today, an astonishing 51% of Russians view Stalin favorably as a person and only 13% dislike him.[97]

Statistics for Chinese leaders are not easily available, but they are likely very similar in the case of Mao Zedong, the Chinese Communist leader. It is estimated that his Great Leap Forward movement killed between 15 million and 55 million Chinese and his Cultural Revolution added up to another 20 million victims. Nonetheless, Mao stands, even today, as a hugely respected leader. (I can confirm from my personal experience of visiting China and talking to ordinary people there that his cult is still alive. I remember an ordinary bus driver explaining to me that Mao was good and Hu Jintao, a former Chinese president, was not.)

This love of authority and strength is not confined to history. We have the same flaw in our business and industry today: We prefer bombastic, larger-than-life characters to quieter, kinder but tamer individuals.

Jack Welsh, a former CEO of General Electric (GE), rose to prominence in the late 1990s and early 2000s, promoting an aggressive management style, binary views, and flashy, short catch-all answers to any problems. Among insiders, it is now a conventional view that Welsh's policies underpin the recent demise of GE. What is good in the short term often does not work for the long term.

Steve Jobs and Steve Wozniak are also great examples. The two Steves represent vastly different management styles. Jobs was aggressive, articulate, and ruthless; Wozniak was quiet, creative, and productive. It was Wozniak who actually created Apple's key products. But Jobs took all the glory while shining on stage as he bullied a lot of people at Apple, refused to share any equity upside with his employees, and was a terrible father to his children, caring more about fame and money. Wozniak, in turn, was building all those incredible products and, in secret, giving grants of his own equity to employees because he felt so embarrassed by Jobs's stinginess.

Which of these two men does the world cherish? Steve Jobs, of course. He exuded confidence and was perceived as strong and authoritative. Same as the bigger alpha male in a wolf pack or musk ox herd.

A most surprising discovery is that this "love of strength" can be inherited or transferred. If you are descended from a strong leader, you benefit from unearned appreciation and goodwill. Basically, people assume you have the character traits of the original creator of this authoritative brand. A perfect example of this is political dynasties. Just the pure fact that you are from the Gandhi family gives you an incredible boost in India, regardless of your individual capabilities. And why were there so many

Kennedys in politics in the US? Because they came from the beloved John Fitzgerald Kennedy, voters gave them the unearned, immediate benefit of the doubt. Robert F. Kennedy Jr. is so much less impressive than JFK was, but some voters subconsciously credit him with the same features as their assassinated leader.

So, we humans are still prone to a romantic view of projected strength. We no longer need such ability in our leaders but are beguiled by this fallacy far too often. Our atavistic instincts still kick in when choosing leaders—both on a personal level and in business and politics. We do not yet trust enough the likes of Jacinda Ardern, the former prime minister of New Zealand, who governed quietly, humbly, and competently. Instead we prefer the flashy, aggressive styles of Donald Trump, Italy's Silvio Berlusconi, or the UK's Boris Johnson. Our savanna-based mental shortcuts still—alas—wire our operating system.

Let millions die but do not kill the leader

Respect for authority has another interesting twist. We prefer to kill millions of a leader's subjects, rather than directly targeting the leader.

Let's bring in Napoleon again to illustrate this point. The Napoleonic Wars resulted in about 10–15 million deaths, the same order of magnitude as in World War I (about 20 million). Few are aware of that fact.

It is clear that Napoleon started several major wars just for the sake of conquest, vanity, and glory. He destroyed huge swaths of Spain, impoverished France, ravished Germany, Poland, and Russia, and plundered Italy. So it would be fair to say that if Napoleon had died of a heart attack, in let's say 1800, the European continent would have been free from devastation, death, and hunger for a decade and a half. It was this one person's ambition that made the difference between war and peace—life and death for more than 10 million people.

Wouldn't it be more rational to let this one person die rather than sacrifice millions?

History teaches us that the overwhelming answer (at least in Western culture) is "no." It is considered more civilized to fight the people of such a leader's country, not the leader himself. Famously, during the Battle of Waterloo, when Wellington, the commander of the allied armies, was asked by his artillery crews whether they should fire at Napoleon when he appeared in their range, he answered: "It is not a business of generals to shoot at one another."

This sums up pretty well the philosophy of the Western world: Big men remain gentlemen while little boys do the dirty fighting in the mud.

Tendency for radicalism

A highly interesting sociological determinant of our stupidity is our innate tendency for radicalism. Basically, we humans easily move from one extreme position to another, forgetting that, in most cases, there is a golden middle.

Around 900 CE, Polynesians settled on Easter Island. A small civilization started flourishing there shortly afterward, facilitated by favorable weather, supportive soil, and a remote location that prevented any trouble from the outside. However, the problems came from the *inside*. Gradually, the locals divided the island into a bunch of fiefdoms, run by powerful chiefs who designated their territory by erecting giant stone statues called *moai*, 113 of which still stand there today. The factions engaged in an arms race (or rather, a face race) of building more and more *moai* to impress their neighbors.

In order to build them, the islanders chopped up trees, which were scarce on the island. In no time, the building fervor resulted in excessive forest harvesting, which peaked around 1400 CE, and led to complete deforestation. Radicalism without limits! This resulted in ecological disaster, as without trees, the sweet water resources diminished, food became scarce, and the island imploded into a civil war for survival. It even came down to cannibalism. A full breakup of society.

Isn't it tragic? The simple concept of *moderation* would have prevented all that. Wouldn't it have been enough to build a handful of those beautiful statues? Why did they go to the extreme of building so many and cutting down all the trees on the island? Isn't that a bit too radical?

Such stories are not confined to distant lands or to our past. They happen all the time across the globe, among societies big and small, of every latitude, race, and culture.

Let's take an example of a dramatic fall from near total peace to a bloody civil war caused by a surprising explosion of radicalism.

In the 1990s, Nepal was a peaceful nation run by a hereditary king. This stunning Himalayan country was famous for its safety and kindness. However, in 1996, a small group of Maoist activists started a brutal rebellion against the monarchy. The nation was not used to violence: shootings, kidnappings, and rapes were almost unheard of until then. However, within just a few years, the whole country was consumed by a brutal spiral of violence. The kindest people of yesterday learned very quickly how to become the cruelest murderers of today. The killings, lynchings, and torture were largely done by ordinary citizens, those who had lived in peace before. My friend's uncle, a respected businessman, was killed by a group of his closest friends, whom he had employed and trusted before rebellion. Within just a few years, many law-abiding, peace-loving villagers turned into bloody beasts, eager to increase their social status by killing the Maoists' opponents.

Ultimately, the rebels successfully overthrew the king and seized power. But they couldn't agree on what to do next. Between 1996 and 2006, around 20,000 people were killed or disappeared. The economy collapsed. All of this because the Maoists preferred to take the extremist, violent route rather than apply more peaceful political pressure to fulfill their goals. The conflict changed the whole construct of Nepal's society from one of the most peaceful on Earth to one of the most traumatized. Ultimately, the Maoists didn't do anything of significance with their ultimate prize—power. This illustrates how terribly susceptible to radicalism we are as humans. We can turn from angels into radical monsters within just a few years.

The tendency toward radicalism often manifests itself through the legal system.

The US is a country that finds it very hard to respond in ways that are commensurate to the problems it is trying to address. Its legal system typically overacts and tends to apply simple, brutal, extreme solutions.

For example, the US has incredibly radical penalties for most inconsequential breaches of law. The US code envisages a penalty of up to six months in jail for ... parking in a spot reserved for disabled people. Once again, you could go to jail for half a year if you park your car in the wrong place. Isn't it crazy? Have you ever seen an American jail? If you go there for six months, you come back as a true criminal, with huge psychological trauma, perhaps having been raped by other inmates. You will never go back to a normal life, as you will not find a decent job: US businesses typically discriminate against citizens with any criminal record. In other words, violating a minor parking rule could completely shatter your life. The same is true for possession of marijuana or other nondangerous drugs. A personal friend knows someone who was sentenced to a minimum five-year prison term in California for offering acid to her romantic partner, as the court considered this a "sale."

At the same time, the US as a country tolerated film producer Harvey Weinstein's regular assault of women, including two rapes, for 20 years. The US system—despite getting a wire recording of him admitting to groping one actress—was not able, or willing, to put him to jail for what he did until the Me Too campaign started. To sum up, the legal system harshly penalizes people for small things but cannot punish the real, big crimes.

Another good example of radicalism is a US law that prohibits government employees from accepting even a coffee from a government contractor. So basically, if you sell T-shirts to the US government, you cannot negotiate your contract over a tea or coffee because it would be considered bribery. In the meantime, it is perfectly legal for Mitt Romney, a US senator from Utah (otherwise a very respectable figure) to pocket $13.6 million—this is an official number, available publicly—from National Rifle Association lobbyists.[98] That is *not* considered bribery.

Even more shockingly, in 2024 the US Supreme Court decided that taking bribes *after* the act is fine. It came as a result of the *Snyder v. United States* case, which involved the former mayor of Portage (a small city in Indiana) taking a $13,000 bribe from a company that supplied five garbage trucks. As Snyder was paid the money after the trucks were delivered, the Supreme Court ruled that it was just a "gratuity" payment. So since 2024, it is totally legal to bribe officials in the United States of America, as long as you pay the bribe after you make the delivery. This is a rational, pro-business decision—why would I pay the criminal before delivery of what's promised? Ludicrous, isn't it?

Is the economy, at least, less susceptible to radicalism? In the end, the Western free market economy, with its invisible power over the market, *should* stabilize it and make it more immune to stupid, dramatic decisions.

Not really.

Humans are terrible at quantifying things and providing a proportionate response across the board. Even when it relates to our economy. In most cases, we overreact and go from one extreme position to another.

Take the response of the US Federal Reserve to the 2020 COVID pandemic. Every student who has taken a macroeconomics class knows that a central bank's response to a deep economic contraction should be to increase the money supply. The only real question is: By how much? The Federal Reserve is full of highly educated, well-remunerated, smart individuals like Fed chair Jerome Powell who wear perfectly cut suits—they should know that answer. That's the whole point of having them. However, those smart people completely screwed up the response to the crisis. They printed too much money, which resulted in high inflation. They went from "Oh shit, we have a liquidity crisis" to "Oh shit, we have an overliquidity crisis." Even the smartest economists in the most powerful country in the world could not escape radicalism.

In the face of big events, we humans completely lose our sense of moderation. Unfortunately, entire rational, well-educated, and generally balanced societies are falling into this radical trap on our watch.

After the 2011 Fukushima disaster, when a tsunami damaged the reactor at a Japanese nuclear power plant, causing leakage of radioactive material, Japan decided to gradually decommission its nuclear-generating capacity, which provided about 30% of the country's electricity. According to domestic and international statistics, the Fukushima disaster caused 1 (!) confirmed death from radiation, and another 18 people suffered physical injuries due to hydrogen explosions or possible radiation burns. So, while the accident was scary, it did not cause major loss of life.

Conversely, the response to the disaster caused massive carnage. The hasty evacuation *after* the accident was the direct cause of 1,232 deaths. Another 1,280 deaths occurred between 2011 and 2014 due to higher electricity prices, which caused people to try to save on heating and led to pneumonia and other terminal diseases.[99] The actual loss of life related to higher electricity prices was several times higher, because the number above accounts only for deaths covering the 21 largest cities in Japan, representing 28% of the total population. If we extrapolate these figures for the whole country and include deaths after 2014, we easily end up with a total death count in excess of 10,000.

This means that the very thoughtful, balanced Japanese society took a radical path to a cure, which only exacerbated the problem by a factor of 10,000. Once again, the cure and response to the problem caused 10,000 more deaths than the actual problem itself....

Surprisingly, half a world away, a bulwark of democracy and rationality went down the same rabbit hole. Following the Fukushima disaster, then-Chancellor Angela Merkel also decided to phase out nuclear energy in Germany. Her decision was completely unsupported by facts: Germany has never had any significant incidents in its nuclear power plants. Nuclear energy, based on actual statistics, is one of the safest forms of energy produced. Figure 44 below shows the number of deaths per terawatt-hour of produced electricity by energy source.

Producing energy from fossil fuels such as coal or gas creates far more deaths, due to higher incidences of cardiovascular diseases. Additionally, coal mining results in accidents, mostly due to methane explosions. By contrast, nuclear power plants have had only two incidents in their entire history in which there were confirmed fatalities: one at Chernobyl and one at

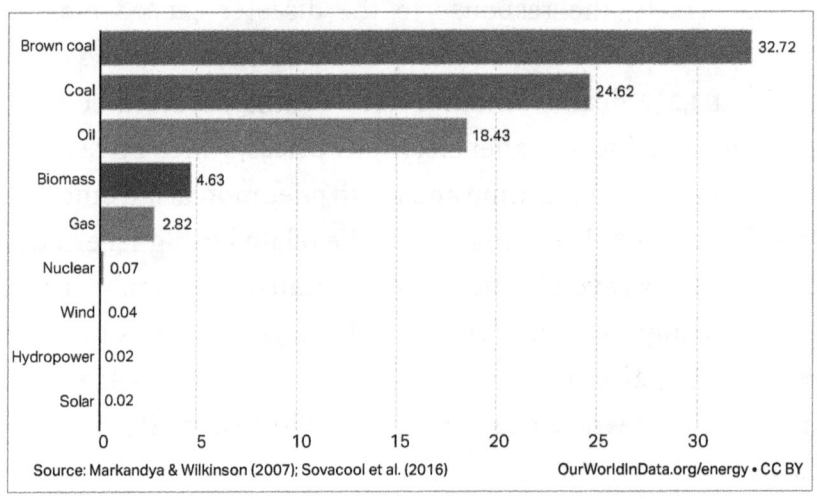

FIGURE 44. Death rates from energy production per TWh[100]

Fukushima. Chernobyl was an example of flagrantly incompetent management coupled with a bad reactor design, which has since been fixed.

Figure 44 above illustrates that nuclear energy is about 350 times safer than coal-based energy. Despite that, Germany phased out all its nuclear-generation capability. Unfortunately, the shortfall could not be fully covered by wind and solar. Germany had to bring old fossil fuel–powered plants back online, which created more pollution, resulting in more deaths.

These examples show how susceptible to irrationality and imbalance we are. Even such seasoned politicians as Angela Merkel could not withstand going radical. The former chancellor was widely respected for her work ethic and rational, pragmatic approach to problem-solving. However, modern Germany's whole political class, cherished for its thoughtfulness and methodical decision-making, was lured into a tragic trap by radicalism. Most of society supported Merkel in this decision.

German elites made decisions based on political momentum, emotions, and prevailing sentiment rather than facts and figures. And the German economy suffers from it to this day—paying very high prices for energy (as opposed to France, which produces 70% of its electricity from nuclear power plants[101]). Additionally, German society is paying a higher price in lives lost due to increased pollution. However, those thousands of people dying quietly in their homes and hospital beds, with "cardiac arrest" as the official cause of death, are far less newsworthy than one person dying from nuclear radiation....

We have become scarily radical—vulnerable to simple, dramatic ideas to solve our problems: Stop nuclear energy! Get rid of immigrants! The extremist traits we humans were born with make us lose our ability to moderate far too easily.

Obsession with Powerful Stories

Do you know the saying "Never let the facts get in the way of a good story"? It pretty much sums up our societal construct. Our culture originated through spending time together around the bonfire, where early humans started telling stories about their past adventures, such as successful hunts or journeys to faraway places. From such stories, we began developing abstract concepts, commonly shared myths, beliefs, and religions. Since those early days, something primal has stayed with us—the love of a powerful, dramatic story.

Just as early hunter-gatherers were attracted to stories of journeys with unexpected encounters—unknown beasts and dramatic escapades—today we love "breaking stories" that mimic such archetypes. Consequently, we are easily manipulated by the media.

Check out Figure 45 below.

In our public life, we often completely overstate the drama. We *like* hearing stories involving murders, terrorism, and suicides. These are memorable stories that catch our attention, and so they sell well. Nobody is mesmerized by repetitive, positive, or benign facts. That's why the media is full of news about terrorism, building a perception of constant threat. An analysis of *The New York Times*'s coverage of death revealed that terrorism takes 35.6% of this paper's attention, while in the real world less than 0.01% of Americans die because of it. Also, homicide is completely overblown in media reporting. *The New York Times* devotes 25 times more coverage to homicide than the actual proportion it represents in real life. You and I will probably die of cardiovascular diseases, not terrorists.

Nonetheless, we underestimate and, frankly, do not care about "non-newsworthy" facts, even if they are objectively very meaningful. We care much more about powerful, "trending" stories that are recognized and appreciated by others. Example?

All Americans have heard of the attack on Pearl Harbor on December 7, 1941, and the D-Day landing on June 6, 1944. These were two bloody battles during the Second World War,

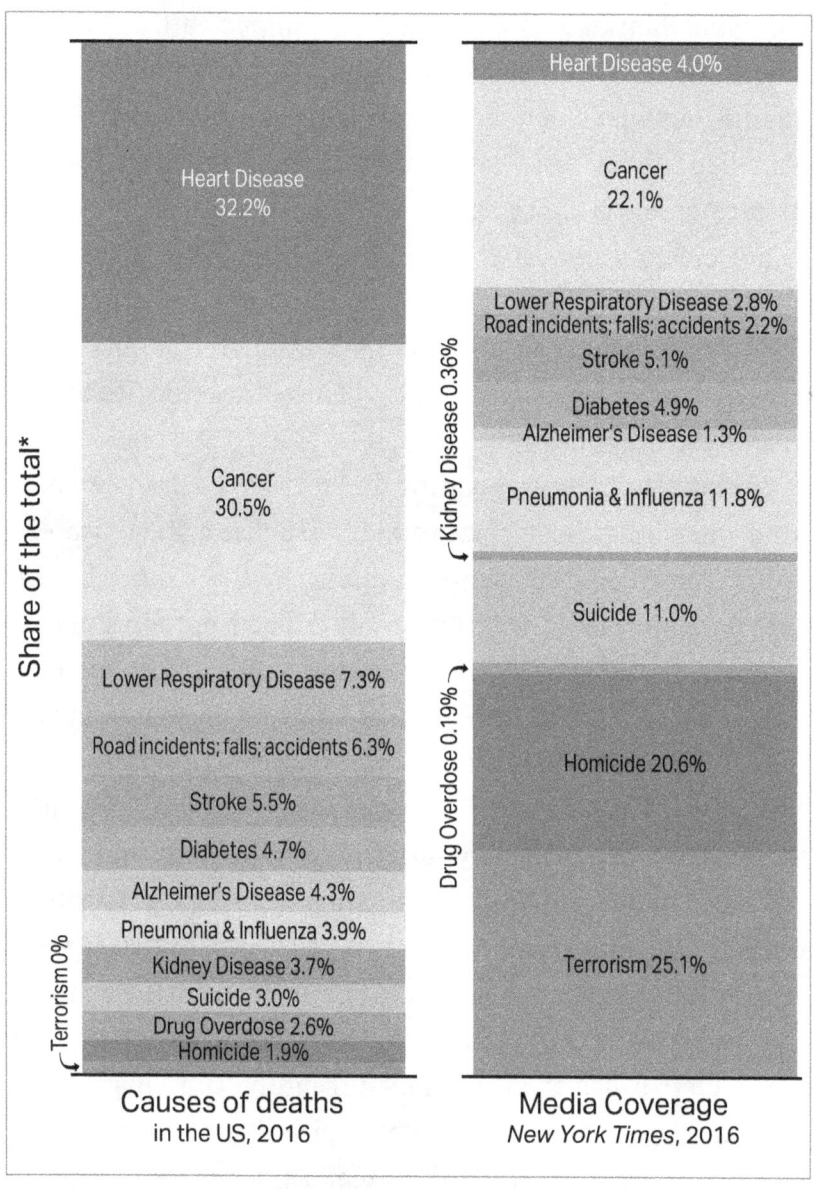

FIGURE 45. Real causes of death in US v. media coverage reports[102]

with respectively about 2,300 and 2,500 American lives lost.[103] However, 15,000 American pilots were killed during World War II while learning to fly.[104] So about six times more people died *in training* than in each of those most famous battles. We celebrate those who died in the Pearl Harbor attack and the D-Day landing, but we do not even know about the many, many more who died under less "newsworthy" circumstances. Nobody cares to mention those sacrifices and tragedies because they do not create a powerful story. Despite their human cost being three times greater than these two battles combined....

The obsession with media is multifaceted. Not only do we crave dramatic stories, but we also believe those stories to a far greater extent than we should.

In short, we like exaggerating the stories we tell, and we don't mind when others exaggerate either. Visualize again our predecessor: The Paleolithic hunter jumping by the red-hot bonfire and telling the rest of the tribe how he killed a buffalo. Probably he will overstate the size of the animal; probably he will add a few details to spice up the storyline; probably he will even omit a few unglamorous acts, such as missing the first bow shot.

We still have so much in common with this Paleolithic hunter. We often color our stories to jazz them up, and we are also tremendously susceptible to such pepping up. Whatever we see in the official media, such as television or newspapers, we too often consider credible, despite evidence to the contrary.

This is why propaganda is so effective. When Russian frontline soldiers called their mothers during the Ukrainian war in 2022 and reported on the dramatic, pitiful circumstances and huge casualties, they were often met with complete disbelief. The phrase that has been repeated across hundreds of intercepted calls: "But ... on television they said that ..." So the mothers had trouble believing their own children, the people closest to them on Earth. Isn't that incredible? People naturally believe television, official online media, radio, and newspapers, even if they are known to be unreliable and even in the face of direct, firsthand information from members of their family.

Since our earliest days, we've been obsessed with stories. Therefore, control over who tells the story is one of the most important instruments of power. What's more, we prioritize bonding and community over rationality and facts. We don't mind being lied to a bit, as long as this makes a compelling story and does not get blown out of proportion. That is the price we eagerly pay for a good time and our needed sense of community.

INSTITUTIONS

Not only are we fighting our own biology, psychology, and society to remain rational, but we also face concerted institutionalized efforts to make us stupider. Yes, you read it correctly, there are organizations—well-functioning and often high performing and respected—that promote "institutionalized" stupidity to help them achieve their own goals.

The Military

A great example of an institution that is highly respected yet programmed to make us irrational is ... the military. One of the fundamental principles of the army is obedience—not questioning orders from above, however stupid they might be. But unconditional obedience inevitably leads to mistakes, irrational actions, and subsequently brutality.

Let's make sure we distinguish here between necessary ruthlessness and unnecessary cruelty. An army's role is to be lethal to its enemies and to be coldly efficient in this role. The military often has to make decisions such as "I am going to let this 300-person battalion die because it will cover the retreat of my 3,000-strong brigade." This is the cold, ruthless mathematics of war. However merciless, it *is* rational.

Institutional cruelty is about enforcing unnecessarily violent, wasteful, or dumb actions such as shooting prisoners, sending thousands of soldiers to certain death for no reason, and torturing civilians. There are countless examples of this, from the infamous 1968 killing of about 400 civilians by American troops in the Vietnamese village of My Lai to the Soviets detonating a test atomic bomb in 1954 at Totskoye in the Ural Mountains and then ordering 45,000 soldiers to advance through this area to check what impact it would have on them.

These cases show institutionalized, chain-of-command, top-down-led stupidity, above and beyond the typical ruthlessness of war.

Most armies follow the absolute principle of obedience, so if your superior is cruel, stupid, or both, you have no choice but to become their tool. A noteworthy exception to this rule is the contemporary German army, which gives the individual soldier the option to disobey an order if—in their opinion—it violates democratic values. This is to ensure there will be no more "I was just following orders" defenses. Seems like we can learn from history!

Religious Organizations

This is a sensitive topic but, in the name of intellectual purity, we have to cover it. Formal religious organizations are another example of institutionalized stupidity. Despite having many positive traits, organized religion also has a dark side, rooted in a desire to prevent people from thinking independently or questioning and to impose obedience and self-sacrifice.

Organized religions operate on the belief in a certain ontological order, despite facts or contrary evidence. Members of religious institutions tend to unquestionably follow the guidance of their leaders—even killing people in the name of God.

The Catholic Church, for example, murdered a lot of innocent people accused of "heresy" by the so-called Inquisition from the 13th to the 19th centuries. Basically, if you acted in ways that did not fit typical societal roles, you were likely to face torture and death. The Inquisition was particularly nasty toward free-thinking, educated women, as it was trying to instill fear, obedience, and adherence to traditional rules and confine women to domestic duties. Independent women in those times had to fear being tested to determine whether they were "witches."

What were those tests?

One of the most ridiculous was weighting: If a woman weighed less than 109 pounds (49.5 kilograms), it meant she was a witch. Why? Because church experts ascertained that only people lighter than 109 pounds could ... *fly on a broom*. And, obviously, witches fly on brooms.

FIGURE 46. Weighing of a witch by Inquisition[105]
Note the seriousness of the whole procedure, rules based, official approach, in short institutional stupidity.

Isn't this just crazily stupid? But this was supported by the most powerful institution of the day—the Catholic Church!

Another brutal test to figure out whether someone was a witch was the water test: A woman would be put into a bag (often with some additional stones) and thrown into the water. If she drowned immediately, this meant she was innocent. If she floated for some time, this meant the devil was helping her and she should be killed.

In both cases, of course, the person under trial died.

Is innocence worth much if you die? Is this a "test" at all? Or an execution with a good or bad postmortem opinion?

Please note that these were not acts of individual barbarity or mental illness. These were institutionalized, formal, society-based rules, enforced with complete brutality by a powerful organization that preached mercy, charity, and pity.

Many institutions of Islam historically advocated for violence as a way to spread the faith. Sadly, this concept is still very much alive in modern times, as evidenced by terrorist attacks against "infidels." The Arabs who flew into the World Trade Center towers on September 11, 2001, were mostly pious, religious men. Most of the fatalities caused by terrorist attacks in Europe in the last 25 years were carried out by Muslims in the name of God—the 2004 Madrid bombings targeting commuter trains that left 193 dead and over 2,000 injured; the 2015 Bataclan theatre massacre in Paris that left 130 dead; the heavy lorry driven into a crowd in the French coastal city of Nice in 2016 that killed 86 people, 15 of them children....

Many Muslim religious leaders across the globe are still advocating for armed violence in the name of God. And many organized religions, from Islam to Judaism, still limit the rights of women, in particular their ability to study, wear the clothes they choose, or marry the person they want.

Even institutional representatives of Buddhist religion have a mixed record—in Japan in the 1930s and 1940s, they strongly supported the military in their quest for domination in Asia and promoted selfless obedience and self-sacrifice.

While your personal relationship with God might be pure, beautiful and idealistic, the institutions that organize religions are often not equally clean....

Corporations

Corporations—and Big Tech, in particular—also represent institutions that don't want you to think too much. Rather, they want you to consume stuff mindlessly. Facebook, Instagram, TikTok, and YouTube are designed to engage you in the pointless, mechanical, passive act of swiping through posts, as long as you physically can, because this allows them to expose you to more advertising. So if you spend time reading a book, learning something new, hanging out with your family, or making friends in the real world, it is not good for them. It takes you away from swiping, and swiping means money.

Recently, Big Tech gained a huge ally in its quest to make you stupider: machine learning. If you have tried TikTok, you know how addictive consuming those short videos can be. You are fed engaging and funny content, which gives you easy, immediate gratification, creating a desire for more and more. This translates into more time with your eyeballs on the screen, which translates into billions of dollars of advertising revenue—$120 billion, to be exact (per the 2023 annual report for ByteDance, TikTok's parent company).

TikTok, however, has a big negative impact on your brain, leaving you with the impression that everything is possible and well-being can be attained immediately and independently of your actions. If you post a lot on TikTok, it can create a perception that you are famous, doing something meaningful, or ... working. I personally know people who went from having 300,000 TikTok followers to attempting suicide when they realized how fake it all was.

Even a company as celebrated as Apple finds it beneficial to feed you idiotic content because it makes more money. Apple News is the primary source of information for millions of people every day. So many people see the world the way Apple presents it to them. In the UK, for example, Apple will typically serve you information about what Meghan Markle ate last week, the drunken starlet that was caught by the paparazzi, and the state of the real estate market; or it might share some moving story of a person who recently died. It will not, however, typically tell you about new research pointing to a breakthrough technology in nuclear fusion, nor will it tell you about critical political events of the day or educate you on large societal trends.

As a result, the younger generations do not have a good overall understanding of the world. Most young Britons are able to enumerate more football clubs than they can countries in Africa. They are more up to date on which celebrities are having affairs with each other than the fact that there is a major war somewhere or that interest rates have doubled, which might soon prevent them from buying a house.

Just note what stupid content it serves up (see Figure 47). It is fluff about supermodels, royals, and criminals. It doesn't tell you about any important political, demographic, or sociological developments; it doesn't enhance your understanding of the world. It feeds you with the lowest common denominator—primitive entertainment for the masses.

FIGURE 47. Apple News feeds from 2022 for the UK
The world as seen by Apple: typical newsfeeds for Britons from June 27, 2022, to July 1, 2022.

Healthcare

One of the ugliest forms of institutional stupidity is the wasteful nature of the healthcare system. The apogee of stupidity in this sector was achieved through grand efforts in America.

The US healthcare system is one of the most convoluted, inefficient, unfair social systems ever designed:

- The United States spends around $15,000 per person per year on healthcare[106] and achieves the worst medical results among the G20 countries.[107] Despite this humongous spending, 60% of Americans suffer from chronic disease and

only 8% of Americans do all prescribed preventive health procedures. The US has two to four times more amputees than western Europe per unit of population, because cutting off an arm or a leg is the easiest, most primitive last resort when other treatment options are not available.[108] US life expectancy was four years lower than comparable countries even before COVID-19, and then it got even worse.[109]
- Top executives at the largest health insurance companies in the US reject preventive procedures that have less than a two-year payback period. Insurers avoid paying, for example, for a $1,600 colonoscopy, even if it could save the person's life and $50,000 in chemotherapy and surgery bills five years later. Why? Because Americans change their medical insurance every 2.7 years on average, so this savings would be passed on to the next insurer. It would not be *that insurer's* savings. Shocking! (I learned this fact firsthand in a face-to-face meeting with a former C-level executive of a large US healthcare insurance company).
- The cost of medicines in the US is the highest in the world. For example, one of the most well-known standard blood-thinning drugs for stroke prevention is called Xarelto, often sold under the same brand name internationally. In 2021, a 30-day supply of Xarelto cost $450–$550 in the US, while in Germany it was $95–$130, and $75–$100 in Poland— *for the same molecule.* I remember studying this topic when sitting on the board of a pharmacy chain in Poland and was amazed at the scale of this discrepancy. Smart pharma executives know that the US is a rich country that can pay three to four times more for the same substance as other countries. They get away with it because the pharma lobby is incredibly well-organized and the industry is highly concentrated.

Big pharma officially spent $159 million on lobbying Congress in 2023 (per official statistics reported by OpenSecrets) to maintain the status quo and keep prices high. Much more is spent informally in ethical "gray zones," such as incentivizing doctors to prescribe particular brands.

- Global consulting company McKinsey estimates that the US spends approximately $1 trillion a year on healthcare administration.[110] Not on medical procedures, but on pushing papers, gathering stamps, sending faxes, issuing invoices, and correcting billing mistakes. For context, this is more than the US spends on defense. It is a waste of epic proportions.

These terrible results are not random. It is really hard to spend more money on healthcare than every other country in the world and have the worst medical results among G20 countries. America has managed to achieve that—it's no accident. How?

It is the result of institutional stupidity, coupled with poor regulation and greed.

The system currently is designed to perpetuate itself to maximize profits and reduce legal risk. In the US, most healthcare players are interested in keeping the cost of healthcare as high as possible, because ... everyone gets a cut. So the higher the total cost, the bigger your cut. If you are a doctor performing a surgery, you will get either a percentage of the revenue from this procedure or a fixed amount per procedure (which ultimately will also depend on the total cost); if you are an insurer, you will get a percentage margin over the cost; if you are a health records administrator or claims processor, you will get a percentage of the volume handled. Are you getting it now?

Individually, the CEOs and senior managers of key healthcare players are not bad people. They are not greedy vampires who are consciously trying to deny the poor access to healthcare. They are simply savvy businesspeople who are following incentives. Over the long term, it creates exactly this tragic result.

Let's identify a few transmission mechanisms of these "good people doing harm" phenomenon.

For Kaiser Permanente, a large and respected healthcare services group out of California, buying smaller players is a sound business decision. It serves two purposes: reducing competition and preventing price erosion. Kaiser's acquisitions almost always result in "rolling out" its standard pricing policies, which in plain language means a price increase. What is a good business call for Kaiser is also a death sentence for an uninsured or underinsured person who cannot fork out $2,000 for an MRI scan at a fancy Kaiser hospital but could potentially have had one for $500 at a small, somewhat run-down clinic. Sadly, the small players in Northern California who were doing MRIs for $500 have already been bought out by the big players.

Similarly, supporting a new regulation that increases the reporting burden is good business judgment for an executive at a big healthcare company. Kaiser has an army of administrative personnel who will always be ready to do one more report/table/study and send it to the federal or state institution that requested it. A small business, meanwhile, will struggle to hire an extra person to prepare such a report. Eventually, the small business will either lose profitability and go bankrupt or will have to sell itself to a large player like ... Kaiser! So the official narrative of "increasing quality of healthcare via better reporting" will have the pleasant benefit of killing off your small competitors. Two birds with one stone!

Finally, any smart executive knows that increasing prices is the best way to improve profitability. While at McKinsey, I learned this principle well. Increasing the volume (the number of patients served) of your business by 10% is a major headache for a hospital chain: You need to find, train, and integrate more nurses and doctors, build more facilities, manage shifts, source more medical equipment, and so on. That's a lot of work! Instead, why not increase prices by 5% a year? The impact on the bottom line will be better than a 10% increase in volume, *and* you don't need to do any work on leading those initiatives mentioned above. You can be home with your family at 5:00 p.m., holding a beer, rather than managing the construction and staffing of a new clinic. The difference for the population, meanwhile, is dramatic—fewer slots for surgery and lower affordability. This innocent, lazy 5% price increase, cumulatively over 14 years, *doubles* the original prices—that's roughly how much higher US healthcare costs are than everywhere else in the developed world. Small changes over the long term add up to a massive difference.

The plethora of arcane, ambiguous regulations creates the need to build an expensive administrative apparatus that can navigate this healthcare labyrinth. While building a preventive medicine business in the United States, I had to hire lawyers for $1,000 an hour (!) to get basic answers and set up the right procedures. Idiocy. Only a few large businesses can afford that, so over time this limits competition, which leads to higher prices. The surprising thing is that US lawmakers do not feel responsible for creating this reporting monster. Federal and state regulations create the burden of reporting, which requires doctors, nurses, and pharmacists to spend 25%–50% of their time on administrative work. A 2020 study found that US physicians spend

44.9% of their time inputting data into electronic health record systems.[111] Well, if you use a doctor who makes $300,000 a year to fill in tables, then no wonder the US has the most expensive healthcare in the world....

Part of this obsession with bureaucracy is caused by institutionalized legal paranoia. A nurse or a doctor typically has to think a lot about the administrative, reporting, and legal aspects of their job instead of about your medical problem. However, having more complete records of what was done and said during treatment helps doctors and hospitals to defend themselves in court in case they are sued. This is where most of their attention is going.

In order to be better positioned in a potential lawsuit, we sacrifice a huge proportion of doctors' time. Wouldn't it make sense for a doctor to take care of almost twice as many patients within the same time frame, rather than spending 45% of their time on building up a defense against potential litigation?

The US healthcare system is rotten, wasteful, and self-serving. It is institutionally designed to be ineffective—but it makes money. A lot of money.

Government and Political Institutions

Ultimately, the most powerful organizations that are trying to make you stupider are states, political parties, and political institutions.

What's their motivation? Simple ...

It makes *Homo idioticus* easier to manipulate and govern.

Research proves that well-educated, prosperous societies are more difficult to direct and control. Poor and uneducated societies are much more moldable and likely to follow inconsistent logic and irrational explanations and tolerate incompetence or graft. Political institutions typically use several techniques to make you stupid.

Create an enemy

Most parties play the common trick of identifying an "enemy of the people." This allows them to rally support and create unity and a perception of them as strong, influential leaders. A playbook example is to pick on a minority and turn the majority of society against them. Then the state has someone to blame for all the problems and an easy way to vent frustration.

Prime Minister Narendra Modi in India has mastered this tactic perfectly. He singled out Muslims as a scapegoat for all the country's problems and mobilized support around the concept of making them second-class citizens. This has tremendous benefits for him: First, frustrated young men have someone to beat up on (semilegally) so they don't turn against the government. Second, having an enemy allows Modi to build a narrative that Muslims are responsible for all the country's problems. Finally, it creates a perception of him as a strong leader. When you are strong and harsh, your ratings go up! (See the earlier "Love of Strength and Authority" section.) Brilliant! Unfortunately, the Indian population has fallen prey to his masterful technique and completely missed that, in the meantime, it is being exploited by incredible corruption and cronyism.

Advocate supremacy

This is another easy trick that most people cannot resist: Tell them they are unique, special, and superior by comparing them favorably with others. Nationalism is the best example. Playing a patriotic leader always wins you applause. Talking up your nation at the expense of other nations is cheap, builds your prestige at home, and doesn't cost you much domestically. Even the most benign, stable countries such as Italy, France, or the UK still explicitly or implicitly support the image of their uniqueness and superiority.

Why not believe in the uniqueness of *both* the French and the Italians at the same time, rather than debating which is better?

Create a myth of "worthy sacrifice"

Nation-states are adept at creating myths to explain policy failures. They often take advantage of our psychological bias toward optimism and hope for a better future to manipulate us. Very sophisticated, very callous—but usually effective.

Take, for example, American intervention in Afghanistan from 2001 to 2021. This was a 20-year-long war: 20 years of blood, sweat, and tears, 2,500 dead and 21,000 wounded American soldiers, 50,000–70,000 dead Afghan civilians, a cost of $2.3 trillion,[112] tens of thousands of people with destroyed mental health, broken marriages, unrealized dreams. However, the underlying state and political narrative is that "their sacrifice was not in vain." Really? Afghanistan is today run by the Taliban, just as it was before the war in 2001. Of the American soldiers who served in Afghanistan, 62% of them will tell you that this war *was* in vain....[113]

Design a faulty educational system

The heavy hand of the state transpires clearly in educational systems, which are often designed to prevent society from thinking independently. In most countries, students are expected to memorize information exactly as it is presented to them. Very few countries teach kids how to think, how to solve problems, how to question the data. Why is it so? Well, rote learning allows one version of reality to be created. Moreover, reciting and repeating something many times makes you (psychologically) more likely to believe in it. Even if it is a lie, and even if, at the beginning, *you know it is a lie*. Brilliant, isn't it?

In 2013, Mexico enacted a reasonable reform of its education system, aimed at solving some obvious pathologies: inability to fire an underperforming teacher, widespread tolerance for not showing up to work, selling teachers' positions, and even paying nonexistent, dead teachers (apparently 300,000 such cases in 2014![114]). A presidential candidate, Andrés Manuel López Obrador (popularly known as AMLO), announced in 2018 that these reforms would be canceled if he won the election—and he did win, given the incredible power of the Coordinadora Nacional de Trabajadores de la Educación and the Sindicato Nacional de Trabajadores de la Educación teachers' unions. AMLO backed a completely underperforming system—teachers did not have to show up for work or prove they had taught anything during class—that made people *less* educated! It is far easier to manipulate the uneducated because they do not know how to check facts, do not have much subject matter knowledge, and cannot benchmark. Great voters for a demagogue like AMLO!

Finally, California suggested removing calculus from the high school program in 2021. This was done in the name of "equity" and removing racial differences. So, instead of bringing children from all backgrounds to a higher level, proponents of the reform suggested lowering the bar for everyone. Again, well-educated voters ask difficult questions. Why bother fostering more of those?

Institutional Stupidity of the Legal System

Imagine you are a middle-income person who wants to start riding horses in California. You want to go on trails to enjoy the extraordinary beauty of the Californian countryside, and you want to ride fast (canter or gallop, in horse jargon). So you start calling all the stables in the Bay Area (of which there are plenty) and explain to them what you want. One by one, all of them refuse you.

This peaceful, relaxing activity is practically beyond the reach of a middle-income person in California because of ... legal paranoia. Commercially run stables do not want to take you horseback riding outside the barn because of the fear of legal liability. They are afraid that, if you fall off the horse, you will sue them for millions of dollars and they will go bankrupt.

This is not a theoretical risk. In 2021, an owner of a brilliant riding school in Sonoma Horse Park in Petaluma was sued for a million dollars by a woman whose chair collapsed beneath her while she was watching her child ride a horse. No real damage, no fall from the horse—just mom's embarrassing fall from the chair. The riding instructor's life is now destroyed because she must spend thousands of dollars and hours of time to protect herself against a senseless lawsuit by an angry, litigious mother.

This is absurd! First, this dramatically reduces the number of people who are horseback riding, because you can only ever ride fast if you own your own horse. Second, it reduces riding instructors' incomes because they have far fewer clients (only the very rich). Third, it reduces the amount of exercise that society as a whole is getting and contributes to the epidemics of obesity and diabetes. Everybody loses, except for injury lawyers.

The US as a country has institutionalized legal stupidity to a degree unheard of among other well-developed economies. In the United States, you can be successfully sued for naming your sandwich a "Footlong" or failing to "energize" someone with an energy drink. Really.

In 2013, an Australian teenager posted a photo on Facebook showing that Subway's Footlong Sandwich was not really 12 inches long, but 11 inches. This culminated in litigation against Subway, and in 2016 a Wisconsin federal judge approved a settlement requiring Subway to adopt quality control measures consistent with "the realities of baking bread" to ensure that its 6-inch and 12-inch sandwiches were those exact lengths.[115]

In 2014, Red Bull was accused of failing to "give you wings," as several customers did not feel so energized by its energy drink. The matter was settled out of court for $13 million (!), and Red Bull had to provide up to $10–$15 worth of its products to customers who bought the company's products between 2001 and 2014.[116]

These examples show how institutionalized stupidity is. You can use the powerful machinery of the court system to pursue ridiculous allegations—and win.

Because we have built and continue to pay for institutions that promote stupidity, we have created a society that has very low trust and no cohesion; it encourages us to find ways to screw other people. And it favors the wealthy—powerful organizations and rich individuals—because in civil lawsuits, you do not get a defender that is paid for by the state. This means you can easily bankrupt your opponent by filing several often-flimsy claims. When your adversary cannot afford lawyers, they will have to represent themselves and will be required to know the law, or they can try to beg lawyers to represent them pro bono. Good luck with that.

WHAT TO DO ABOUT IT?

All that is necessary for the forces of evil to win in
the world is for enough good men to do nothing.

Edmund Burke (allegedly)

Hopefully by now, dear reader, you agree with me that we are surrounded by stupidity on an epic scale. The natural question is: What to do about it?

Basically, our duty to ourselves and humanity as a whole is to fight it! Tooth and nail. As Winston Churchill said in his famous speech, "*We shall fight on the beaches, … we shall fight in the fields and in the streets, we shall fight in the hills, …*"—with resilience, humor, and kindness—"*… we shall never surrender.*"[1]

EDUCATION

As you will remember from our opening story about a six-year-old boy named Dina Sanichar who was found living with a group of wolves, the difference between us and animals can be practically indistinguishable in the absence of culture. In Dina's case, just six years without education and access to civilization made him behave like an animal well into his adulthood. It prevented him from developing deep relationships with people or learning how to read, write, or even talk. For all intents and purposes, he behaved similarly to non-human primates such as gorillas or chimpanzees.

This story highlights that *education* is the critical differentiator. So it is not surprising that, in the most basic terms, the solution to human stupidity is three-fold: education, education, and more education.

Education is the ultimate driver of progress. More educated societies are more difficult to manipulate and less likely to become extremist. They are wealthier, less violent, and have a more efficient state apparatus. They are more generous to the weak, sick, and underprivileged, and have better respect for women and minorities.

And education doesn't just help to combat stupidity. It also dramatically increases the wealth of nations. A study at Georgetown University showed that American individuals with bachelor's degrees earn an average of $1 million more over their lifetimes than those with only high school diplomas. China's rapid economic growth was fueled by a massive upgrade of its workforce. In 1990, tertiary education enrollment in China was at 3%.[2] By 2020, it had reached 58%—it grew by a factor of 19! This speed of improvement is much bigger than anything else observed in the Western world during this time (e.g., in the same period, the US improved from 71% to 79%, an increase of only 10%).

In the long term, education is a panacea for almost all of our problems!

Improve Quantity *and* Quality

Both the quality and quantity of education in the world today are woefully inadequate. The wave of positivity about the world's progress in the 2010s, trumpeted by famous statisticians like Hans Rosling, missed an important point: Educational progress cannot be equated merely to *literacy*. It is simply the wrong metric to use. Being able to read and write (which can typically be achieved with three years of schooling) is an extremely low bar and under no circumstances can be used as proof of a good education.

A person who can read and write might still not be able to understand basic mathematics, physics, chemistry, or biology. Nor will they understand how to spot the difference between opinion and fact, or how to isolate and compare opposing viewpoints.

Let's look at a better proxy for global education levels: the number of years of schooling. Obviously, this is not an ideal statistic either. Many countries use ineffective methods or curricula, with teachers not showing up to work (e.g., in Mexico) and school time used for rote memorization of religious texts or patriotic songs, which are of little use in the contemporary world. Often, one year of schooling in some countries is worth two or even more in others. However, years of schooling is still a better metric than literacy.

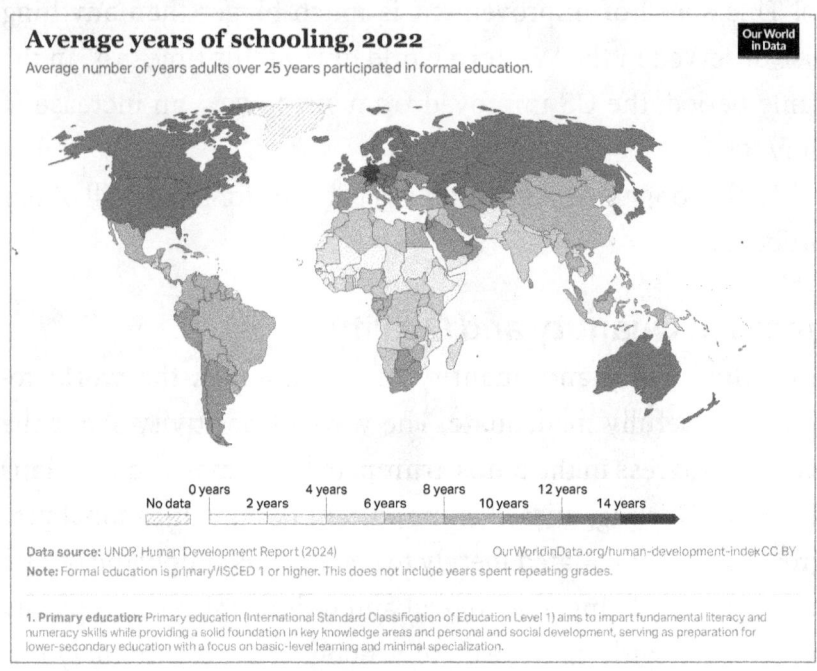

FIGURE 48. Average years of schooling for people aged 25+ in 2022[3]

Take a look at Figure 48. This graphic shows that outside of North America, Europe, Japan, and Australia, most people around the world receive less than six years of education in their lifetimes.

Globally, the population-weighted average number of years of schooling is just below nine. This means that, assuming most people start school at age 6, most do not continue beyond age 15. Even after including all those PhDs from Harvard, MIT, Oxford, and many other institutions. Stunning....

So the first worldwide priority in the fight against stupidity should be increasing the years of schooling!

Second should be increasing the *quality* of education. Most countries run schools very poorly—with underpaid staff, an outdated curriculum, excessive focus on building national pride and subjects such as religion, history, and their own country's literature. There is nothing wrong with teaching history. I love history! However, if you have two hours of history a week and one hour of religion but only one hour of math, something is wrong.... Also, if you know only poets and writers in your own country and do not know anything about the world's most celebrated authors, your education was incomplete or too heavily localized.

As cofounder of the top high school in Poland, I also know how badly public school systems teach the art of studying.

Most countries do not teach *how* to learn, even though teaching two simple techniques—fast reading and fast memorization—could rapidly improve how quickly students can learn. These are proven, easy-to-learn skills that should be taught early to make students' later educational years more productive. Do you know these methods?

- **Fast reading.** This technique focuses on training your eyes to consume written text in groups of words (sections), typically two or three per line of text, instead of reading words one by one. It also teaches you to eradicate subvocalization. Once you learn those two habits, you will read 30%–300% faster.
- **Fast memorization.** This technique is based on teaching you to create in your mind visual stories that are vivid, dynamic, and dramatic. This allows you to remember almost an infinite number of words in a sequence.

Mastering these two techniques can reduce study time by 10%–25%, which can boost productivity by a similar proportion. It should be mandatory for our schools to teach these skills early in a student's education. (If you don't know these tricks as an adult, don't worry. Find an online course and start today! It is never too late to learn!)

Another intervention that can radically accelerate the speed and quality of teaching is combating "summer learning loss" or "summer slide." Research has proven that over the long summer holidays, students lose about 20%–30% of their learning.[4] It's as if after starting a new school year in September, by the end of October you have done nothing more than return to where you left off in June. Frustrating, isn't it? The decline is steeper in math skills than in reading.

Unfortunately, this problem does not have an easy, cheap solution. The best way of handling it would be to extend the duration of the school year. Spending, let's say, one month longer in school would not only prevent the "summer slide" of about 20% but would allow another 10%–15% of new material to be introduced.

However, this is obviously hard to implement, as any reform along those lines would meet strong resistance from teachers (who want more free time) and parents (who want more flexibility regarding holidays), not to mention the children themselves. The second-best option would be to enroll students in rich summer programs, which could partly offset such a decline. That is an inferior alternative, as it is more optional and selective. Typically, only kids of wealthier parents participate in such programs, which further deepens the class divide.

Harness the Power of Artificial Intelligence

The ultimate power to improve the quality of education, though, lies in artificial intelligence (AI). The promise of AI-assisted schooling is mind-boggling.

Thanks to personalized teaching via individual interaction with the study material on a tablet, children can advance three times faster on average than in traditional classrooms. This builds on the "two sigma" phenomenon that had already been observed in the 1980s by educational psychologist Benjamin Bloom, who concluded that children tutored individually score an average of two standard deviations (two sigma, in statistical jargon) better than in a traditional setup. Today AI can replace one-on-one tutors, which have been prohibitively expensive. With careful, thoughtful design of online, AI-driven courses, children can move ahead at their own pace. This benefits both students who move faster than the rest and those who struggle with the material, as they can easily go back to an earlier stage and repeat what they missed. Sometimes the fastest way forward is to go back to earlier material, and AI is best at serving the right content at the right time, based on observation of a student's interactions. This is not sci-fi. Such schools already exist (e.g., Alpha School in Texas), and they achieve phenomenal results: reducing the time needed to master the curriculum from six hours to two hours per day and achieving results in the top 1%–2% nationally.

These three ideas—teaching students how to study (through fast reading/memorization techniques), extending the school year and/or providing rich summer programs, and deploying AI for personalized tutoring—could improve educational outcomes dramatically. Children could learn two to three times faster. And all of this is available to us today! We are just used to doing things the old way.

Teach Critical Thinking

Increasing the number of years of schooling alone—or even teaching students how to learn—is not enough to overcome human stupidity. We need additional tools: the skills to identify stupidity and insulate ourselves from it. In short, we need critical thinking skills.

Systemically, the best way to teach these skills would be to introduce a mandatory one-year, one-hour-per-week class on critical thinking to all high school students. Such courses sometimes exist at various British schools, but their programs are different from what I am proposing. The ideal class should include the following curriculum:

Biases

Teach students about the biases and heuristic shortcuts we are susceptible to, and how to guard against them:

- Review and discuss confirmation bias, availability bias, priming, framing, and omission bias. Ask students to provide their own examples of each of these.
- Develop a toolkit for staying independent and unbiased—teach specific procedures and skills for staying well-informed and in touch with reality.
    - Introduce the concept of how social groups perceive data differently when fed different news:
        - Show examples of videos from CNN and Fox News that cover the same topic but point to completely different conclusions.

- » Show written coverage of certain facts, summarized differently by various journalists.
  - ○ Encourage students to:
    - » Read news from various sources and recognize the signs of typical high-quality journalism (showing both sides' opinions, facts, etc.).
    - » Fact check—create a habit of verifying information and the best sources for it.
    - » Verify actors—create a habit of evaluating people by their track record and consistency with facts.

Manipulation

Review the basic tools of manipulation:

- **Reciprocity rule.** The expectation of receiving something in return after giving a gift or favor.
- **Social proof.** When the sheer number of people who have a certain viewpoint makes it more appealing to you.
- **Persecution of minorities.** Finding a common enemy and directing the public's frustrations at them; blaming problems on someone else.
- **Extreme nationalism.** Nationalism used as a tool to rally support for confronting some other nation or group. Show how the narrative of "them" versus "us" can easily lead to aggression and violence and explain the biological background for this manipulation technique.
- **Cult of personality.** When you see this, you know that something is going wrong.

Logic

Review the fundamental logical paradigms that are overlooked by millions in their daily lives:

- **Long-term versus short-term effects.** Study this at length at the national and individual level. Go through examples such as the introduction of generous gasoline subsidies and ask students to give short-term and long-term cost-benefit analyses. Develop the concept of vastly different short-term and long-term outcomes.
- **Correlation versus causation.** Teach that sometimes events have surprising correlations with each other, but this doesn't mean that one caused the other. Give funny examples, such as the nearly perfect correlation between the divorce rate in Maine and the price of margarine.
- **Economic cyclicality.** Explain that economic performance is often not correlated with politicians' actions, as it naturally undergoes stochastic cycles, sometimes boosting incompetent politicians or harming competent ones.
- **Value of consumption over time.** Explain the concept of deferred gratification. This can be illustrated on a personal level by discussing what premature, excessive consumption (e.g., partying or computer gaming) would do to you as a person. Show examples of real students who went for easy pleasures too early and compare them to the more fulfilling lives of those who aimed for more painstaking, long-term gratification. Discuss the same concept on a national level, focusing on short-term boosts to economic growth versus long-term damage to the economy. Examples could include:
    - Hugo Chávez's early success and his subsequent total destruction of the Venezuelan economy
    - Universal handouts versus thoughtful incentives
- **Compound interest.** Explain the power of compound interest, showing that regular saving over a long period is "the eighth wonder of the world" (a quote attributed to Einstein).

Give students concrete examples with real numbers, such as Tony Robbins's story of two friends named Joe and Bob: Joe saves $300 a month starting at age 19 and continues for only eight years, until he is 27. By age 65, he will have saved more for his pension than Bob, who contributes $300 a month starting at age 27 and continues saving throughout his career.[5]

- **Preventive health.** Illustrate in medical and financial terms how preventing disease is better than fighting it, showing the benefits of preventive medicine versus the cost of surgeries, cancer therapies, and other expensive medical procedures. Ask students to write short essays illustrating when they or their family members were hurt by not understanding those mechanisms.

Complexity

Introduce the concept of balanced thinking and nonbinary evaluation of people and situations.

- Teach students that the world is not black and white; people and events have both good and bad sides simultaneously (e.g., while John F. Kennedy was considered a great president, he was also a womanizer who often cheated on his wife).
- Ask students to write a brief (less than one page) essay on a person they admire but whom they've discovered have negative characteristics.

This entire program—giving students specific examples, internalizing their learnings through short essays, and intriguing them with controversial discussions—could be done within one year, in just one hour per week. You would be shocked at what a huge positive difference it would make to the formation of young people.

MINDSET

We cannot bet on the idea of a critical thinking class to eliminate stupidity. Some governments might implement it many years from now, some likely never will. As we know, most countries institutionally *are interested* in keeping their population stupid, manipulable, and susceptible to propaganda.

So what can we do today?

Reading this book and creating awareness of all those traps we fall into is a good first step. Changing your mindset is a good second step.

We should, every day, fight the battle against stupidity. This should be our default mindset. Such a state of mind by itself can make a huge difference. What if you identify, expose, and attack stupidity on a daily basis? Well, over time, things will get better.

Cultivate the Will to Fight

Most of the time, we lack the willpower to change things and grudgingly accept the small stupidities in life. The problem, of course, is that small stupidities always grow into bigger ones, and we end up with more and more of them. So we need to fight them during every meeting, every human interaction, every instance, however small they may be.

Therefore—whenever you have a chance—attack stupidity with absolute fervor. When you see a stupid behavior, bureaucratic procedure, or pointless requirement, make it known that you disagree with it. Go further and ask to talk to a manager or supervisor about it. Send a complaint email. Fight back.

Swiss, Switzerland's national airline carrier, has devised a system whereby making complaints is almost impossible. It (very smartly) designed its online form so it cannot accept numbers or typical symbols such as hyphens or bullet points. It also hides "call to action" buttons such as Send and Next. This makes submitting a claim very difficult. Few people have the patience to review the text again and again, figuring out how to move forward, removing various characters they typically use. The right approach there is to fight. *Do* take the time to submit the claim, tell all your friends how bad the airline is, don't fly with them again. In the long term, unless the company improves its system, Swiss will lose because people will gradually move their business elsewhere.

Why don't we have enough quarters in the US? From 2020 until at least early 2023, the US (or at least San Francisco) experienced a chronic shortage of $0.25 coins. How can a country that maintains a million-soldier army, has intercontinental ballistic missiles, and can send people to the moon, not mint enough quarters? We need to talk openly about the incompetence of the chair of the Federal Reserve. He was able to print trillions of dollars in paper money and shower it on the economy, causing huge inflation, but he was incapable of minting enough quarters. Millions of normal people cannot get change in the store, cannot operate a laundromat, because of the Fed's incompetence. We need to criticize it and demand action.

These are examples of small stupidities in everyday life that we have to deal with regularly. However, complacency is what allows those stupidities to grow and flourish. Ultimately, it is our mindset—the willpower to change—that makes the difference. It took more than half a century to ban lead-heavy wall paint, which caused so much damage to children's brains in the late 1800s and early 1900s, and it took about two decades to ban smoking indoors in public spaces in most Western nations.

History provides excellent examples of progress being made by applying the constant-fight mindset. The "no tolerance for stupidity" approach simply works.

Here's a powerful example: Commercial jet flights have become incredibly safe over the last 50 years, due to a meticulous and relentless focus on rooting out every single smallest stupidity. One by one, step by step, the industry has implemented a myriad of rules that has eliminated most accidents due to reckless behaviors of the crew, maintenance failures, bad air traffic control procedures, risky takeoffs and landings, and the like. As a result of detailed investigations and permanent redefinition, most of the areas for potential failures have been eradicated. This has resulted in an unprecedented improvement in safety. Your chance of dying in a flight accident on a commercial airline is 1 in 1.2 million. Your chances of dying in a car crash are 1 in 5,000. This all happened because some people decided they would not tolerate stupidity, human mistakes, and "bad days" on the job. It is all in the mindset.

Another example provides an even better illustration, as it provides a direct comparison between action and inaction, tolerance and intolerance of stupidity.

Both the United States and the Soviet Union (and later Russia) have large submarine fleets. Both countries also suffered a series of high-profile submarine losses of their conventional and nuclear submarines during the 1960s. In response, the US implemented a strict operations protocol for its fleet, resembling in depth and scope the regulations developed for commercial aviation. As a result, the US has not lost a single submarine since 1968. On the other hand, the Soviet Union and Russia continued to tolerate procedural shortcomings, deviations from standards, training deficiencies, and human mistakes. Consequently, since 1968, the Soviet Union/Russia has lost a staggering nine state-of-the-art submarines! That's the price they've paid for tolerance of stupidity![6]

Saying no to double standards and privileges is another manifestation of the fight against stupidity. My friend was asked to leave the bar in a fancy San Francisco members' club to make room for the city's then-mayor, London Breed, who had arrived with her entourage of personal pals. My friend objected. On what grounds is London Breed allowed to take precedence over other citizens in a bar, outside of her official duties? Why should she have more rights than others? I am very proud of my friend for fighting for her rights. Too often, politicians eat our lunch—*and* take our seats.

Unfortunately, we do not oppose often enough the people who want to eat our lunch. Famously, Nancy Pelosi was able to build a $170 million fortune on stock trading via her husband. As a speaker of the US House of Representatives, she has access to nonpublic, sensitive information well ahead of anybody else. Somehow, miraculously, her husband made a large number of brilliant trades on the stock exchange over several decades while she was in office.

For example, in June 2022, he exercised options to buy $5 million in shares of Nvidia, a famous chip manufacturer, just weeks before the House of Representatives—led by Pelosi—approved legislation to grant more than $50 billion to US chip manufacturers, with Nvidia being one of the beneficiaries. A politician who pretends to represent ordinary citizens, benefiting from her privileged position—isn't that disgusting?

The right response here is to fight—ideally, creating a movement to ban members of the House and Senate from trading, with the exception of mutual funds and exchange-traded funds.

Complacency about stupidity is everywhere, in everyday life, in small events that make our lives worse, even in the intellectual capitals of the world.

Take New York, for example. The traffic jams in New York City are grossly aggravated by drivers' practice of driving into the crossroads to avoid waiting for another cycle of lights, even if there is no space to clear the crossing. When the traffic lights change, vehicles therefore block traffic moving in a perpendicular direction, which causes additional chaos and makes the whole situation far worse. Everyone honks, people get mad, cortisol goes up, mayhem ensues. However, there is a simple solution to this situation—a $500 fine for driving into a crossroad if you have no space to fully cross it. A few months of merciless enforcement of this rule would quickly eradicate the problem and significantly alleviate New York's traffic situation. The traffic fines would also generate a lot of money to help solve the homelessness problem. Do you think New York lacks the intellectual capital to come up with such a solution? No, it is simply too complacent, too lazy.

Be Vigilant

Fighting stupidity is never-ending. We cannot ever lower our guard, because stupidity is like a hydra—it has a phenomenal ability to resurrect and regrow. As we learned in an earlier chapter about "wokeism," even good ideas can get corrupted and be used as a vehicle for stupidity. So we need to be vigilant all the time.

Take the example of Just Stop Oil activists who in 2022 attacked Van Gogh's iconic painting *The Sunflowers* in the National Gallery in London. How would the destruction of Van Gogh's masterpiece help to advance their cause? Would it create sympathy for their movement? And why would an organization called Just Stop Oil attack Van Gogh's painting to protest … world hunger?

While protecting the environment and ending hunger are highly commendable causes, it seems that some of those ideals were hijacked by moronic individuals who just want more likes on their social media. Even if someone is riding the wave of a noble movement, we need to be able to call out stupidity and stigmatize it.

Being vigilant might be most difficult while addressing stupidity in the culture we grew up in. In particular, when it has benevolent or well-intentioned roots.

Let's say you are a salesperson who grew up in the warm, personable, informal Brazilian culture. It fosters human connection and prioritizes friendships and family. However, you might miss that Brazilian culture typically tolerates an inefficient use of time, including being extremely late. This cultural trait might cause you to earn only half of what your cold, punctual Swedish friend makes. Why? While you can meet three clients a day (because you or your client is late to every meeting), she does six meetings a day (because everything starts and finishes on time).

Conversely, the amazing and laudable transparency of the Swedish culture can lead to stupidity as well. Sweden makes a summary of personal tax returns available online to anyone. This means that everyone can check how much money you made last year. Incredible, right? However, when you check the income of your date *before* going for dinner, doesn't it destroy romance? Doesn't it create a judgmental environment, a classist approach, and inaccurate perceptions? Well, why should my worth be measured, and publicly displayed, in Swedish krona?

You see a pattern here? These are stupidities built on top of good roots—positive traits such as warmth or a culture of transparency. This highlights that not everything with good origins will remain good. It might *become* stupid, and we need to be vigilant about that possibility.

Travel and Talk to People

Traveling and experiencing other cultures is a great stupidity-prevention tool. Learning directly from other people's behaviors allows you to see different perspectives, appreciate local sensitivities, and see unfamiliar phenomena with your own eyes.

Perhaps talking to Chinese people in China will open your eyes to the feeling of humiliation they harbor due to their treatment by European powers in the early 1900s, when French, English, and German troops drowned the Boxer Uprising in blood and burned icons of Chinese architecture, such as the Summer Palace, to the ground. During your trip there, you might hear about the Opium Wars, which are not well covered in history classes taught in the West. In short, the UK waged war with China between 1839 and 1860 to force it to buy opium from British plantations in India. Yes, the British Empire acted like a drug lord—forcing the Chinese government to give unfettered access to this devastating drug to its own citizens—because it made a lot of money for the UK.

Perhaps a visit to the two sides of the wall between Israel and Palestine will give you a glimpse of the depth of the conflict in the Middle East. Perhaps a visit to Cuba will give you a lesson in economics: how heavy subsidies for gas (petrol) are destroying its economy. You might spot huge lines in front of gas stations and learn about massive corruption—gas bought at government prices and sold on the black market, while farmers still plow their fields with oxen because they cannot get gas for tractors. So Cubans are going hungry for lack of food because, despite having good soil, there is no gasoline for tractors to help harvest the crops.

Perhaps a visit to Bhutan will teach you about how the nation applies four basic questions to every single decision it makes. Since the 1970s, Bhutan has focused on gross national happiness (GNH) instead of GDP, and every decision is based on its effect on (a) sustainable development, (b) preservation of cultural values, (c) conservation of the natural environment, and (d) good governance. You might also see how a poor nation can be extremely happy, close-knit, and supportive at the same time.

Be Humble, Be Honest

Admitting your weaknesses and stupidity is a first step to improvement. When I realized my own layers of stupidity, it taught me where my blind spots are and what I should avoid doing in the future.

I am not a good real estate investor, as I too often mix aesthetics with business. This is a recipe for disaster. My conclusion: Do not to invest in real estate, or let others do it for me.

I also am overly optimistic. While generally this is a good approach to life, at times it creates unnecessary stress because of the discrepancy between reality and my expectations.

Being honest with yourself—removing rigidity and fakeness—prevents the buildup of stupidity.

Use Mathematics to Reason

Mathematics provides a universal language that can help expose irrationality and enable good decision-making. We do not use it enough in our public discourse. Too often we get carried away by beautiful, catchy phrases that have universal appeal but, in reality, are not true.

Let's pick one that appears universally true: Human life is invaluable. Almost nobody would oppose that. However, unfortunately, this statement is not correct.

We ascribe value to human life *every day* in our lives:

- We decide as a society which procedures are medically reimbursable and which are not, choices that lead directly to life or death.
- We pay very specific amounts of insurance for death under specific circumstances.
- We evaluate drugs' effectiveness based on how many years they can extend life.

Based on such implied calculations, various US government agencies value human life, for all practical purposes, at around $7–$10 million, and one extra year of life at around $100,000.[7]

In November 2022, US courts awarded the families of eight victims of the 2012 Sandy Hook shooting punitive damages totaling $1.44 billion. This was the result of a defamation lawsuit brought against Alex Jones, a ridiculous far-right conspiracy theorist who claimed, through his website and radio program, that the shooting was "a false flag operation planned by the government using 'crisis actors' to undermine gun rights." The families were awarded, on average, $180 million per person.

However, there were many other school shootings in the same year and many more before and after. Compensation for lives lost in those shootings was far lower (often below $1 million per person, or even minimal).

In the meantime, the US government refused to pay $5,000 per year for insulin strips for diabetics, which has caused many amputations of legs or arms. Hundreds of such people can be seen in the streets of San Francisco. Thousands of people die every year in the United States who could be saved by a $50,000 coronary artery bypass procedure.[8] Thousands more die every year who could be saved by a $20,000 bariatric surgery.[9]

So as a society, on one hand we agree to compensate one child's life lost with $180 million and another child's life with less than $1 million or close to nothing. And we do it in the context of refusing to spend a mere $50,000 to prevent the death of another human being? Mathematically, wouldn't $180 million save 3,600 people's lives if we paid for their coronary artery bypass procedures? Why do we compensate someone for a life that is already lost instead of helping 3,600 people whose lives can still be saved?

This is the dark side of the "human life is invaluable" statement, which we just debunked with mathematics. As a society, we do not use mathematics enough for real-life decisions, which leads to incredibly inconsistent and illogical choices.

I know how hard this sounds, but isn't the mathematical logic behind it difficult to question?

Fight for Freedom of Speech

Open-minded deliberations—such as the one we just had about the value of human life—are increasingly rare. People today are afraid of talking about difficult topics because of the fear of being canceled. There are more and more taboo subjects. People are afraid of asking the right, logical questions, because it may be considered disrespectful, or not in line with the progressive line of thinking or the conservative line of thinking, or will touch too closely on religion, sexuality, or race.

If we stop asking tough questions and stop having open debates, where views can be expressed freely, we will turn into even more polarized, atomized tribes who believe in parallel realities. Eventually, we will deliberately stop access to the flow of information. We will stop criticism of our views and actions, when it is only in the openness of public debate that we can uncover our own fallacies.

We get offended so easily in debates these days. Since when have we become so thin-skinned?

Be Ready for a Lonely Fight

If you are planning on fighting stupidity, be ready for a lonesome fight. History has proved over and over again that smart and rational ideas are supported by only a few. You might need to fight alone for a long time before your common-sense views are adopted by the general public.

Any major social change in the last 200 years probably took at least 20 years to ripple successfully through society. So if you are totally right about something, you will likely need to be really patient.

Can you imagine how frustrating it was for the early abolitionists, let's say in 1813 (20 years before slavery was abolished in the UK)? At that time, if you mentioned your views at a fancy cocktail party in London high society, you would be laughed at and called unpatriotic or economically illiterate.

Can you imagine being a European man who supported suffrage rights for women in 1898? You would be derided by most of your male peers and considered socially awkward. In 1918, however, universal voting rights for women were moving into the mainstream in Europe.

Can you imagine how civil rights movement activists in the US felt in 1944, when they were getting very little traction for their ideas? In 1964, President Lyndon Johnson outlawed race-based segregation.

Social progress is typically made by brilliant individuals working in small groups or even alone. Societies, as a whole, rarely bring positive change spontaneously on their own.

Take the example of Dr. Ignaz Semmelweis, a Hungarian doctor who worked in a hospital in Vienna in the 1840s and noted a substantial difference in mortality between two obstetrics clinics. One, where both doctors and students worked, had a mortality rate of 10%, while the other had a mortality rate of 4%. He deduced this must have to do with students performing autopsies and then coming into contact with the blood of multiple patients later the same day. The concept of germs was not yet known, so Semmelweis called the agent of the problem "cadaverous particles," and in 1847, he logically advised his staff to wash their hands with chlorinated lime.

The results were stunning! Mortality declined to below 1% across both wards. This was an amazing success, but nonetheless, Semmelweis was universally mocked by his colleagues and then-respected, moronic figures such as the powerful Rudolf

Virchow. Virchow was a famous and influential physician who was nicknamed the Pope of Medicine, and his strong opposition to Semmelweis's ideas destroyed the Hungarian doctor's reputation. Semmelweis was fired from his hospital in 1849, and he was disowned by the medical establishment. The rejection caused him to suffer a mental breakdown, and he died.

He paid the ultimate price for opposing stupidity. He was right—he saved many lives—but he was also alone. And he was about 20 years too early with his idea.

Evaluate Your Input Data

The scariest part of human stupidity today is that various segments of society have started living in parallel realities in which we no longer can agree even on facts. Donald Trump's supporters claim that he is fiscally conservative (he isn't; during his first presidential term, he created the biggest increase in the federal debt in US history during one term, totaling almost $8 trillion!), and progressives claim that somehow defunding the police reduces crime (it doesn't; just the opposite).

If we cannot agree on the facts, there is no hope for building a well-functioning society.

Therefore, it is imperative to curate, clean up, and constantly evaluate the data inputs we receive. Have you heard the saying "We are what we eat?" It applies not only in a physical sense but also in an intellectual sense. If we consume only one-sided, polarized propaganda, we will quickly degrade intellectually and become easy objects of manipulation. If we take in data from various sources, however, we preserve a balanced point of view and are unlikely to be fooled by skilled manipulators.

In the US, a good example would be reading (or watching) both Democratic-leaning and Republican-leaning media.

Adding high-quality, paid journalism, which always presents two sides of the debate, to your information diet is a great idea. Fact-checking should become part of our routine. Now that we have constant internet access on our smartphones, it is relatively easy, as long as we know how to pick unbiased sources.

Over time, fact-checking allows us to form views on politicians, journalists, and other opinion leaders, depending on whether or not they stick to the facts. By fact-checking media that express various opinions, we can verify which ones are reliable.

Even if we have established which sources are dependable, it is still worthwhile from time to time to visit sources that present opposing opinions. This practice allows us to self-reflect and autocorrect, in case our usual sources get corrupted over time.

Exercise Your Brain

Your brain has incredible neuroplasticity. This means that it can reorganize its structure, functions, and neural connections even in adulthood. The brain is like a muscle—the more you use it, the stronger it gets. So make your brain spend some time at the gym! Read, do crossword puzzles, pick up a musical instrument, try learning a bit of a new language, attend a lecture, drive or walk without GPS from time to time to train your spatial thinking, and, most importantly ... dance!

Partner dance, to be specific. A 21-year-long study at the Albert Einstein College of Medicine in New York City, published in *The New England Journal of Medicine*, concluded that partner dancing has an off-the-charts impact on preserving brain function.[10] Scientists measured the cognitive status of subjects 75 years old or older who participated in various activities that were expected to help preserve cognitive acuity and prevent dementia. The findings (see Figure 49) were startling.

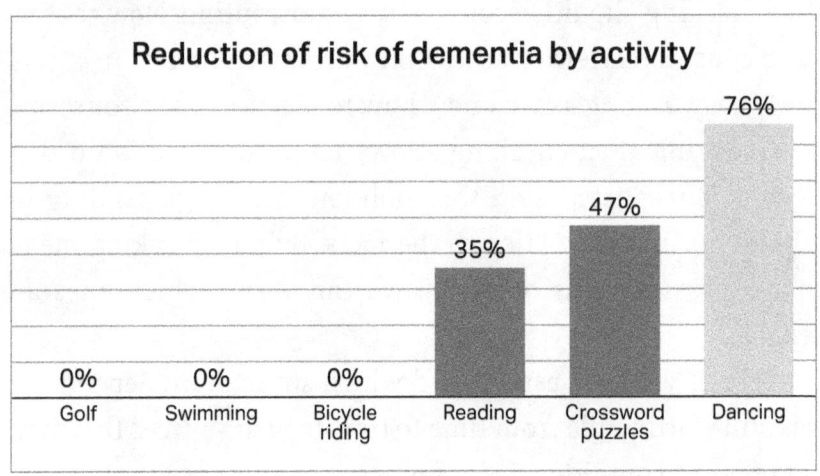

FIGURE 49. Reduction of dementia risk by activity[11]

Partner dancing completely outperformed any other activity in preventing dementia. Why dancing? Scientists believe it is because dancing requires a lot of split-second, rapid-fire decision-making. It demands multidimensional thinking, such as spatial planning, following rhythm and music, remembering steps, feeling and reading your partner's emotions, and coordinating movements. The brain needs to process a huge amount of data in a rapidly changing spatial environment and make rapid neural connections, rather than habitually doing the same thing.

This is a hell of an exercise for your brain! So make a gift to the world this weekend—grab your partner or friend and go dancing ... together!

STRUCTURAL SOLUTIONS

Imagine you're a benevolent dictator of a country, one in which you have total power to change anything. How would you fight stupidity? Some of you, my dear readers, may even happen to be running a country already, or be in a position of influence, so this knowledge might be helpful to you. The rest of us might simply want to know what to demand from our politicians to make our lives better.

So let's continue on this exciting journey of an imaginary benevolent dictator who has all the power to do the right things and reduce the amount of stupidity we face!

Ensure Adequate Food

We should probably start where our track record is most shameful—feeding our children. As you might remember from the "Biology" chapter, a lack of food in the early stages of a child's development can lower IQ by as much as 15 points. Implementing a targeted school meal program and even a preschool food distribution system would have, therefore, an incredibly high return for society. In poor countries that typically have a low calorie intake, any help would make a big difference.

In rich countries, it is more about food quality. However, even a rich country like the US falls short in this area. About one-sixth of the US population relies on governmental food subsidies via its Supplemental Nutrition Assistance Program (SNAP, commonly known as food stamps). SNAP subsidizes retailers that sell unhealthy, low-quality foods, which the US Department of Agriculture recommends that Americans avoid. Why? These foods are characteristically very salty or high in sugar. More than half of SNAP benefits are used for meats, sweetened beverages, snacks, and desserts.[12] One study scored the healthiness of food obtained via food stamps at 47 (out of 100), compared to the average American score of 58 (which is still very low). Only 24% of food stamps are spent on fruits, vegetables, grains, and other healthy foods.

So, as a benevolent dictator, your first role would be to implement an appropriate assistance package that allow recipients to buy food that has enough caloric value but is not composed of pizza and french fries. In the US, simply readjusting what food stamps can be used for and targeting healthier foods would make a huge difference.

Reform Education

A second high-impact task would be reforming the education system. We should stop requiring a lot of rote memorization and teach students how to learn and think. Remember our fast reading and memorization techniques in the "Education" chapter? This will create time savings, which we can reinvest in high-yield new subjects such as coding, computer science, biology, and robotics. Let's not forget our one-year critical thinking course!

Promoting interdisciplinary thinking should be high on your "dictatorial agenda." Most innovation comes at the intersection of two different disciplines, as it combines the benefits of one technology or domain with another, diverse one. Therefore, studying more than one field and smooth transitions between disciplines should be encouraged.

Reduce Pollution

With total power to do the right thing, we could address the problem of pollution. We noted that dirty air can have a 2%–5% negative impact on test outcomes, as evidenced by both Chinese and Israeli studies. Lead, mercury, and other pollutants have an even greater negative effect. Pollution levels cannot be changed overnight, unfortunately. They typically result from electricity generation (more fossil fuels mean worse air), car traffic, and local weather conditions. Our idealistic state, run by you, would likely run on nuclear power, photovoltaics, and other renewables, and our cars would predominantly run on electric and hydrogen batteries.

Clean Up the Legal System

Any benevolent dictator running a country should have a deep look into its legal system. We have pointed numerous times to the law as a quagmire of complexity, irrationality, and outright stupidity. A good starting point would be to implement a rule requiring that one law be rescinded whenever a new one is implemented. A lot of stupidity is caused by laws piling one on top of another, with nobody understanding the relationships between them and nobody able to learn, remember, and obey all the rules. Why are we notionally subject to a threat of six months in prison for parking in a disabled parking spot? Why are you notionally liable for up to 20 years in prison, under chapter 272, section 34, of the Massachusetts General Laws, for having oral sex in private with your partner in Boston?

A good dictator would also change how the legal system operates and what its incentives are. What reasonable society should tolerate for-profit prisons run by private, returns-driven companies? And how about removing the plague of frivolous litigation? We need to get rid of the stupid system of injury lawyers and incentivization to claim disproportionate damages.

Fix Bureaucracy

An adjacent area requiring immediate attention of our benevolent dictator is our bureaucracy. Most developing and especially many already-developed countries have antiquated, inefficient, slow bureaucracies that offend our intellect and waste our time. Why do so many Americans spend two to three days a year working on their taxes? Why do they have to provide the same name, address, and Social Security number on every form, over and over again? Why do people require three days of work to apply for the most basic social support program?

If, every day, you are fighting with the mundane stupidity of your own administrative office, you start accepting mediocrity and stupidity on a daily basis. This permeates to what you expect in human interactions and what you expect of yourself. It is like osmosis—the more you have it around you, the more it will get inside you. In essence, over time, it makes you stupider.

The solution would be to employ a group of high-powered, intellectually top-notch minds to simplify the bureaucracy. These would have to be well-remunerated, smart people rather than the usual "not my problem" type of bureaucrats who populate most government administrations today. Singapore and the United Arab Emirates have proved that this approach works. They have very well-paid top graduates staffing many critical functions of the state's administration—who run it as if it was a high-powered, efficient enterprise. Things simply work in those countries, saving people tons of time and frustration.

Reform the Political System

Any structural fight with stupidity must involve reform of the political system itself, in particular in the US. Most developed countries have iterated and evolved their political systems, often coming up with a relatively well-functioning model in which simple concepts such as proportional representation work. This means that the candidate who gets elected is the one whom people actually voted for at the ballot box.

The basic concept of proportionality, well-understood already in ancient Athens, is not applied in the US. In the 21st century, we have had two presidents who lost the general election but took office anyway (Donald Trump, with 2.9 million (!) fewer votes than Hillary Clinton in 2016, and George W. Bush, with half a million fewer votes than Al Gore in 2000).

Because of the American obsession with its Constitution and an unwillingness to modify something that was developed nearly 250 years ago, the US has a broken political system. One voter in Wyoming is worth three times more than a voter in California. This is because of the Electoral College—an archaic system in which a group of unnecessary intermediaries elect the president after you have cast your vote. The problem is that it takes about 193,000 people to get one Electoral College vote in Wyoming and over 700,000 in California.[13] So, we are discriminating against many states and unfairly favoring others.

Nor does the system allow people with nonpolarized views to have decent representation in Congress. If you do not like voting for Democrats or Republicans, in practice, you really have nobody else to vote for. There is no credible third party, as the system is built to support this duopoly.

The US primary system is the birthplace of many quandaries. In essence, if you want to run for office, there is a prequalification race within your own party called the "primary." If you get the highest number of votes in this prequalification race, you become an official candidate. Once you become an official candidate, in many states you will be pretty much guaranteed to win, because people always vote the same way (Democrat or Republican) in those areas.

The trick is to get enough votes to win the primary, and it's not that difficult if you galvanize a determined group of supporters. On average, the turnout in primaries is around 10% for Republicans and 20% for Democrats. So let's go through the math for electing a very visible, divisive, outspoken person who wants to represent a two-million-person state (a quarter of US states have a population of two million or fewer). Out of two million people, approximately 76% are eligible voters (above 18 years of age, etc.). Of this number, around half will be supporters of your party only (Democrats or Republicans), and you need to care only about that half. Out of this partisan group, only 10% will show up at the primaries, and you need to secure the top (or second-best) result, so often that means you need to get as little as 25% of the vote. Alas, two million multiplied by 0.76 (the eligibility ratio), multiplied by 50% (the Democratic versus Republican split), multiplied by 10% (the primary turnout), multiplied by 25% (the share of votes) gives 19,000 voters. Yes, you need only 19,000 votes to get elected and represent a two-million-person state! Only 1% of the state's population! This is because the population of most states always votes the same way (Republican or Democrat) in general elections. So if you win your primary and get on the ballot for the general election, your ticket to Congress is guaranteed.

So, how to get those 19,000 votes? Well, you have to be visible, controversial, outspoken, and radical. If you have extremist views, some people will hate you for it, but you will become very appealing to others. Even if twice as many people hate what you say as love what you say, you might still get elected, because it is all about getting this tiny, determined group of voters to show up on primary day. (Others don't matter—they are from the opposing party or do not vote in the primaries because they have real life to deal with.) These disciplined voters typically have fewer responsibilities—they may not have to pick up a kid from school, go to work, or take care of aging parents. Therefore, primary voters represent a more radical demographic—extremely progressive or conservative, woke or far-right, susceptible to manipulation, insulated from facts and blindly following their leaders.

That is why the US has been electing more and more radical, non-middle-of-the-road leaders to its Congress and as president.

If US citizens want to change these outcomes, they will have to change the Constitution. Only such a level of change will allow equal representation of voters, a president elected by popular vote, and representation by more parties in the House of Representatives and Senate. The US Constitution is not a divine document; it is not a bible. It can be changed, and it has been done already 27 times before! We can do it again.

An equally important element of reforming the political system is changing how campaigns are funded. The system—which allows big corporate donations—creates instant, high-level political corruption because of the implicit game of favors: I give you money for your campaign, you make sure to take care of me in legislation regarding topic X later. The current campaign-funding system is also extremely costly. It is estimated that in the 2022 midterm elections (the less important ones, where we don't choose the president) the cost was still about $9.3 billion.[14]

What if we limited the amount of donations candidates can receive (just as in most European countries) and saved two-thirds of that amount? We could build a lot of homes for low-income families with $6 billion, or save 120,000 lives by funding their coronary artery bypass procedures, or even build a new airport! And we can do this every other year (as the US has rolling elections every two years)!

Finally, enacting campaign-funding reform would limit the financial power of political parties. This would leave fewer opportunities for manipulation—less money for political advertising, less expensive PR, and so on. Of course, such a reform will not come from the politicians—they will oppose it. It has to come from a grassroots movement, the demands of all citizens to reduce the privileges of the ruling political class and their access to easy money. Again, this is not an impossible task. Most European and many Asian countries have such legislation, which makes their political systems less corrupt and wasteful.

Fixing the stupidity of the US political system would also entail getting rid of the filibuster rule, which requires 60% of the vote, rather than 50% plus one vote, to approve any legislation through the Senate. With the US's polarized, partisan politics, achieving 60% is extremely difficult for anything. This prevents getting things done.

Gerrymandering, which we discussed in the "Political Stupidity" chapter, is a ridiculous remnant of an old era that should be eliminated too.

I know these are all extremely difficult things to do. But remember, we are on an unconstrained intellectual journey exploring what we would do if we had unlimited power to eradicate stupidity!

Remove Gender Imbalance

If you were the almighty ruler of a country with high gender imbalance, you would need to sort out the problem of aborting female fetuses. As you will remember, every 0.1% increase in gender imbalance increases the odds of men committing violence with a weapon, from 1.0 to 1.59. It is a difficult task, but the combination of effectively measuring gender-specific abortions, increasing women's profile in society, and discouraging the social cost of being a woman should ultimately prevail. This will take many years to overcome and should involve sweeping social campaigns, such as a celebrity-sponsored movement against the antiquated institution of dowries.

Reform Healthcare

Structurally, we are incredibly stupid in our approach to healthcare. Today, in almost all countries, the system is designed around "sick care"—caring for people who already have symptoms, when the sickness is in full swing. As a benevolent dictator, you should create a *health*care system that prevents diseases before they develop. Why? Because it is more effective medically and financially.

Here is a typical situation: A 68-year-old man reports to a doctor with abdominal pains.[15] Colorectal cancer is diagnosed; the discovery is made too late, and the cancer is in an advanced stage (3 or 4). The patient had never done any preventive screening. Within five years, the patient dies, as 35% of people diagnosed with colorectal cancer do. The total cost of a failed treatment adds up to $60,000. In the US alone, 52,000 people die just this way each year from this disease. And 40% of them have never done any preventive screening.[16] Adding in all other similar conditions, including other cancers and cardiovascular diseases, it is estimated that 48% of deaths in the US are largely preventable.

Here's what a typical situation would be in a country under your enlightened dictatorship:

A typical man reports for a free preventive procedure called a colonoscopy at age 50. A few small polyps are discovered and are immediately removed as part of the procedure. Cancer is prevented for 10 years, after which there is another colonoscopy, which removes further polyps. This same person lives a relatively healthy life until age 82. The cost of the three colonoscopies adds up to $5,000.

The difference between healthcare and sick care in this example is life and death, and an extra $55,000 in the bank.

A few specific ideas on how to reorient the healthcare system more toward prevention rather than merely reaction:

- **Make information about preventive procedures more easily available and easy to understand.** Use free, government-sponsored apps that provide individualized preventive plans based on factors such as age, gender, ethnicity, height and weight, diet, medical history, DNA, and exercise. These apps need to be beautiful, easy to navigate, and connected to medical records *and* biometric wearables. This is no science fiction. These apps already exist—I built one like that in my previous career and know it is perfectly doable, and the results are very encouraging.

- **Make all preventive procedures ... free.** While Obamacare in the US mandated a number of free preventive procedures, most people do not know those procedures are available at no cost. Also, Americans are intrinsically afraid of going to the doctor because this opens a floodgate of bills: doctor bill, hospital bill, facilities bill, administrative fees, and on and on. We need to eliminate this fear by clearly saying that preventive procedures are *always free*.
- **Make booking appointments easy.** A large number of people are aware of what they need to do, yet they are never able to go through the pain of setting up the actual screening. This is because they need to do more research about the procedure: availability, which provider does it when and where, what the co-pay is, and so on. Making this process simple and easy to navigate via a government-sponsored app will increase compliance with preventive testing.
- **Use a stick.** Very often in life, a "carrot" is not enough to entice someone to do something—even a good thing. Perhaps we should think of the "stick," as well, and introduce (*alongside* financial incentives) an actual penalty for not doing preventive procedures. For example, if you avoid a scheduled preventive screening of your lungs, you should pay a penalty of $500 per year. In several countries, such a penalty system exists already for not showing up to vote (e.g., in Australia). Why not extend it to preventive healthcare?

Healthcare reform must take advantage of serious financial analysis. In particular, the concept of return on investment should be popularized. In healthcare, as in business, in order to reap the benefits over a long period of time, it is often necessary to invest up front. A high up-front investment often results in an ultimate reduction in total cost.

So if you were the enlightened benevolent dictator, interested in structurally solving healthcare stupidity, you would probably pay attention to the data shown in Figure 50.

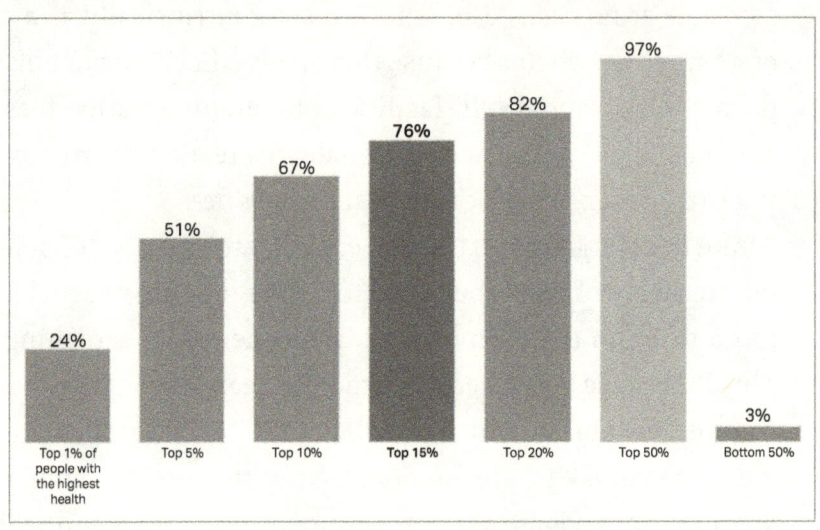

FIGURE 50. Contribution to health expenditures by individuals in 2015[17]

Basically, this means that 5% of the population generates more than 50% of the total cost of healthcare in the US. This is the super-Pareto rule: a very small share of the sickest members of society creates disproportionate costs.

What if we could target these 5% in a personalized, high-touch manner, with a combination of preventive medicine and aggressive treatment so we can address the issues before they become big and costly? What if we could reduce these costs by one-third?

This is entirely possible. Here is how it can be done.

Medical "war rooms"

The top 1% of healthcare spenders (who generate 24% of costs) become covered by a personalized health monitoring body, which sets up medical "war rooms" with constant monitoring of these high-risk citizens. These are literally command centers, with a multitude of screens and real-time flowing data, that measure and alert staff about the health conditions of the most vulnerable people. It is staffed 24/7 by a mixed, skilled group of administrators, dispatchers, nurses, and doctors who decide immediately what to do. Imagine the following scenarios:

- John (age 65) just received a very bad lipid test result. His results are automatically sent to the central health command center via a lab company. John's name, age, location, and telephone number pop up on one of the screens with a prioritization number. A doctor from the command center calls John that same day to investigate possible reasons for this abrupt change. Given that John has low IT literacy, the doctor mails him an engaging paper-based pamphlet that explains natural methods for reducing LDL cholesterol, with practical examples. John picks up a few new habits and reduces his "bad" cholesterol level within three months.
- Rebecca (age 45) didn't pick up her prescription insulin from the drugstore. Her records point to the fact that she is a diabetic and takes insulin regularly. This data flows directly from the pharmacy's IT system, which notes that her previous supply seems to be exhausted (as calculated by an AI algorithm). In response, an administrative associate calls Rebecca to find out why she didn't pick up her prescription. If it is a money problem, the insulin might be delivered free of charge or on credit. If it is a logistical issue, the administrative staff might authorize the pharmacy to send the drug by Uber to Rebecca's home. It would be much cheaper than treating her a few days later in the intensive care unit.

- Maria (age 70) tests her blood pressure at home with an intelligent blood pressure monitor, which sends the data automatically to the medical war room. Her most recent reading of 60/180 — much higher than her last three readings — is extremely worrying. Something out of the ordinary must have happened recently. Immediately, she receives a call from the dispatcher at the command center, but Maria does not pick up. The command center dispatches a doctor to her house, as the system evaluates the probability of a heart attack at 20% within 48 hours. The doctor arrives just in time. Maria has just had a tremendous shock, having learned that her daughter had lost her job, and suffered a heart attack. This immediate intervention saves her life, and Maria continues on to support her daughter through her own difficult time.

These might seem like scenarios from sci-fi movies. Well, they are not. Actually, those scenarios and protocols are already in existence at several sophisticated Medicare Advantage systems in the US, such as Alignment Healthcare.

I had a chance to visit one such center, talk through their protocols, and encounter stories similar to those described above. We only need to scale this solution to cover the most vulnerable parts of society, make procedures more standardized and cost-effective — and secure funding. A lot of work also needs to be done on integrating the healthcare IT needed to make the data flow more seamless. But with enough determination and some heavy-handed regulation, a solution can be in place within five years.

Targeted prevention

Okay, once we've covered the top 1% of healthcare spenders, it's time to look into the next 4%, who generate another 27% of costs.

These citizens should be covered by a range of targeted preventive programs such as selective food delivery, diabetes reversal, and weight loss.

Selective food delivery

Many patients end up with terrible health conditions because they eat unhealthy foods. Often this is caused by financial distress—poor people tend to maximize their calorie intake with cheap fast-food sources such as pizza or hamburgers, rather than purchasing quality food. Weekly delivery of free healthy ingredients such as broccoli, brussels sprouts, asparagus, berries, nuts, beans, lentils, peas, and fish could help augment their diets. This, in turn, would have a major impact on their health.

Again, this is not sci-fi. Such a program was piloted by Geisinger, a well-respected integrated healthcare provider in Pennsylvania, who in the late 2010s delivered more than 175,000 meals using this model, at a yearly cost of only $2,400 per patient. Over 18 months, this resulted in a more than 40% decrease in the risk of death or serious complications. Probably the single most important metric for this project was hemoglobin A1c (HbA1c), which dropped by 2.1 on average for the covered population, compared to the typical 0.5–1.2 decrease achieved through administration of costly drugs!

Sending food to our most vulnerable people is also a wise financial decision. Healthcare costs for Geisinger's test group declined by 80% because there were much fewer cases of urgent interventions, ambulance dispatches, unscheduled operations, and multiple hospital visits, which generate high system costs.

Food is medicine. We simply need to scale all of this up.

Diabetes reversal programs

The direct cost of diabetes was over $306 billion in 2022 in the US.[18] It is estimated that one-third of Americans will develop diabetes sometime in their lifetime. As an enlightened dictator, you could make diabetes reversal programs mandatory for every person with type 2 diabetes, as science has shown that this type can be reduced—or even fully reversed—by diet and exercise alone.

Several innovative firms, such as Virta Health, have proved that such programs work. Through providing timely advice, well-organized oversight, equipment, and mental support, Virta takes its patients on a journey to improve their eating patterns and physical activity. Within one year of starting the program, 63% of participants eliminated the need for diabetes medication altogether. They also lost on average 30 pounds and their HbA1c levels declined by 1.2—results equivalent to what could be achieved through the permanent intake of medicines!

Subsidized weight loss

Obesity (defined as a body mass index (BMI) above 30), typically reduces life expectancy by 5–20 years and causes heart attacks, strokes, diabetes, and musculoskeletal disorders. The cost of obesity in the US alone is a staggering $170 billion per year.[19] A new class of drugs called GLP-1 has become available recently and in most cases is capable of reducing body mass by 20% within just a few months. If confirmed safe, such drugs could be manufactured at mass scale and prescribed at subsidized rates to those who cannot lose weight in the traditional ways.

A certain proportion of the population needs assistance in dealing with obesity through so-called bariatric surgery. This typically involves sewing shut a part of the stomach, which reduces the perception of hunger and slows down absorption of nutrients. Patients who have this surgery lose a substantial amount of weight (often 30%–50%[20]), which results in a dramatic improvement in health. The mortality rate within 30 days of the surgery is very low (around 0.08%)—yet BMI decreases on average by 12–17.[21] In the US, only about 0.4% of the eligible population undergoes bariatric surgery.[22] In our ideal, nonmoronic country, you could make this procedure freely available and strongly encouraged for a greater proportion of society.

Preventive health app

Finally, for the remaining 95% of society, a government-sponsored preventive health app could be made available, one that should be linked to medical records. Regular preventive screenings should be encouraged or even required, with moderate financial penalties for noncompliance. This would create a habit of taking care of one's health and unearth problems early, allowing them to be addressed before they become full-blown diseases. The savings generated by these steps would reduce the overall cost of healthcare while fully funding all the other initiatives we've discussed and provisioning of "seven-day healthcare."

Encourage Competition

Many of the contemporary world's problems result from limited competition. Capitalism as a system has a strong tendency to self-destruct through monopolization. A monopoly is the most comfortable economic position for business owners, generating the highest profits, but is bad for everyone except the monopolists.

A cousin of a monopoly that's almost as bad is an oligopoly (a market shared by a small number of producers). I observed one at work firsthand when we launched a third mobile operator in Latvia (which had a population of two million at the time), and prices declined by 50%! That's the power of competition!

Therefore, if you were a benevolent dictator, it would be worthwhile to consider aggressive antitrust laws to promote competition. Study after study has shown that countries with multiple strong players in any given sector experience more innovation and lower prices. Poland had a fiercely competitive banking system (before the Law and Justice Party (PiS) gained control of the government and damaged it), with several larger and many smaller banking groups fighting ferociously for clients by offering better and better products: world-class online banking, free bank transfers, money arriving in your bank account within hours or minutes of the moment you sent it. Meanwhile, the British retail banking system is dominated by half a dozen banking groups, which operate antiquated systems with terrible customer service—where it costs £25 to send a single wire, and signatures for larger transfer requests must be submitted by ... paper mail.

Installing and enforcing aggressive antitrust rules would benefit society as a whole. This includes introducing serious regulations to curb the power of Big Tech.

Enact Gun Laws

Structurally, we can reduce the amount of stupidity caused by avoidable gun violence in the US. As you might remember, Americans own 46% of all the world's guns, while constituting only 4% of the world's population. Gun violence in the US is 40 times higher per person than in the UK.

Many people believe that America is such an exception—due to its history, geography, and demographics—that nothing can be done about guns. Really? Look around and do the benchmarking work. How about we look at Australia—also a continent of its own, also populated by an immigrant population that prides itself on its self-determination, with even more dangerous wildlife than in the US—which until quite recently had relatively lax gun laws?

After a massive school shooting in 1996, in which 35 people died, Australians decided that something needed to be done.[23] They enacted a comprehensive piece of legislation that made obtaining new guns much harder. Semiautomatic weapons and pump-action shotguns were banned. In addition, the government started to buy out existing stocks of guns from its citizens, who turned them in voluntarily for cash. As a result, gun ownership declined—and gun violence plummeted. See Figure 51.

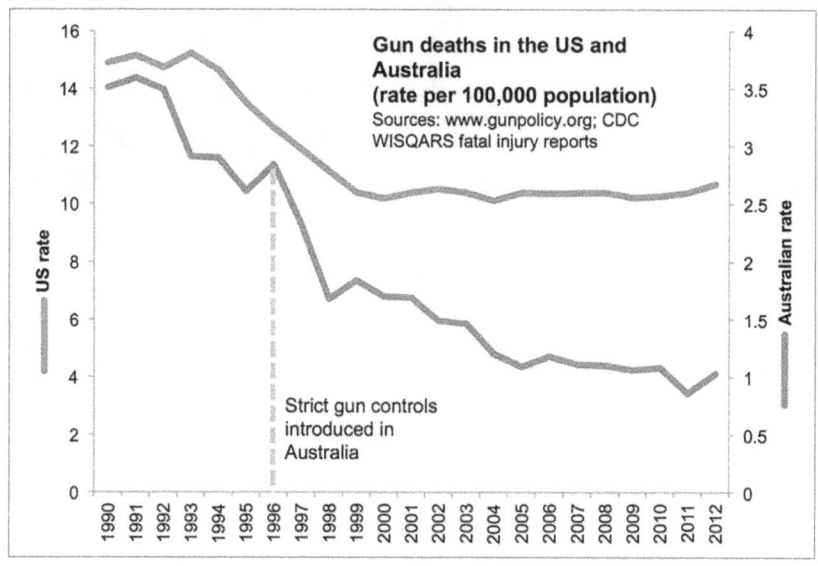

FIGURE 51. Firearm-related deaths in Australia[24]

Gun violence can be reduced dramatically, just by deploying three measures: (a) stricter background checks, (b) a ban on semiautomatic weapons, and (c) voluntary purchases of guns by the state.

Australia's example from the 1990s proves that point decidedly.

Why Care About These Structural Changes at All?

Why bother making all these structural changes? Well, if we did, we would not only live happier, longer, fuller lives, but we would also have more time and more resources at hand. In the US, it might be possible to fully fund college educations or dramatically lower the costs of healthcare for everyone. And we could go to Mars sooner!

Imagine all the savings that would result from reducing the amount of stupidity—less money spent on bureaucracy and administration, lower cost of policing, less money lost through crime, a higher tax base due to higher productivity, less violence. Fighting stupidity will make us much more financially secure.

As an economist, I am salivating at the prospect of putting all this money to good use!

CONCLUDING THOUGHTS

Biology

Our environment has been evolving much faster than our bodies. Our individual "software" (the algorithms for operating our bodies and the skills acquired through learning) and "hardware" (the physical constructs of our bodies) are outdated compared to the joint achievements of modern civilization. Thus, a "stupidity gap" has opened up between the high-tech culture we've created and the bodies and brains we've inherited.

Biology bears a lot of the blame for this gap. We are simply not designed for the modern world. Nature lags behind the rapid progress of civilization because it typically does its work over a period of thousands or millions of years. It takes time for biological change—which occurs chiefly through the brutal yet effective process of natural selection, with cultural coevolution as a supporting driver—to happen in response to a new environment. But this adjustment has been disrupted recently by the explosive growth of technology and rapid advancements in our civilization. The modern era that began about 400 years—a mere 20 generations—ago arrived far too quickly for us to adapt and improve biologically through natural selection.

A phenomenon called prepared learning allows us to identify potentially lethal dangers thanks to associations we've inherited over millions of years of evolution. This is why we react reflexively against snakes, spiders, and predatory animals.

However, we do not typically have such natural defenses against cars or disgruntled coworkers, which are far bigger killers in the contemporary world. Basically, because these dangers are so recent, nature hasn't had enough time to reprogram us.

This biological determinism has also equipped us with ancient mechanisms that we have named "beautifully stupid": sometimes we behave like colonies of ants or bees that will do everything for their hive, prioritizing the greater good without consideration for their own safety. We create art, whose most spectacular examples are often completely irrational and illogical, yet beautiful.

Whatever biology prompts us to do, there are always those few magical seconds between any action and reaction. This magic time between stimulus and reaction opens a whole world of possibilities. It totally depends on us. We can react with uncontrolled fury or aggression, or we can take a deep breath, regroup, and do the right thing. Our software, in this respect, works well if we have the patience to train it (in other words, be patient and thoughtful).

In the decades to come, our biology will change because of technology. We will become a bionic species—we will have non-biological body parts, designed with features such as additional sensors and brain-to-computer interface links. Will they make us better? Probably more efficient; but there is also a risk that it will make us even stupider and more reliant on technology. Already today, we do not do simple calculations in our heads or remember phone numbers; we do not know how to get from A to B without GPS, although we have already covered that route 10 times.

Psychology

Our psychology is built around the principle of conserving our brain's computing power, similar to the overarching concept in physics of returning to the lowest energy state. We have—both consciously and subconsciously—developed a lot of tricks and biases to deal with information overload. Those heuristics make us susceptible to manipulation and blunt our appetite for learning.

As humans, we are not good at acknowledging correct but conflicting facts, such as appreciating that coercion can be good and bad. (A police force might be a force for good or evil, depending on how its response is calibrated.) We always look for simplifications. We have a tendency to search for patterns, even if there aren't any. We cannot appreciate the magnitude of long-term, distributed problems. We consistently miscalculate risk, either by radically understating or radically overstating it.

On a personal front, we waste all our health by working extremely hard in the first few decades of our careers to make a lot of money—and then we spend all that money to get back our health, which we lost while making it.

Sociology

As a society, we have developed a tremendous number of stupid rules that might have been useful some time ago but have since become unnecessary or even perilous. These include conformity, group behavior, and respect for authority. Our modern rules are erratic and random at best. In the US, one can legally buy an AR-15 to kill people at age 18 ... but cannot buy a beer or rent a car.

Our social systems are torn between the two conflicting models of authoritarian rule and democracy. One model is based on an atavistic bias toward following a pecking order, similar to the hierarchical structure of a pack of wolves or a troop of chimpanzees. That's why we are so obsessed about the next royal baby, why we tolerate a caste system in India, why we cherish brute power. The other model gives decision-making power to average members of society rather than privileged elites. However, this can result in mediocrity and stupid decisions made by the undereducated masses. As Winston Churchill famously said, "The best argument against democracy is a five-minute conversation with an average voter." While the democratic model seems to be more advanced and effective in the long term, we are struggling with calibrating it exactly, often falling into populism.

Any organization or idea decays and corrupts over time. However, because of our high respect for the very institution of society, we tend to continue respecting those organizations, despite their decline. In general, we believe that if something is legal, it is also moral. Throughout modern history, many atrocities have been committed by mobs empowered to do so by that same belief. We have entered into large-scale conflicts between societies—wars fought by young boys for old men—and repeat this same pattern of waging pointless wars again and again. History teaches us only that people don't learn from history.

There are bad actors around us (organizations, states, etc.) that intentionally want to keep us stupid. This allows them to control us better or extract higher profits. We are very poor at recognizing long-term effects and are often led by bad leaders who happened to ride the wave of positive circumstances or macroeconomic trends. We too often value authority and good storytelling over authentic competence.

A Dangerous Fight

You should know that it is dangerous to fight stupidity.

Giordano Bruno, an astronomer who supported the Copernican view that Earth orbits the sun, got into serious trouble with the Catholic Church. After claiming the universe is infinite and has no center, he was imprisoned and then sentenced by the Pope to be burned at the stake. He died a martyr—of reason and science—at age 52, fighting stupidity until the very end. He was right and got killed for that.

Whole swaths of society have paid the ultimate price for opposing stupidity. In Cambodia during the Khmer Rouge rule, everyone who had any semblance of intellectuality (even wearing glasses) was summarily executed. Almost two million people were killed between 1975 and 1979 (a quarter of the population!). China had a similar movement during its Cultural Revolution, when most "intellectuals" were resettled to farms and had to work there to undergo "reeducation." In Poland, during World War II, the country lost about 18% of its prewar population (the highest proportion in the world). However, the losses among the most educated groups were far higher: 39% of doctors, 33% of teachers, 26% of lawyers.[25] Both German and Russian occupiers had targeted programs (such as the German Intelligenzaktion mass murders) specifically designed to eliminate the intellectual elites of Polish society. Teachers—who often organized secret, underground courses for students (because German occupiers forbid education)—often paid the highest price for their fight against stupidity.

Two Paths Ahead

We have, therefore, two paths ahead: We can choose complacency, or we can fight back.

Tolerating stupidity will lead to a dystopian society in which the divide between the poor and the rich will grow exponentially. The rich will take advantage of the poor, bureaucracy will eat up our time, dampening our productivity and happiness, and violence will rise as the healthcare system implodes.

Option 1: Accept stupidity as is
Imagine your day like this: You walk out of your home and see that your car window was shattered overnight by a homeless person (quite a typical sight on a San Francisco morning). You start the day angry and waste two hours of your most productive morning time dealing with the police and insurance company, and arranging a repair.

Then you sit in the office and spend an hour preparing some irrelevant report that some federal agency has requested. During your lunch break, you talk to your colleagues about Kim Kardashian's performance as the current president of the United States, and how she has completely mismanaged the economy. Your vote in the last election didn't matter anyway, because the districts were drawn in a ridiculous way (read: gerrymandered). At the end of your lunch break, you finally feel a bit relaxed, and you compliment a female colleague on her new haircut. To your astonishment, she says your comment is inappropriate and vows to complain about you to HR.

Resigned, you stop by Walgreens to pick up some ointment for a small skin lesion and are surprised that it costs $150. You come back home, feeling too tired and stressed to talk to your wife. Then you chat with your eight-year-old daughter, who tells you about the patriotic song she learned today and how supremely better America is than any other country in the world.

Then you force yourself to spend one extra hour on your tax return. This eats into the time you have to visit the gym.

In search of some positivity and social connection, you rush instead to a nearby bar, where you were supposed to join a couple of pals for a quick drink. You realize, at the doors, that you don't have your ID, and the stubborn bouncer will not let you in, despite your obvious age, 52.

You come back home totally angry and, just before you go to sleep, open the overdue results of a health test you hadn't done for three years because you never had time for it. The results are very worrying, a potential cancer. You go to bed in fear and despair, anxious about your health and tomorrow's discussion with HR. Will they fire me? Am I going to die soon?

Option 2: Fight stupidity

Alternatively, imagine a day when we all stand up to stupidity: You walk out of your home in the morning, drive safely to work (because the police work well and any aggressive homeless people are in mandatory rehab or jail, and those needing help are in decent, temporary housing) and you make great progress at work. You prepare a presentation on a new idea that came to your mind that might get you an early promotion. Then you focus on other important matters, not wasting much time on routine reporting, as the new government's requirements are rather slim and mostly done automatically by AI.

During lunchtime, you comment on a new program that promotes bike transport within cities, which has been advocated by the new technocratic, boring president, who gets things done. She was chosen by a small margin of votes, following election reform that allowed the popular vote, and she has proven spectacularly effective, albeit somewhat bland. Toward the end of lunch, you compliment your female colleague, and she thanks you with a big smile.

On your way home, you pick up an ointment for $30, and since you have plenty of spare cash, you decide to buy a bouquet of flowers for your wife. You come back home a hero, making a positive impression on her when she gets back from work, and receive a big hug and a kiss. In a winning mood, you start chatting with your eight-year-old daughter, who is excited to discuss today's class at school about DNA and her ideas about how we might use that knowledge to do new and exciting things.

As you don't spend any extra time on tax calculations (they are simple and done semiautomatically by a federally authorized app), you have time for a gym session. Then you stop in for a quick drink with your pals, and although you don't have your ID, the bouncer lets you in because you clearly look 52 (well, you look 42 because you've been taking such great care of yourself with diet and preventive care). At the bar, you randomly meet a person who gives you a great piece of advice on the project you worked on in the morning. This advice proves the magic final touch you needed for this idea to be brilliant!

Just before going to bed, you squeeze in 30 minutes to read up on epigenetics, the concept that various genes are activated by factors such as life events, food, and stress. You can't wait for round two of the discussion with your daughter tomorrow. Also, you receive a message from your doctor congratulating you on your stellar lab results. You had a cancer scare about two years ago, but because it was detected so early, the problem was solved in no time. You go to bed happy and fulfilled, excited to meet your boss tomorrow and talk to your daughter again.

This is how different a day in our lives could be. In the first scenario, we accept stupidity; in the second, we fight it. It is not a theoretical concept—it touches every moment of our lives.

Stupidity Is a Choice

Indeed, rampant stupidity exists because we allow it. We have numerous examples that prove no tolerance for stupidity will eventually eliminate it. Remember the story of dramatic improvements in commercial aviation's safety record? Remember the stories of the American submarine fleet having zero tolerance for mistakes, and the opposite approach of the Russian submarine fleet?

History shows that we can reinvent ourselves as a society within a short period.

The China of 2010 is unrecognizable from the China of 1990, just two decades earlier. Its economic and technological progress has been unprecedented in human history, lifting millions out of poverty and hunger. Moving from chasing sparrows to creating the second largest economy in the world and leading in several critical technologies is no small feat. A real improvement on fighting stupidity.

The Poland of 1990 and 2020 seem like a different countries as well—much stronger economically, very safe, without petty corruption, and zero tolerance for drinking and driving (despite cultural acceptance of it in the past). Both countries eliminated various levels of stupidity (ideological, economical, societal, technological), which unleashed hidden creativity and dynamism that has elevated the lives of millions in almost every dimension.

We can make similarly beautiful progress in other areas and other geographies. Actually, we will have to do it in the next 10 years to face the upcoming great battle of our generation: climate change. Very likely, we will need to mobilize huge resources to combat this phenomenon. The Intergovernmental Panel on Climate Change (IPCC) estimates that the cost of limiting global warming to 1.5°C will be up to 2.3% of GDP by 2100. That's a lot of money that nobody wants to spend right now. However, we have proved that as a society, we can do grand things—when we feel the pinch.

There is good precedent for it. The US stepped up its military spending from 1% of GDP in 1939 to a staggering 43% of GDP by 1943 to combat the existential risk from Nazi Germany and Imperial Japan.[26] Hopefully, we can mobilize again to fight another existential risk—this time from global warming. This time around, we will probably require 10 times less resources.

It is our choice whether or not we want to live in a world of stupidity. But it is a choice.

Coin shortage? Yes, the United States of America is capable of minting more $0.25 coins. People dying in America for lack of a $5,000 per year insulin supply? Yes, we can afford it. Violence and homelessness ruining San Francisco? Yes, we can solve it, and quickly.

It is scientifically rational to believe that humankind can change. The incredible paradox is that humans have a natural resistance to change while, in fact, being one of the most adaptable species that ever existed! This is a normal, expected state of things, per the laws of physics: Systems naturally tend toward a state of minimum energy. But we totally can change, if we can just overcome our laziness.

Final Recommendations

Dear reader, thank you so much for taking this epic journey with me through human stupidity. I would like to leave you with some final thoughts:

- You can be highly intelligent, even brilliant, but you can, at the same time, be simply stupid! Remember Napoleon in Russia? Objectively the greatest commander of all time, famous for his memory and intellect, a great logistical mind—overwhelmed by basic logistics. Stupidity is a state of mind. It happens when we are overly self-confident or lazy, when we do not listen to feedback. It requires constant vigilance and self-evaluation to prevent stupidity. Stupidity can happen even to geniuses.
- Fight bureaucracy, read from different sources, think critically, question the status quo, be interdisciplinary, travel to different countries. Learn forever.
- Remember how little things make a big difference—30 minutes of reading a day, small gestures of goodwill or unexpected kindness, small change in your daily routine can make waves long term.
- Follow the Voltairean principle: "I disapprove of what you say, but I will defend to the death your right to say it."
- Be ready for a long fight—it can sometimes take years to prevail in even the simplest fights with stupidity.
- We come to this world to die. We have full awareness of this fact from the get-go—but we keep going, anyway. Isn't it stupid? Yes, it is, but it is also courageous, romantic, and magical. Stupidity can carry beautiful colors as well....

The funny thing is, you have just read a book written by someone with limited authority: a person who is divorced; who, as an economist, made a terrible bet on a Swiss franc-denominated mortgage (which blew up); and who turned down a job that would have produced tens of millions.

In other words, you've just read a book on idiocy written by a person who confirms he is an idiot himself. Isn't it ironic?

Welcome to the world of *Homo idioticus*!

ACKNOWLEDGMENTS

This book would never have been published if not for the encouragement of a few people who gave me a positive nudge at the right time. Mercedes Blanco, thank you for making me believe this book was good enough to share with the world, and for your amazing support during the publishing process. Olga Serhiyevich and Zain Latif, your opinions and specific comments on the manuscript were invaluable. Olga, the debate on guns you organized sparked my interest in the topic and encouraged me to do all the research! Violet Abtahi, thank you for your critical encouragement early in the process. Thank you, Tony Llaya, for reviewing the chapter on the Argentinian economy; Nachi Gupta, for sharing terrific insights on gene editing; Barbara Jop, for inspiration for the right materials on psychology; John Mills, for teaching me about wildfires; Ash Shrivastav, for explaining the history of Nepal; Joe Liemandt and MacKenzie Price, for inspirational discussions about education; and Akiko Tamano, for an incredible line editing job. Krystyna and Beata Pietrasik, thank you for your polite nudging about the publishing date!

NOTES

INTRODUCTION

1. Paul Reber, "What Is the Memory Capacity of the Human Brain?," *Scientific American*, May 1, 2010, https://www.scientificamerican.com/article/what-is-the-memory-capacity/.
2. Lawrence Hamilton, "Conspiracy vs. Science: A Survey of U.S. Public Beliefs," University of New Hampshire Carsey School of Public Policy, April 25, 2022, https://carsey.unh.edu/publication/conspiracy-vs-science-a-survey-of-us-public-beliefs.
3. John Hands, *Cosmosapiens: Human Evolution from the Origin of the Universe* (Abrams Press, 2017), 12.
4. Daniel Ellsberg, *The Doomsday Machine: Confessions of a Nuclear War Planner* (Bloomsbury USA, 2017), 222–237.

PART I: HOW?

1. "6.7% of World Has College Degree," *The Huffington Post*, May 19, 2010, https://www.huffpost.com/entry/percent-of-world-with-col_n_581807.
2. Einar H. Dyvik, "Education Worldwide—Statistics & Facts," Statista, July 3, 2024, https://www.statista.com/topics/7785/education-worldwide/.
3. "Literacy," Our World in Data, last updated March 2024, https://ourworldindata.org/literacy.
4. Niall Ferguson, *The Ascent of Money: A Financial History of the World* (Penguin Books, 2008), 13.
5. Réka Vágvölgyi, Andra Coldea, Thomas Dresler, Josef Schrader, and Hans-Christoph Nuerk, "A Review About Functional Illiteracy: Definition, Cognitive, Linguistic, and Numerical Aspects,"

Frontiers in Psychology 7 (November 2016), https://doi.org/10.3389/fpsyg.2016.01617.

6. Wikipedia, "Functional Illiteracy," last updated January 10, 2025, https://en.wikipedia.org/wiki/Functional_illiteracy.
7. Wikipedia, "Functional Illiteracy," last updated January 10, 2025, https://en.wikipedia.org/wiki/Functional_illiteracy.
8. Barbara Wegenschimmel, Ulrike Leiss, Michaela Veigl, Verena Rosenmayr, Anton Formann, Irene Slavc, and Thomas Pletschko, "Do We Still Need IQ-Scores? Misleading Interpretations of Neurocognitive Outcome in Pediatric Patients with Medulloblastoma: A Retrospective Study," *Journal of Neuro-Oncology* 135, no. 2 (2017): 361–369, https://doi.org/10.1007/s11060-017-2582-x.
9. Peter Dockrill, "IQ Scores Are Falling in 'Worrying' Reversal of 20th Century Intelligence Boom," *ScienceAlert*, June 13, 2018, https://www.sciencealert.com/iq-scores-falling-in-worrying-reversal-20th-century-intelligence-boom-flynn-effect-intelligence.
10. Richard Gray, "British Teenagers Have Lower IQs Than Their Counterparts Did 30 Years Ago," *The Telegraph*, February 7, 2009, https://www.telegraph.co.uk/education/educationnews/4548943/British-teenagers-have-lower-IQs-than-their-counterparts-did-30-years-ago.html.
11. Glenn Wilson, "Infomania" study of Porter Novelli employees, sponsored by Hewlett-Packard, 2005, http://drglennwilson.com/Infomania_experiment_for_HP.doc.
12. Source: Graphic from Matthew Kendrick, "34% of Americans Can Find Ukraine on a Map. They're More Likely to Support an Aggressive Posture Against Russia," Morning Consult, February 9, 2022.
13. Zoe Strozewski, "10 Percent of Americans Don't Believe in Climate Change, 15 Percent Unsure: Poll," *Newsweek*, October 26, 2021, https://www.newsweek.com/10-percent-americans-dont-believe-climate-change-15-percent-unsure-poll-1642747.
14. Mayumi Okuda, Julia Picazo, Mark Olfson, Deborah S. Hasin, Shang-Min Liu, Silvia Bernardi, and Carlos Blanco, "Prevalence and Correlates of Anger in the Community: Results from a

National Survey," *CNS Spectrums* 20, no. 2 (2015): 130–39, https://doi.org/10.1017/s1092852914000182.

15. *Violence Against Women Prevalence Estimates, 2018*, World Health Organization, March 9, 2021.
16. United Nations, *Global Study on Homicide: Gender-Related Killing of Women and Girls*, (United Nations Office on Drugs and Crime, 2018), 10, https://www.unodc.org/documents/data-and-analysis/GSH2018/GSH18_Gender-related_killing_of_women_and_girls.pdf.
17. "El Salvador: Health Data Overview for the Republic of El Salvador," World Health Organization, accessed January 30, 2025, https://data.who.int/countries/222; "Number of Homicides in El Salvador in 2018, by Department," Statista, accessed January 30, 2025, https://www.statista.com/statistics/696155/el-salvador-number-homicides/.
18. Rachel Kleinfeld, "Why Are Some Societies So Violent, and Can They Be Made Safe?," November 19, 2018, Carnegie Endowment for International Peace, https://carnegieendowment.org/2018/11/19/why-are-some-societies-so-violent-and-can-they-be-madesafe-pub-77749.
19. Jennie B. Gamlin and Sarah J. Hawkes, "Masculinities on the Continuum of Structural Violence: The Case of Mexico's Homicide Epidemic," *Social Politics: International Studies in Gender, State & Society* 25, no. 1 (2017): 50–71, https://doi.org/10.1093/sp/jxx010.
20. "A 'Responsible' Start," *Newsweek*, updated March 13, 2010, https://www.newsweek.com/responsible-start-135197.
21. Wikipedia, "Sodomy Laws in the United States," last updated January 29, 2025, https://en.wikipedia.org/wiki/Sodomy_laws_in_the_United_States.
22. Dana Liebelson, "Why Do So Many States Still Have Anti-Sodomy Laws?," *The Week*, updated January 8, 2015, https://theweek.com/articles/465821/why-many-states-still-have-antisodomy-laws.
23. *The Economist*, Politics This Week, August 12, 2021.
24. Source: "Gun Ownership by Country 2024," World Population Review.
25. Source: "Gun Ownership by Country 2024," World Population Review.

26. Ian Bremmer (@ianbremmer), tweet dated July 8, 2022, 5:57 a.m., Twitter (now X).
27. "School Shootings by Country 2024," World Population Review, accessed February 26, 2022, https://worldpopulationreview.com/country-rankings/school-shootings-by-country.
28. "17 Facts About Gun Violence and School Shootings," Sandy Hook Promise, accessed January 30, 2025, https://www.sandyhookpromise.org/blog/gun-violence/16-facts-about-gun-violence-and-school-shootings/.
29. Source: "Gun Ownership by Country 2024," World Population Review.
30. Katelyn Brown, "Tax Code Is So Long That Nobody's Really Sure of Its Length," Politifact, October 17, 2017, https://www.politifact.com/factchecks/2017/oct/17/roy-blunt/tax-code-so-long-nobodys-really-sure-its-length/.
31. Jonathan Haidt, *The Righteous Mind: Why Good People Are Divided by Politics and Religion* (Pantheon Books, 2012), 14.
32. Jonathan Haidt, *The Righteous Mind: Why Good People Are Divided by Politics and Religion* (Pantheon Books, 2012), 21.
33. Source: Rob Oechsle Collection
34. Wikipedia, "Foot Binding," last update January 20, 2025, https://en.wikipedia.org/wiki/Foot_binding.
35. "Female Genital Mutilation (FGM): Over 230 Million Girls and Women Worldwide Have Undergone Female Genital Mutilation," UNICEF Data, accessed January 22, 2022, https://data.unicef.org/topic/child-protection/female-genital-mutilation/.
36. Michael Shellenberger, *San Fransicko: Why Progressives Ruin Cities* (Harper, 2021), 63.
37. Michael Shellenberger, *San Fransicko: Why Progressives Ruin Cities* (Harper, 2021), 35.
38. Sharon Bernstein, "Explainer: Marijuana Pardons in U.S. Help Thousands, Leave Others in Prison," *Reuters*, October 8, 2022, https://www.reuters.com/world/us/us-marijuana-pardons-help-thousands-leave-others-prison-2022-10-09/.

39. "The Right Way to Do Drugs," *The Economist*, February 13, 2016, https://www.economist.com/leaders/2016/02/13/the-right-way-to-do-drugs.
40. Joe Knight, "Napoleon Wasn't Defeated by the Russians," *Slate*, December 11, 2012, https://slate.com/technology/2012/12/napoleon-march-to-russia-in-1812-typhus-spread-by-lice-was-more-powerful-than-tchaikovskys-cannonfire.html.
41. Paul Scharre, *Army of None: Autonomous Weapons and the Future of War* (W. W. Norton, 2018), 156.
42. Source: Photo by Rick Wilking.
43. Source: Photo by Reuters / Alberto Lowe / Bridgeman Images.
44. Eugeniusz Tarle, *Napoleon* (Malopolska Oficyna Wydawnicza, 1991), 156.
45. Richard Hargreaves, *The Germans in Normandy* (Pen & Sword Books, 2006), 280.
46. Josh Hoxie, "Trump's Tax Cuts Are the Biggest Wealth Grab in Modern History," *Fortune*, November 3, 2017, https://fortune.com/2017/11/03/trump-gop-tax-plan-cuts-2017/.
47. Source: Maps (*top left and top right*) from Census.org; photo of duckling (*bottom left*) by Frankhuang / Getty Images; photo of earmuffs (*bottom right*) AI-generated.
48. Wikipedia, "Gerrymandering," last update January 21, 2025, https://en.wikipedia.org/wiki/Gerrymandering.
49. Nachi Gupta, CIO of Kriya Therapeutics, in discussion with author, March 2022.
50. Source: Photos by Cezary Pietrasik and Mercedes Blanco.
51. Safi Bahcall, *Loonshots: How to Nurture the Crazy Ideas That Win Wars, Cure Diseases, and Transform Industries* (St. Martin's, 2019), 20.
52. Source: Photo by Fairfax Media / Getty Images.
53. Jane Ridley, "One in 10 People Checks Their Phone During Sex: Survey," *New York Post*, June 7, 2018, https://nypost.com/2018/06/07/one-in-10-people-checks-their-phone-during-sex-survey/.

54. Source: Graph from Lyman Stone, "More Faith, Less Sex: Why Are So Many Unmarried Young Adults Not Having Sex?," *Institute for Family Studies* (blog), November 11, 2021.
55. "Most Popular Websites in the World—1996/2021 + Top Websites in the US by Traffic," Statistics & Data, accessed January 22, 2022, https://statisticsanddata.org/data/most-popular-websites-in-the-world-1996-2021/.
56. Source: Will MacAskill, "What We Owe the Future," virtual lecture, April 2020, posted June 5, 2020, by Global Priorities Institute, YouTube, at 17 min, 53 sec.
57. Source: Will MacAskill, "What We Owe the Future," virtual lecture, April 2020, posted June 5, 2020, by Global Priorities Institute, YouTube, at 18 min, 14 sec.
58. Source: Toby Ord, *The Precipice* (Grand Central Publishing, 202).
59. Jennifer McDermott, "Nearly $100 Billion Stolen in Pandemic Relief Funds, Secret Service Says," PBS News, December 22, 2021, https://www.pbs.org/newshour/nation/nearly-100-billion-stolen-in-pandemic-relief-funds-secret-service-says.
60. Jutta Bolt and Jan Luiten van Zanden, "Maddison Style Estimates of the Evolution of the World Economy. A New 2020 Update," Maddison Project Database 2020, University of Groningen, https://www.rug.nl/ggdc/historicaldevelopment/maddison/releases/maddison-project-database-2020.
61. Robert Plummer, "Argentina Records Sharp Rise in Poverty," *BBC News*, September 27, 2024, https://www.bbc.com/news/articles/ceqn751x19no.
62. "How to Deal with Venezuela," *The Economist*, July 29, 2017.
63. Nick Miroff, "Venezuela Nears End of the Road for Gasoline Subsidy," *The Guardian*, January 27, 2014, https://www.theguardian.com/world/2014/jan/27/venezuela-petrol-subsidies-cheap-gas.
64. Wikipedia, "Hugo Chávez," accessed January 16, 2025, https://en.wikipedia.org/wiki/Hugo_Chávez.
65. "How to Deal with Venezuela," *The Economist*, July 29, 2017.

66. *Singapore Food Statistics 2021* (Singapore Food Agency, 2021), 3, https://www.sfa.gov.sg/docs/default-source/publication/sg-food-statistics/singapore-food-statistics-2021.pdf.
67. "Food Security," UK Parliament Commons Chamber, March 21, 2024, https://www.parallelparliament.co.uk/debate/2024-03-21/commons/commons-chamber/food-security.
68. "Japan Sets New Record Low for Food Self-Sufficiency on a Production Value Basis," *Japan.com*, August 22, 2023, https://www.nippon.com/en/japan-data/h01758/.
69. Capt. Benton at Washington arsenal for—warded a report of Master Armorer J. Dudley re the condition of small arms received from the battle fields, National Archives, record group 156, entry 201, vol. 40, letter W28, January 4, 1864.
70. Paul Scharre, *Army of None: Autonomous Weapons and the Future of War* (W. W. Norton, 2018), 241.
71. "The Story of the 'Mad' Highland Piper of World War II," *The Scotsman*, March 16, 2016, https://www.scotsman.com/whats-on/arts-and-entertainment/story-mad-highland-piper-world-war-ii-1480752.
72. Haroon Siddique, "Policeman Tells How He Fought London Bridge Attackers with Baton," *The Guardian*, June 28, 2017, https://www.theguardian.com/uk-news/2017/jun/28/policeman-fought-london-bridge-attackers-baton-wayne-marques.
73. Emily Pennink, "Hero Police Officer Stabbed by London Bridge Terrorists Relives His Fight for Life," *Daily Record*, June 28, 2019, https://www.dailyrecord.co.uk/news/uk-world-news/hero-police-officer-stabbed-london-17273406.
74. "Kirsty Boden: Queen's Bravery Award for Australian Nurse Killed In London Bridge Terror Attack," ABC News, July 20, 2018, https://www.abc.net.au/news/2018-07-20/kirsty-boden-bravery-award-for-nurse-london-bridgeattack/10016658.
75. Source: Graph from Esteban Ortiz-Ospina, Max Roser, and Pablo Arriagada, "Trust," Our World in Data, updated April 2024.

76. Source: Graph from Luke Lanskey and Conor O'Loughnan, "300 Years of UK Public Finance Data," Office for Budget Responsibility, July 20, 2023.
77. Niall McCarthy, "Which Countries Constructed the Most Skyscrapers In 2019? [Infographic]," *Forbes*, January 16, 2020, https://www.forbes.com/sites/niallmccarthy/2020/01/16/which-countries-constructed-the-mostskyscrapers-in-2019-infographic/.
78. Source: Martin Shields / Alamy Stock Photo.

PART II: WHY?

1. Ann Gibbons, "Bonobos Join Chimps as Closest Human Relatives", *Science*, June 13, 2012, https://www.science.org/content/article/bonobos-join-chimps-closest-human-relatives.
2. Niall Ferguson, *The Ascent of Money. A Financial History of the World* (Penguin Books, 2008), 19.
3. Source: Graph based on Mark Follman, Gavin Aronsen, and Deanna Pan, "US Mass Shootings, 1982–2004: Data from Mother Jones' Investigation," *Mother Jones*, updated September 4, 2024.
4. United Nations, *World Population Prospects The 2019 Revision—Volume I: Comprehensive Tables* (United Nations, 2019), https://doi.org/10.18356/15994a82-en.
5. Amanda Arnold, "69 Percent of Men Don't Wash Their Hands After Using the Bathroom?!," *The Cut*, March 6, 2020, https://www.thecut.com/2020/03/69-of-men-dont-wash-their-hands-after-using-the-bathroom.html.
6. *Utilization of Ambulatory Medical Care by Women: United States, 1997–98*, Vital and Health Statistics, series 13, no. 149 (U.S. Department of Health and Human Services, 2001), https://www.cdc.gov/nchs/data/series/sr_13/sr13_149.pdf.
7. Jonas M. Fuks, Romanico B. G. Arrighi, Jessica M. Weidner, Suresh Kumar Mendu, Zhe Jin, Robert P. A. Wallin, Bence Rethi, Bryndis Birnir, and Antonio Barragan, "GABAergic Signaling Is Linked to a Hypermigratory Phenotype in Dendritic Cells Infected by *Toxoplasma gondii*," *PLOS Pathogens* 8, no. 12 (2012).

8. George Monbiot, "Yes, Lead Poisoning Could Really Be a Cause of Violent Crime," *The Guardian*, January 7, 2013, https://www.theguardian.com/commentisfree/2013/jan/07/violent-crime-lead-poisoning-british-export.

9. Wikipedia, "Lead Paint," last modified January 11, 2025, https://en.wikipedia.org/wiki/Lead_paint.

10. Source: Graph from Rick Nevin, "How Lead Exposure Relates to Temporal Changes in IQ, Violent Crime, and Unwed Pregnancy," *Environmental Research* 83, no. 1 (2000): 1–22.

11. George Monbiot, "Yes, Lead Poisoning Could Really Be a Cause of Violent Crime," *The Guardian*, January 7, 2013, https://www.theguardian.com/commentisfree/2013/jan/07/violent-crime-lead-poisoning-british-export.

12. Jonathan Haidt, *The Righteous Mind: Why Good People Are Divided by Politics and Religion*, (Pantheon Books, 2012), 299.

13. Yulong Chen, "Air Pollution and Academic Performance: Evidence from China," Iowa State University (November 1, 2018), http://dx.doi.org/10.2139/ssrn.3341008.

14. Avraham Ebenstein, Victor Lavy, Sefi Roth, "The Long-Run Economic Consequences of High-Stakes Examinations: Evidence from Transitory Variation in Pollution," *American Economic Journal: Applied Economics* 8, no. 4 (2016):36–65.

15. David Wallace-Wells, *The Uninhabitable Earth: Life After Warming* (Tim Duggan Books, 2019), 104.

16. Source: Graph from Avraham Ebenstein, Victor Lavy, and Sefi Roth, "The Long-Run Economic Consequences of High-Stakes Examinations: Evidence from Transitory Variation in Pollution," *American Economic Journal: Applied Economics* 8, no. 4 (2016): 36–65.

17. Jianghong Liu, Adrian Raine, Peter H. Venables, Cyril Dalais, and Sarnoff A. Mednick, "Malnutrition at Age 3 Years and Lower Cognitive Ability at Age 11 Years," *Archives of Pediatric and Adolescent Medicine* 157, no. 6 (2003): 593–600.

18. Ohio State University, "Fast-Food Consumption Linked to Lower Test Score Gains in 8th Graders," *ScienceDaily*, December 22, 2014, https://www.sciencedaily.com/releases/2014/12/141222111605.htm.

19. Shai Danzinger, Jonathan Levav, and Liora Avnaim-Pesso, "Extraneous Factors in Judicial Decisions," *Proceedings of the National Academy of Sciences of the United States of America* 108, no. 17 (2011): 6,889–6,892.
20. Gregory Clark, *A Farewell to Alms: A Brief Economic History of the World* (Princeton University Press, draft version), 56.
21. Samara Joy Nielsen, Brian K. Kit, Tala Fakhouri, Cynthia L. Ogden, "Calories Consumed from Alcoholic Beverages by U.S. Adults, 2007–2010," National Center for Health Statistics Data Brief, no. 110 (November 2012).
22. Sendhil Mullainathan and Eldar Shafir, *Scarcity: The True Cost of Not Having Enough* (Penguin-Highbridge, 2014), 15.
23. "Study Ties I.Q. Scores To Stress," *The New York Times*, May 31, 1983, https://www.nytimes.com/1983/05/31/science/study-ties-iq-scores-to-stress.html.
24. Patrick Baylis, "Temperature and Temperament: Evidence from a Billion Tweets," working paper, Energy Institute at Hass, November 2015.
25. Source: Graphs from Matthew Ranson, "Crime, Weather, and Climate Change," *Journal of Environmental Economics and Management* 67, no. 3 (2014): 274–302.
26. Source: Graphs from Solomon M. Hsiang, Marshall Burke, and Edward Miguel, "Quantifying the Influence of Climate on Human Conflict," *Science* 341, no. 6151 (2013).
27. Source: Graph from Marshall Burke, Solomon M. Hsiang, and Edward Miguel, "Global Non-Linear Effect of Temperature on Economic Production," *Nature* 527 (2015): 235–239.
28. Marshall Burke, Solomon M. Hsiang, and Edward Miguel, "Global Non-Liner Effect of Temperature on Economic Production," *Nature* 527 (October 2015): 235–239.
29. Nadia Diamond-Smith and Kara Rudolph, "The Association Between Uneven Sex Ratios and Violence: Evidence from 6 Asian Countries," PLOS One 13, no. 6 (2018), https://doi.org/10.1371/journal.pone.0197516.

30. Simon Denyer and Annie Gowe, "Too Many Men," *The Washington Post*, April 18, 2018, https://www.washingtonpost.com/graphics/2018/world/too-many-men/.
31. *Brittanica*, "Physiology," last updated January 2, 2025, https://www.britannica.com/science/information-theory/Physiology.
32. Annamari Patja, Irja Davidkin, Tapio Kurki, Markku J. T. Kallio, Martti Valle, and Heikki Peltola, "Serious Adverse Events After Measles-Mumps-Rubella Vaccination During a Fourteen-Year Prospective Follow-Up," *The Pediatric Infectious Diseases Journal* 19, no. 12 (2000): 1,127–1,134.
33. Wikipedia, "Measles," last updated December 24, 2024, https://en.wikipedia.org/wiki/Measles.
34. Daniel Kahneman, *Thinking, Fast and Slow* (Farrar, Strauss & Giroux, 2013), 57.
35. "Pop Music Exposes Kids to Positive Portrayals of Drug, Alcohol Use, Pitt Study Finds," *Pitt Chronicle*, February 11, 2008, https://www.chronicle.pitt.edu/story/pop-music-exposes-kids-positive-portrayals-drug-alcohol-use-pitt-study-finds.
36. "Pop Music Exposes Kids to Positive Portrayals of Drug, Alcohol Use, Pitt Study Finds," *Pitt Chronicle*, February 11, 2008, https://www.chronicle.pitt.edu/story/pop-music-exposes-kids-positive-portrayals-drug-alcohol-use-pitt-study-finds.
37. J. S. Jenkins, "The Mozart Effect," *Journal of the Royal Society of Medicine* 94, no. 4 (2001): 170–172, https://doi.org/10.1177/014107680109400404.
38. Jafar Rezaei, Alireza Arab, and Mohammadreza Mehregan, "Equalizing Bias in Eliciting Attribute Weights in Multiattribute Decision-Making: Experimental Research," *Journal of Behavioral Decision Making* 35, no. 2, (2021), https://doi.org/10.1002/bdm.2262.
39. Eliza Relman and Azmi Haroun, "The 26 Women Who Have Accused Trump of Sexual Misconduct," *Business Insider*, May 9, 2023, https://www.businessinsider.com/women-accused-trump-sexual-misconduct-list-2017-12.
40. Amos Tversky and Daniel Kahneman, "The Framing of Decisions and the Psychology of Choice," *Science* 211, no. 4481 (1981): 453–458.

41. Source: Gumroad, "A Penny Saved: Psychological Pricing," Medium, April 22, 2015.
42. The Conversation.com, accessed on February 15, 2025, https://theconversation.com/the-trolley-dilemma-would-you-kill-one-person-to-save-five-57111
43. Tom Hale, "The Trolley Problem Has Been Tested in Real Life, and the Results Are Surprising," IFLScience, May 11, 2018, https://www.iflscience.com/the-trolley-problem-has-been-tested-in-real-life-and-the-results-are-surprising-47646.
44. Source: Trolley problem concept from Judith Jarvis Thomson, "Killing, Letting Die, and the Trolley Problem," *The Monist* 59, no. 2 (1976): 204–217; illustration © by Cezary Pietrasik.
45. Dan Pilat and Sekoul Krastev, "Why Is It So Hard to Change Someone's Beliefs?," The Decision Lab, accessed February 26, 2022, https://thedecisionlab.com/biases/cognitive-dissonance.
46. Frans B. M. de Waal, "Food Sharing and Reciprocal Obligations Among Chimpanzees," *Journal of Human Evolution*, 18, no. 5, (1989): 433–459.
47. Source: Photo by Michele and Tom Grimm / Alamy.
48. Richard Wrangham, *The Goodness Paradox: The Strange Relationship Between Virtue and Violence in Human Evolution* (Pantheon, 2019), 14.
49. Richard Wrangham, *The Goodness Paradox: The Strange Relationship Between Virtue and Violence in Human Evolution* (Pantheon, 2019), 150.
50. "Intentional Homicides (per 100,000 People)—Country Ranking," Index Mundi, updated December 28, 2019, https://www.indexmundi.com/facts/indicators/VC.IHR.PSRC.P5/rankings.
51. Wikipedia, "Estimated Number of Civilian Guns per Capita by Country," accessed February 26, 2022, https://en.wikipedia.org/wiki/Estimated_number_of_civilian_guns_per_capita_by_country.
52. *Brittanica*, "Honor Killing," August 3, 2016, https://www.britannica.com/topic/honor-killing.
53. Robert M. Sapolsky, *Behave: The Biology of Humans at Our Best and Worst* (Penguin Press, 2017), 458.

54. Saul McLeod, "Solomon Asch Conformity Line Experiment Study," Simply Psychology, updated October 24, 2023, https://www.simplypsychology.org/asch-conformity.html.
55. Source: Illustration created by Cezary Pietrasik based on "Solomon Asch Conformity Line Experiment Study," Simply Psychology, updated October 24, 2023.
56. Bartholomew Sawicki, "Uprawnienia do Emisji CO2. Ile Kosztuje nas Polityka Klimatyczna?," *Rzeczpospolita*, February 6, 2022, https://energia.rp.pl/co2/art35648731-uprawnienia-do-emisji-co2-ile-kosztuje-nas-polityka-klimatyczna.
57. "Minister Klimatu: 45 Tys. Polaków Umiera Co Roku z Powodu Złej Jakości Powietrza," *Business Insider*, December 30, 2019, https://businessinsider.com.pl/polityka/zanieczyszczenie-powietrza-w-polsce-ilu-polakow-umiera-zpowodu-smogu/8qr37r4.
58. "Eksperci: W Polsce Koszt Emisji CO2 Trzy Razy Większy Wyższy od Średniej Unijnej," *Dziennik Gazeta Prawna*, September 10, 2022, https://serwisy.gazetaprawna.pl/energetyka/artykuly/8533723,polska-wyzszy-koszt-emisji-co2-niz-w-ue.html.
59. "Górnicy Znajdą Zatrudnienie w Energetyce Odnawialnej," *Infor*, August 6, 2021, https://kadry.infor.pl/wiadomosci/5302493,Gornicy-znajda-zatrudnienie-w-energetyce-odnawialnej.html.
60. Wikipedia, "Port Said Stadium Riot," last updated January 7, 2025, https://en.wikipedia.org/wiki/Port_Said_Stadium_riot.
61. Wikipedia, "2017 Military Police of Espírito Santo Strike," last updated January 27, 2025, https://en.wikipedia.org/wiki/2017_Military_Police_of_Espírito_Santo_strike.
62. Hogg A. M., Adelman J. (2013). Uncertainty–identity theory: extreme groups, radical behavior, and authoritarian leadership. J. Soc. Issues 69, 436–454.
63. Robert Sapolsky, *Behave: The Biology of Humans at Our Best and Worst* (Penguin Press, 2017), 456.
64. "Retired U.S. General Wesley Clark: Wars Were Planned, Seven Countries in Five Years," posted September 28, 2013, by People Over Politics, YouTube, 2 min., 12 sec., https://youtu.be/z8ityboIps4?si=TUC0_mmQ6JlBK_DE.

65. Source: Graphs from Anthony H. Cordesman, "Strategic Competition and Foreign Perceptions of the United States," Center for Strategic & International Studies, June 14, 2021.
66. Paulina Cachero, "US Taxpayers Have Reportedly Paid an Average of $8,000 Each and over $2 Trillion Total for the Iraq War Alone," *Business Insider*, February 6, 2020, https://www.businessinsider.com/us-taxpayers-spent-8000-each-2-trillion-iraq-war-study-2020-2.
67. Jill Kimball, "Costs of the 20-Year War on Terror: $8 Trillion and 900,000 Deaths," Brown University, September 1, 2021, https://www.brown.edu/news/2021-09-01/costsofwar.
68. Source: Graph from "Homicide Rates over the Long Term," Our World in Data.
69. Source: Graph from Max Roser, "Global Deaths in Conflicts Since 1400," Our World in Data.
70. *Enquete Aupres des Temoins ou Recit du Vecu Personnel* (Robert Schuman), Reperes: Partneriats Educatifs Grundtvig 2009–2011, Centre Virtuel de la Connaissance sur L'Europe, 2011.
71. Malcolm Graham, *Oxford in the Great War* (Pen & Sword Military, 2015), 12.
72. Mark Harrison, "Was the Soviet 1923 Male Birth Cohort Doomed by World War II?," *Mark Harrison's Blog*, *Warwick Blogs*, December 13, 2014, https://blogs.warwick.ac.uk/markharrison/entry/was_the_soviet/.
73. Hedrick Smith, *The Russians* (Ballantine Books, 1984), 150.
74. Marian F. MacDorman, Fay Menacker, and Eugene Declercq, "Cesarean Birth in the United States: Epidemiology, Trends, and Outcomes," *Clinics in Perinatology* 35, no. 2 (2008): 293–307, https://doi.org/10.1016/j.clp.2008.03.007.
75. Emily Oster and W. Spencer McClelland, "Why the C-Section Rate Is So High," *The Atlantic*, October 17, 2019, https://www.theatlantic.com/ideas/archive/2019/10/c-section-rate-high/600172/.
76. Christopher Ingraham, "What's a Urinal Fly, and What Does It Have to Do with Winning a Nobel Prize?," *The Washington Post*, October 9, 2017, https://www.washingtonpost.com/news/wonk/wp/2017/10/09/

whats-a-urinal-fly-and-what-does-it-have-to-with-winning-a-nobel-prize/.

77. In case you are not a bureaucrat: An 83(b) is an IRS form that enables you to pay 23.8% on your capital gains rather than 39.3% in the US, and *Miranda v. Arizona* is your right to be informed about your rights before the police can question you. You might not have understood either of those terms. Don't you think unfamiliarity with the jargon could have played a role there?

78. Lukas Schwingshackl, Carolina Schwedhelm, Georg Hoffmann, Anna-Maria Lampousi, Sven Knüppel, Khalid Iqbal, Angela Bechthold, Sabrina Schlesinger, and Heiner Boeing, "Food Groups and Risk of All-Cause Mortality: A Systematic Review and Metaanalysis of Prospective Studies," *The American Journal of Clinical Nutrition* 105, no. 6 (2017): 1,462–1,473.

79. "Time Required to Start a Business (Days)—Country Ranking," Index Mundi, last updated December 28, 2019, https://www.indexmundi.com/facts/indicators/IC.REG.DURS/rankings.

80. David Austin and Tamara Hayford, Research and Development in the Pharmaceutical Industry, Congressional Budget Office, April 8, 2021, https://www.cbo.gov/publication/57126.

81. Daniel Pincus, Bheeshma Ravi, David Wasserstein, Anjie Huang, J. Michael Paterson, Avery B. Nathens, Hans J. Kreder, Richard J. Jenkinson, and Walter P. Wodchis, "Association Between Wait Time and 30-Day Mortality in Adults Undergoing Hip Fracture Surgery," *JAMA* 318, no. 20 (2017): 1,994–2,003.

82. W. L. Palmer, A. Bottle, C. Davie, C. A. Vincent, and P. Aylin, "Dying for the Weekend: A Retrospective Cohort Study on the Association Between Day of Hospital Presentation and the Quality and Safety of Stroke Care," *Archives of Neurology* 69, no. 10 (2012): 1,296–1,302.

83. Lu Han, Rachel Meacock, Laura Anselmi, Søren R Kristensen, Matt Sutton, Tim Doran, Stuart Clough, and Maxine Power, "Variations in Mortality Across the Week Following Emergency Admission to Hospital: Linked Retrospective Observational Analyses of Hospital Episode Data in England, 2004/5 to 2013/14," *Health and Social Care Delivery Research* 5, no. 30 (2017), https://doi.org/10.3310/hsdr05300.

84. Source: Photo of AR-15 (*left*) and photo of pistol (*right*) from Wikipedia Commons.
85. Danny Hooley, "How to Buy an Assault Rifle in North Carolina," *Indy Week*, June 15, 2016, https://indyweek.com/news/buy-assault-rifle-north-carolina/.
86. Wikipedia, "2017 Las Vegas Shooting," last updated January 24, 2025, https://en.wikipedia.org/wiki/2017_Las_Vegas_shooting.
87. Jim Yardley, "Soaring Above India's Poverty, a 27-Story Home," *The New York Times*, October 28, 2010, https://www.nytimes.com/2010/10/29/world/asia/29mumbai.html.
88. Jake Johnson, "Since 1978, CEO Pay Has Risen 1,322%. Typical Worker Pay? Just 18%," *Common Dreams*, January 24, 2025, https://www.commondreams.org/news/2021/08/10/1978-ceo-pay-has-risen-1322-typical-worker-pay-just-18.
89. Lawrence Mishel and Jori Kandra, "CEO Pay Has Skyrocketed 1,322% Since 1978," Economic Policy Institute, August 10, 2021, https://www.epi.org/publication/ceo-pay-in-2020/.
90. Source: Graph by John B. Donaldson and Hyung Seok Eric Kim, "Executive Compensation: Inconvenient Truths," ResearchGate, June 25, 2022.
91. Source: Photo by Karl Höcker / US Holocaust Memorial Museum.
92. United States Holocaust Museum, "Auschwitz Through the Lens of the SS: The Album—Photograph," Holocaust Encyclopedia, accessed March 2022, https://encyclopedia.ushmm.org/content/en/gallery/auschwitz-through-the-lens-of-the-ss-the-album-photographs.
93. Gregg R. Murray, "It's Weird, Candidate Height Matters in Elections," *Psychology Today*, October 30, 2012.
94. Wikipedia, "Excess Mortality in the Soviet Union Under Joseph Stalin," last updated January 18, 2025, https://en.wikipedia.org/wiki/Excess_mortality_in_the_Soviet_Union_under_Joseph_Stalin.
95. Wikipedia, "Excess Mortality in the Soviet Union Under Joseph Stalin," last updated January 18, 2025, https://en.wikipedia.org/wiki/Excess_mortality_in_the_Soviet_Union_under_Joseph_Stalin.

96. Wikipedia, "Death and State Funeral of Joseph Stalin," last updated January 27, 2025, https://en.wikipedia.org/wiki/Death_and_state_funeral_of_Joseph_Stalin.

97. "Stalin's Approval Rating Among Russians Hits Record High—Poll," *The Moscow Times*, April 16, 2019, https://www.themoscowtimes.com/2019/04/16/stalins-approval-rating-among-russians-hits-record-highpoll-a65245.

98. Andrew Naughtie, "Mitt Romney Attacked for $13m NRA Donation as He Tweets About Uvalde Attack," *The Independent*, US Edition, May 26, 2022, https://www.independent.co.uk/news/world/americas/us-politics/mitt-romney-nra-donation-uvalde-b2087971.html.

99. "Japan Nuclear Shutdown Did 'More Harm Than Good', Study Finds," World Nuclear News, October 29, 2019, https://www.world-nuclear-news.org/Articles/Japan-nuclear-shutdown-more-harm-than-good-study-f.

100. Source: Graph from "Death Rates per Unit of Electricity Production," Our World in Data.

101. "Nuclear Power in France," World Nuclear Association, accessed January 30, 2025, https://world-nuclear.org/information-library/country-profiles/countries-a-f/france.aspx.

102. Source: Graphic from "Causes of Death in the US," Our World in Data

103. Dave Roos, "How Many Were Killed on D-Day?," History, June 3, 2024, https://www.history.com/news/d-day-casualties-deaths-allies.

104. Robert Blanchard, "Sobering Stats: 15,000 U.S. Airmen Killed in Training in WW II," Real Clear History, February 12, 2019, https://www.realclearhistory.com/articles/2019/02/12/staggering_statistics_15000_us_airmen_killed_in_training_in_ww_ii_412.html.

105. Source: Illustration from *Die Gartenlaube* (1884), Wikimedia Commons, public domain.

106. "NHE Fact Sheet," U.S. Centers for Medicare & Medicaid Services, last updated December 18, 2024, https://www.cms.gov/data-research/statistics-trends-and-reports/national-health-expenditure-data/nhe-fact-sheet.

107. "National Health Expenditure Data: Historical," U.S. Centers for Medicare & Medicaid Services, last updated December 18, 2024, https://www.cms.gov/Research-Statistics-Data-and-Systems/Statistics-Trends-and-Reports/NationalHealthExpendData/NationalHealthAccountsHistorical.

108. Christian-Alexander Behrendt, Birgitta Sigvant, Zoltán Szeberin, Barry Beiles, Nikolaj Eldrup, Ian A. Thomson, Maarit Venermo, Martin Altreuther, Gabor Menyhei, Joakim Nordanstig, Mike Clarke, Henrik Christian Rieß, Martin Björck, and Eike Sebastian Debus, "International Variations in Amputation Practice: A VASCUNET Report," *European Journal of Vascular and Endovascular Surgery* 56, no. 3 (2018): 391–399, https://doi.org/10.1016/j.ejvs.2018.04.017.

109. Claire Klobucista, "U.S. Life Expectancy Is in Decline. Why Aren't Other Countries Suffering the Same Problem?," Council on Foreign Relations, September 8, 2022, https://www.cfr.org/in-brief/us-life-expectancy-decline-why-arent-other-countries-suffering-same-problem.

110. Nikhil R. Sahni, Prakriti Mishra, Brandon Carrus, and David M. Cutler, "Administrative Simplification: How to Save a Quarter-Trillion Dollars in US Healthcare," McKinsey & Company, October 20, 2021, https://www.mckinsey.com/industries/healthcare-systems-and-services/our-insights/administrative-simplification-how-to-save-a-quarter-trillion-dollars-in-us-healthcare.

111. Fabrizio Toscano, Eloise O'Donnell, Joan E. Broderick, Marcella May, Pippa Tucker, Mark A. Unruh, Gabriele Messina, and Lawrence P. Casalino, "How Physicians Spend Their Work Time: An Ecological Momentary Assessment," *Journal of General Internal Medicine* 35 (August 2020): 3,166–3,172, https://doi.org/10.1007/s11606-020-06087-4.

112. Deirdre Shesgreen, "'War Rarely Goes as Planned': New Report Tallies Trillions US Spent in Afghanistan, Iraq," *USA Today*, September 1, 2021, https://www.usatoday.com/story/news/politics/2021/09/01/how-much-did-war-afghanistan-cost-how-many-people-died/5669656001/.

113. Carroll Doherty and Jocelyn Kiley, "A Look Back at How Fear and False Beliefs Bolstered U.S. Public Support for War in Iraq," Pew Research Center, March 14, 2023, https://www.pewresearch.org/politics/2023/03/14/a-look-back-at-how-fear-and-false-beliefs-bolstered-u-s-public-support-for-war-in-iraq/.
114. "Mexico's Crucial Education Reform Risks Being Unwound," *The Economist*, May 31, 2018.
115. Jonathan Stempel, "'Worthless' Subway 'Footlong' Sandwich Settlement Is Thrown Out: U.S. Court," *Reuters*, August 25, 2017, https://www.reuters.com/article/us-subway-decision-footlong/worthless-subway-footlong-sandwichsettlement-is-thrown-out-u-s-court-idUSKCN1B52H6.
116. "Red Bull Puts Up $13m to Settle False Advertising Suit," Morelli Law Firm (blog), accessed January 30, 2025, https://www.morellilaw.com/red-bull-puts-up-13m-to-settle-false-advertising-suit/.

PART III: WHAT TO DO ABOUT IT?

1. Winston Churchill, "We Shall Fight on the Beaches," speech, House of Commons of the Parliament of the United Kingdom, June 4, 1940.
2. "School Enrollment, Tertiary (% Gross) — China, United States," World Bank Group, September 30, 2024, https://data.worldbank.org/indicator/SE.TER.ENRR?locations=CN-US.
3. Source: Graphic from "Average Years of Schooling, 2022," Our World in Data.
4. Ashley Austrew, "How to Prevent Your Kids from Losing What They Learned in School During Summer Vacation," Scholastic, August 2, 2022, https://www.scholastic.com/parents/books-and-reading/raise-a-reader-blog/summer-slide.html.
5. Tony Robbins, *Unshakeable: Your Financial Freedom Playbook* (Simon & Schuster, 2017), 22–23.
6. Wikipedia, "List of Lost Russian or Soviet Submarines," last updated September 19, 2023, https://en.wikipedia.org/wiki/List_of_lost_Russian_or_Soviet_submarines#After_World_War_II.

7. Austin Frakt, "Putting a Dollar Value on Life? Governments Already Do," *The New York Times*, Mayy 11, 2020, https://www.nytimes.com/2020/05/11/upshot/virus-price-human-life.html.

8. "Coronary Bypass Surgery Cost and Coronary Bypass Surgery Procedures Information," New Choice Health, accessed January 30, 2025, https://www.newchoicehealth.com/coronary-bypass-surgery-cost.

9. Mitzi S. Morris, "How Much Does Bariatric Surgery Cost?," GoodRx, August 24, 2022, https://www.goodrx.com/conditions/weight-loss/bariatric-surgery-costs.

10. Joe Verghese, Richard B. Lipton, Mindy J. Katz, Charles B. Hall, Carol A. Derby, Gail Kuslansky, Anne F. Ambrose, Martin Sliwinski, and Herman Buschke, "Leisure Activities and the Risk of Dementia in the Elderly," *The New England Journal of Medicine* 348, no. 25 (2003), https://doi.org/10.1056/NEJMoa022252.

11. Source: Graph from Joe Verghese, Richard B. Lipton, Mindy J. Katz, Charles B. Hall, Carol A. Derby, Gail Kuslansky, Anne F. Ambrose, Martin Sliwinski, and Herman Buschke, "Leisure Activities and the Risk of Dementia in the Elderly," *The New England Journal of Medicine* 348, no. 25 (2003).

12. "Make Food Stamps Healthy," Physicians Committee for Responsible Medicine, accessed January 30, 2025, https://www.pcrm.org/good-nutrition/nutrition-programs-policies/make-food-stamps-healthy.

13. "Representation in the Electoral College: How Do States Compare?," USAFacts, accessed January 30, 2025, https://usafacts.org/visualizations/electoral-college-states-representation/.

14. Taylor Giorno, "2022 Federal Midterm Election Spending on Track to Top $9.3 Billion," OpenSecrets, September 26, 2022, https://www.opensecrets.org/news/2022/09/2022-midterm-election-spending-on-track-to-top-9-3-billion/.

15. "Colorectal Cancer Risk Factors," American Cancer Society, last updated January 29, 2024, https://www.cancer.net/cancer-types/colorectal-cancer/risk-factors-and-prevention.

16. "QuickStats: Percentage of Adults Aged 50–75 Years Who Met Colorectal Cancer (CRC) Screening Recommendations—National Health Interview Survey, United States, 2018," *Morbidity and Mortality Weekly Report 69*, no. 11 (2020): 314, http://dx.doi.org/10.15585/mmwr.mm6911a7.

17. Source: Graph from Matthew McGough, Gary Claxton, Krutika Amin, and Cynthia Cox, "How Do Health Expenditures Vary Across the Population?," Peterson-KFF Health System Tracker, January 4, 2024.

18. Emily D. Parker, Janice Lin, Troy Mahoney, Nwanneamaka Ume, Grace Yang, Robert A. Gabbay, Nuha A. ElSayed, and Raveendhara R. Bannuru, "Economic Costs of Diabetes in the U.S. in 2022," *Diabetes Care* 47, no. 1 (2024): 26–43, https://doi.org/10.2337/dci23-0085.

19. "About Obesity," Centers for Disease Control and Prevention, January 23, 2042, https://www.cdc.gov/obesity/php/about/.

20. Eat, Inject, Repeat: Curing Obesity, Worldwide," *The Economist*, March 4, 2023, 15.

21. Su-Hsin Chang, Carolyn R. T. Stoll, Jihyun Song, J. Esteban Varela, Christopher J. Eagon, and Graham A. Colditz, "The Effectiveness and Risks of Bariatric Surgery," *JAMA Surgery* 149, no. 3 (2014): 275–287, https://doi.org/ 10.1001/jamasurg.2013.3654.

22. Oliver A. Varban and Justin B. Dimick, "Bariatric Surgery: Safe, Effective, and Underutilized," *Family Medicine* 51, no. 7 (2019): 552–554, https://doi.org/ 10.22454/FamMed.2019.289449.

23. S. Chapman, P. Alpers, K. Agho, and M. Jones, "Australia's 1996 Gun Law Reforms: Faster Falls in Firearm Deaths, Firearm Suicides, and a Decade Without Mass Shootings," *Injury Prevention* 12, no. 6 (2006): 365–372, https://doi.org/10.1136/ip.2006.013714.

24. Source: Graph from Volutin, "Gun Deaths over Time in the US and Australia," Wikimedia Commons, October 3, 2015, licensed under Creative Commons Attribution-Share Alike 4.0 International (CC BY-SA 4.0).

25. Wikipedia, "Straty Osobowe Polski w Czasie II Wojny Światowej," last updated September 4, 2024, https://pl.wikipedia.org/wiki/Straty_osobowe_Polski_w_czasie_II_wojny_światowej.
26. Mark Harrison, *The Economics of World War II: Six Great Powers in International Comparison* (Cambridge University Press, 2009), 34.

ABOUT THE AUTHOR

CEZARY PIETRASIK is a co-owner of Synerise, the #1 AI company globally in human behavior prediction. Previously, he was founder and CEO of Healthdom, a preventive medicine company in San Francisco. Cezary started his career at McKinsey, and then joined the investment banking team at JPMorgan in London. He then went on to become a private equity investor at Warburg Pincus, progressing from associate to head of Central Europe. A graduate of the London School of Economics, SGH Warsaw School of Economics, and Wirtschaftsuniversität Wien, he was named the Best Economics Student of Poland. He is also the founder and president of the Butterfly Effect Foundation, which helps children from underprivileged rural areas, a former member of the Future Leaders Initiative, the author of a book on defense doctrine for Poland, and an ex–board member of large healthcare and technology companies. In his free time, Cezary is an avid traveler, swimmer, and horseback rider.

www.ingramcontent.com/pod-product-compliance
Lightning Source LLC
Chambersburg PA
CBHW020532030426
42337CB00013B/816